MY LIFE
WITH THE PENTECOSTALS
and Other Stuff

MY LIFE
WITH THE PENTECOSTALS
and Other Stuff

STEVE L. MORGAN

Two Harbors Press
Minneapolis, MN

TWOHARBORS
WWW.TWOHARBORSPRESS.COM

Two Harbors Press
212 3rd Avenue North, Suite 290
Minneapolis, MN 55401
612.455.2293
www.TwoHarborsPress.com

ISBN - 978-1-936198-90-0
ISBN - 1-936198-90-8
LCCN - 2010935145

Cover Design by Alan Pranke
Typeset by Melanie Shellito

Printed in the United States of America

When I realized I was actually going to get this book published
I decided to ask the Lord what he thought of it.
You know what he said?
"Everyone is entitled to his own opinion."
That was good enough for me.

DEDICATION

This book is dedicated to all those kids who grew up
in a Fundamentalist, Pentecostal environment, silently questioning
the teachings of the Church—hoping for restful sleep at night but
fearful of giving in to the temptation.

May we all rest in peace.

TABLE OF CONTENTS

INTRODUCTION

Over the years I've told stories about my childhood and my upbringing: about life on the farm and my parents and grandparents, and about my brother and sister.

As I've gotten older, the stories have become more vivid. Possibly this is due to the fact that as we age we appear to be wiser and people are more willing to listen, or maybe just because we've been on earth long enough to believe we have something to say that people will listen to. Whatever the case, friends and colleagues have been saying: "Steve, you have got to write a book!" And I've done that—in a conversational, vignette-filled style—as if I'm sitting across from you while I spin my yarns. I've told them as if I'm starting each tale with "Have I ever told you about the time…?" I've always liked this sort of writing. I trust you will, too.

I'm not delusional enough to believe that I'm the next Stephen Ambrose or Joseph Ellis, or whoever, but I am a good storyteller and I have a story that I want to tell. It's a story that, as I've mentioned, my friends and even some of my relatives have encouraged me to write. What I want to tell is not an indictment of my childhood but an essay on what I went through. It's not a witch-hunt, for that would serve no purpose and that's not my personality. It's not intended to offend anyone. But, if it must, I hope it offends everyone equally. It's my recollection of the events that shaped my life. It's *my* memory of these events. It may not be exactly as my childhood friends, or relatives, brother and sister, mother and father, or others remember it to have been, but it's my recollection and opinion, with a *dash* of artistic license. And if they take exception to what I've written, let them write their own books!

The dichotomy that I have tried to illustrate is that I loved these Pentecostals dearly, for they were my *family*. They meant no harm. For it's as if they were swept up by an ocean current. Even though I may take exception to their philosophies and opinions about things in general, they weren't—and aren't—bad people. Most of my relatives and those I grew up with have come to terms and are at peace with, or even embrace, the sensation of growing up in the environment I describe. I believe I have, too. But, in the back of my mind, there's a little cabinet that I only open now and then, that contains questions on the mysteries of the unknown: "What's beyond the beyond? What's past the end of the Universe? What happens after eternity? Where is Heaven? Where the hell is Hell!?" And those questions have always intrigued me.

In my mind, any unnatural pursuit requires imagination to successfully convince others that what a person is expounding upon is based in fact. In other words, for the adults in the Assemblies of God Church to convince us kids that we needed to be good took a big stick—and that was the threat of Hell. But *my* contention is that we worship a loving God. That's what it says in the Bible, after all. But man corrupts the incorruptible.

THE END OF MY LIFE

So I died and I packed my bags and headed out, toward Heaven. I thought I might as well give it a shot. It took me a while but I finally reached the outskirts and encountered a long procession that I was told was filled with people waiting to get through the Pearly Gates. I joined in with the others and finally made it to the head of the line and came face-to-face with St. Peter. A big man, he asked me my name and when I gave it to him he replied back with unbridled disgust, and in a loud voice, "Yah, you're on the list!" He handed me a Google-Heaven map and indicated that I could enter and, with a sigh of relief, I passed through the gates. I traveled over the streets that were paved with gold and past the mansions, through the *bad* part of town, the suburbs, and then out into a desert area north of the city.

I'm not sure how far it was. Time and space are hard to measure in Heaven but, following the map, I eventually came upon a tent encampment. It appeared to hold a pretty rough-looking crowd. A little different than I'd expected. But, at the moment at least, the flames of Hell weren't nipping at my heels. I wandered through the makeshift town until I came upon a tent that had a number stenciled on it that was the same as the one on the map St. Pete had given me.

Setting down my bag, I slowly opened the flap to the tent. It took a few seconds for my eyes to adjust to the light and when they did I was gazing upon Jimmy Swaggart and Jerry Falwell. Jimmy was seated at a piano, crying while he played, and Jerry was sitting on a cot, mumbling. I pulled up a camp chair across from him. He didn't look good. And, staring him in the eye I asked, "So this is it, huh, Jerry?" He shrugged his shoulders and replied back, "It looks like it, Steve." Then he turned and, opening his bag, pulled out a bottle of Jack Daniel's and three glasses and poured each of us a drink. Jimmy, having heard the tinkle of the glass, stopped his crying and playing and came over and sat down on the cot.

Then Jerry raised his glass and proposed a toast. "Here's to eternity!"

ACKNOWLEDGMENTS

My wife, Annette, for putting up with my stories and my secrets.

My daughter, Natalie, for being my cheerleader and confidante.

My sons, Jason and Neil, for being there for me.

My parents, brother and sister, cousins, aunts and uncles, and friends who provided the fodder for the book.

Susan Ladue and her husband, Peter, who had faith in my dream.

I

A Pentecostal by Birth

I grew up in the 1950s on a small farm that my father had bought from my mother's parents. It was a hard-scrabble farm: a small dairy, pasture, corn, broken-down equipment, and bad fences. My father was a hard worker who had no, or very little, concept of business planning. Decisions were made to solve problems for the moment with no attention to the effect, good or bad, that the current resolution might have on the future. My mother's parents were of German descent and had emigrated from the Ukraine area of Russia and had joined with other Germans to settle in eastern Washington state and then moved on to northern California in the early 1920s. Lutherans by religion, they were generally a happy lot, save for my mother's father, Grandpa, who was the poster child for hard-headed unreasonableness. They were hard-working—but poor as church-mice—and God-fearing and generous with what little they had. In spite of my mother's father. (Whom I also refer to as "Papa" later on in this book.)

Then something happened in the late 1940s. They became Pentecostals. Where in the world it came from my parents, aunts and uncles, or anyone who would listen couldn't tell me. Lutheran to Pentecostal?! My grandparents would tell stories of the "old days." Of stomping grapes for wine in the basement of the farmhouse I grew up in, and of the gatherings of neighbors to celebrate the harvests and sample the fruit of the vines. Pentecostal? Now we could barely say the word "wine," unless of course it was in a biblical sense. What happened? I remember asking my parents and Sunday School teachers how it was that Jesus—having attended a wedding ceremony and learning that the assembled had run out of wine— took water and turned it into the stuff! Now we couldn't even talk about it. Lutherans were reasonable folk who treated people fairly, worked hard, paid their taxes, didn't cheat their neighbors, took a little nip of the fermented grape, and were forgiven of their sins— *normal* people. And now Pentecostal, for cryin' out loud! Now we were judge, jury, and executioner. The grape had gone bad and sin was everywhere! And there was "Church." Lest we dared attempt to forget, or forgive, our own sinning, there was Church on Sunday morning, Sunday night, and at Wednesday night prayer meeting, Thursday night youth group, and Saturday prayer breakfasts. These gatherings were used, I'm convinced, to remind us of the sinning and to erase all doubt in our minds that we were anywhere near "normal." We all yearned for the Lutheran days, although we had never experienced them.

Then came the traveling Evangelists. News of their arrival sent chills through my brother and me. I'm the oldest child with a brother sixteen months younger than I, and a sister eight years my junior. The impact of this craziness I'm describing had more of an effect on my brother and me than it did on my sister. As with most unnatural human pursuits they tend to lose steam, as a rule. By the time my sister was old enough to know better, my parents were somewhat less "preachy Pentecostal" about things. But the traveling Evengelists were still scary. Some came with tents and set up in the gravel parking lot of the church; some just used the church sanctuary for their tirades. "Sanctuary" is a funny word for the structure that housed these Pentecostals. That housed us. For a complete change, a noticeable glow, even a smile, came over even the most ardent disciple of this sect when they left the confines of that space and walked into the open air. We could feel it. Away from the judgment of *sin*. Only to sin again, but free for a moment. *Normal.*

The Evangelists came for two weeks, on average, and preached about sin and the end of the world for fourteen straight days, and we had to attend *every* last service. Being a typical naïve youngster, and in spite of possibly increasing the temperature of my eventual home in Hell—which I surely knew would be my final destination, of course—I would feign illness in an attempt to avoid these gatherings. But it was usually to no avail, for my parents, especially my mother, would seize the opportunity to have this traveling "man-of-god" lay hands on me. A sure edification of the healing power of their version of God. This meant that I not only felt guilty for having even suggested or thought about this ruse, but that I might have denied the others in the congregation the blessing of seeing me *rise up and walk!* But, even worse, several times it completely backfired when—upon hearing me describe the illness—my mother would light up like a Christmas tree and proclaim "We'll have Brother Seamans come to the house and pray for you!" My heart stopped. "Brother" Seamans was the worst of the lot. I believe to this day that if there is anyone on the face of the earth who has been possessed, it was him. He was absolutely crazy. All of us kids could see it, but the adults couldn't. For some reason he had them. He was one of the Evangelists who preached in the sanctuary—maybe because it was harder for the devil to get in.

Brother Seamans was a man in his early sixties, short and pudgy and sweaty, balding with one of the most incredible comb-overs I have ever seen. He would start out like a small foreign car and end up like a freight train. In between, he was incredible. To this day I'm amazed that those seated in the first ten rows were not drowned by his onslaught. To avoid it, my brother and I, and those buddies with any guts, sat in the back rows, although it was frowned upon by the adults. The comb-over varied, depending on how much pomade he had slathered on it, but a few minutes into his sermon/tirade the comb-over would start to slip. It moved ever so slightly at first, until it built up momentum and gravity took over. Watching this was worth the price of admission. Every kid in the place had their eyes riveted on Brother Seamans's head. Even the adults would begin to become uncomfortable, for it was impossible to not notice this phenomenon. However, it never seemed to wake my father up from his nap.

There were two kinds of performances of this event. One we placed bets on, and one we just enjoyed. The first was the game of betting amongst ourselves on how long it would take for the comb-over to start to unravel and fall to his shoulders—and if he would notice or not. This was lightweight stuff. The other was big time: Would the brother remain so involved in his judgmental frothing that he wouldn't notice the movement of the comb-over and it would completely lose its center and tumble onto his shoulders, there to remain for the rest of the sermon? Or would it flail about as if the hair was trying to whip the head to death. This was the best. For we absolutely were beside ourselves with laughter that we tried to control, but we could not keep ourselves from cracking up. Anyone in his right mind would have thought it hilarious. I realized much later that the term "right mind" did not apply to these people, but laughing also elicited the most stern reprimand from our parents. Not so much during the sermon, as we were somewhat protected by the fact that they couldn't do much without causing a stir, but when we got home. How could we be so disrespectful of Brother Seamans? After all, he was preaching the "Word of God." There was that *sin* again. And all throughout these sermons Mrs. Seamans would perch in a chair up on the stage behind and to the right of the brother, wearing a mumu and knitting. And she would not miss a stitch. They were pure insanity! What a team. What a piece of work.

There's one particular session with Brother Seamans that stands out in my mind. A married couple in the Church had a daughter named Lois—only four or five years old—who had contracted leukemia and was near death. The doctors had done all they could. Desperate for some sort of miracle from God, they brought her to a Sunday morning service, during which Seamans would be laying hands on the sick in a faith healing ritual. The poor couple brought Lois's little, almost lifeless, body to the front of the church and laid her on the altar. Seamans went to work and the congregation started their chaotic chanting and frothing and falling down and praying, and the heartsick parents cried and wept. The beautiful little girl died a few days later. That image will never leave my mind.

*****

In the Pentecostal religion, pastors tend to come and go. Some hear the voice of God; some go into other, more profitable, lines of work; and some run off with the pianist or whatever. In my early teens, our minister had left under one of these scenarios—which one I can't remember—and a lay person, which was another word for a church board member, filled in for several Sundays while a search was conducted for another "shepherd of the flock." I remember the Sunday that this lay person happily announced that the search was over and a new pastor would assume the duties beginning with the next Sunday. The congregation was all a-twitter.

Our farm was about a half mile from the church. The land the church sat on had been donated by my grandparents, my mother's parents. Most of the parishioners lived a greater distance from the church than our family did and so, therefore, it fell to my brother and me to mow and water the lawn and do general maintenance. A couple days before the new pastor was to arrive, my mother, and probably my father, too—although my mother normally handled these matters—announced to my brother and me that we would be helping the new "Shepherd" move into the parsonage. As strange as it may seem, the parsonage is where the parson and his or her family live. In this case it was a *she*. Maude Coulter and her husband Speedy were our new ministers. (I'm not kidding!) Maude was probably sixty (although as kids we think everyone is older), stoutly-built with the most amazing head of hair I had seen to date wound in a spiral that must have been at least a foot high. And it was blue. (Really!) Later on, after Maude and Speedy had been in town for a while, we heard rumors that some time in the past a black widow spider had made its home in her hair but was found before it could bite her. (Darn!)

Then there was Speedy. I'll never forget the first time I laid eyes on him. My mother had brought my brother and me to help with the move-in and was introducing him and Mrs. Coulter to us. It was like a cartoon. Here was Maude Coulter, just what her name implies, and Speedy standing dutifully beside her. She was easily 10 inches or a foot taller than he was, not including her hair, and outweighed him by seventy-five pounds, which was probably all muscle. As for being what his name implied, he was as slow as molasses.

Maude, that's what we'll call her, carried things on around the church much as those before her had…although she did add a little spice to things. Speedy did his best to pitch in, but he never could get out of his own way. Brother Seamans kept showing up now and then, as crazy as ever. He had lost a good portion of what had been his hair and he wasn't nearly as much fun to watch. And he seemed to have lost his zest for theatrics, although he did lay hands on the sick and infirm from time to time. But he just wasn't his old self. We needed a new act. And we got it.

One Sunday, Maude announced that we would be graced by Evangelists for the next two weeks. My brother and I had been almost giddy for the past two or three months, as we hadn't had to bear the burden of the fourteen-day prison sentence. But now it was back. And sin. And repentance. Could I resurrect my phony illnesses? Ones that my mother would buy? Maybe, just maybe. The next night, Monday (thankfully, this was before Monday Night Football), we finished our chores, cleaned up and, at seven o'clock, we all went to the first revival meeting. But this one was different. In the back corner of the parking lot a brightly-painted, somewhat hippie-looking van was parked. Ooooh. That was good for starters. This had to be the Evangelists' rig. We entered the church; we were a little early (which was unusual) and the only congregation members there. We knew there were going to be two preachers and we assumed they would be men.

We weren't prepared for what we encountered. Keep in mind that we were country boys and hadn't gotten out much and had been raised and taught by people who believed the world was flat and was made in six days. Before us, setting up their musical instruments and other props were the two biggest bull dykes we had ever seen.

Although we didn't know if we had ever seen one, but if we had these were the biggest. The only reason we knew they were women? They were wearing what passed for dresses. But we learned later the dresses were all a cover. My parents were at a complete loss about what to do or how to greet them. Thankfully, just then Maude came in a side door, with Speedy in tow, and began the introductions. This was Ms. Maupin and Ms. Rathoe, and they were scheduled to minister to us for the next two weeks. Every night.

My brother and I retreated to our customary seats in the back row and were unusually silent. This encounter had visibly shaken us. Really. This is why. (Follow me on this.) Our mother had an older brother who, with his wife and young children, were missionaries to Ceylon (now Sri Lanka). They had just returned to "the States" (that's what missionaries called the United States). This terminology was new to us. "We're returning to the States," they'd say. Remember, now, according to these people the earth is flat. The wife of my mother's older brother, the missionary, had just paid us a visit with her "friend" and had announced that she was a lesbian, would be divorcing my uncle, and marrying this person. You can't imagine what shockwaves were sent through our family. My mother was on the phone for hours with the news to everyone she could reach in the family as well as several telephone operators. Prayer groups gathered.

Even our neighbor Wilma, not religious—but nosy—and who never got off the party line, pitched in when my mother grew tired and continued announcing the news. It was even in the "Did you hear?" section of our little newspaper. We could hardly show our faces. What's a "lesbian"? We didn't know, but our aunt surely was one. Now, inside the sanctuary where Brother Seamans held forth against sin and the devil were, not lesbians, but "bull dykes." Or so our father said to us under his breath. Mom jabbed him in the ribs. Dad said he'd tell us later, giving us a little smile. This was almost too much for two country boys to handle. Wasn't this sin?

The church filled up and the service began in the usual manner, with Maude leading a prayer and then introducing our guests. We were informed that not only would we be ministered to, but graced with the musical talent of, the pair. (Tilley, bar the door!) What's interesting is that these...well whatever they were...were very entertaining. They both played every hillbilly instrument known to man, including a washboard and a saw, and there wasn't a foot that wasn't stomping or tapping for all fourteen days. Sin took a backseat for a change. We never saw them again. Other than Maude wishing them Godspeed nothing further ever was said. But my brother and I still wondered, and looked over our shoulders.

2

Mom's Family on the Farm

Back to my mother's family: Grandma and Grandpa, aunts and uncles, cousins. (Incidentally, I originally wasn't going to use actual names in this little ditty in an effort to protect the guilty, but decided I must to reflect historical accuracy.)

When the great religious migration from Lutheran to Pentecostal took place within my mother's family and spread, in varying degrees, to relatives far and wide, all of my mother's ten siblings crossed over save one: Aunt Elsie, my favorite. Elsie was witty, kind, shy, quiet, and deep. But we talked about her behind her back. "She is *Lutheran*. They're almost like *Catholics*, you know…whisper, whisper. She's surely *lost*, but we'll pray for her." Elsie married a Norwegian, Olaf Dragseth, who was a wonderful man. One of my heroes. An avid 49er and Giants fan. He lived to be ninety and loved his golf. He shot his age at eighty-five, although he kiddingly said he kept his own score, like Nixon, because he played better that way. He was in my foursome when I recorded my only hole-in-one. Elsie lived to be ninety-three, living in her own house until a few days before the end.

*****

Even though my mother and her family grew up in the country, my parents were the only ones who remained on a farm, my grandparent's former farm, and our place became the center of get-togethers over the years, especially at Thanksgiving. In the late 1950s, my father had raised some turkeys for no commercial reason and, therefore, it was decided that this celebration would be held at our farm. As time went along and my brother and I were old enough to begin hunting—you had to be fourteen—cousins and uncles would gather on Thanksgiving morning for "The Great Pheasant Hunt." Corn stubble and newly-planted wheat or oats gave excellent cover and, with the help of a couple good hunting dogs, we would typically all get our limit of two male pheasants each and retire—after picking and cleaning them—to the living room of the farmhouse to watch one of the day's football games; after we got our black and white Packard Bell television, that is. Even back then the NFL carried two games that day.

During these hunting events there were many examples of crack shooting. Dead-eye shooting. I wasn't one of the really good shots, but my Uncle Manuel Muster was. One of the highlights of these occasions was watching my uncle's shooting exhibitions. Uncle Manuel was one of the last of the true "Mountain Men." He lived with my Aunt Minnie, Mom's older sister, and my cousins in the gold country of northern California. He never really had a regular job, a fact lamented by the family but exciting to us kids.

He would take us fly fishing into wilderness areas and we'd see mountain lions and bears and bobcats and rattlesnakes and all manner of critters. It's said that he was bitten more than seven times by rattlers, so much so that he had built up an immunity. Who knows if that's true. It's not important. We enjoyed the stories and his company. He worked for the Forest Service off and on, doing who knows what, but made most of his and my aunt's living mining for gold. He would set up his operation in the backwoods of the old gold country and disappear for days or weeks. It was rough on my aunt, but that's the way it was. When he'd come to our place for the hunting, or some other gathering, he would bring a vial of gold nuggets with him and let us kids hold them. It was neat stuff. We got to see the romantic side of him, but he and his family actually led a pretty rough life. He was a smoker, although the family gave him a hard time about it—mostly for religious reasons, as smoking was not really taboo yet in society. He rolled his own. One handed, perfectly symmetrical. Try that sometime. It can't be done. But he did it. He also played the guitar. Every year, from the time I was a little kid, I can remember my mother's family has had a summer reunion, generally in northern California. Manuel would bring out his guitar and lead all of us, at least those who knew the words, in the singing of German songs. I remember at his funeral all of us gathered around and sang. The service wasn't inside, but out in the woods where he spent his time.

You probably haven't heard our family, my cousins, aunts and uncles sing. It's incredible to hear. I don't believe there's a finer group of voices than those of our family that gathers anywhere. It gives me goosebumps just thinking about it. My cousin, Dan, will usually start, at first with no accompaniment. Then another voice will join and another and another until all of us join in—incredible, clear tenor, baritone and bass singing from the diaphragm. Just like my high school choir teacher, Mr. Kwate, would have wanted. It still brings tears to my eyes. This group ranges from deeply religious to agnostic to people who "just don't know". But, for those moments we are all joined in song, song that takes the world's problems away for a time and brings us together. I remember that when my grandparents passed away, especially my grandmother—my mother's mother who was a saint—the service was held out in the country at a beautifully-maintained cemetery not far from where I grew up. It was almost like a heavenly choir as we sang those songs, songs from days long ago, when my grandparents were young people in Russia. They never forgot to give thanks for what they had—even my bull-headed grandfather never forgot. It was a good example for all of us to follow.

3

Uncle Maynard

My mother's older sister, Ann, one of the siblings** who left Lutheran for Pentecostal, married a fellow by the name of Maynard Bean. Now, Maynard was different. (Just as an aside, I use the first names of my older aunts and uncles, not to be disrespectful or smart-like, but because that's what all of us in the family called them. It is probably a western thing unlike in the East or South where addressing one's elder by a first name would be disrespectful.)

It's hard to describe what was different about Maynard. From the kids' viewpoint it would probably be his goofiness. The word in the family was that, having fought in the South Pacific during World War II, he had contracted jungle fever and suffered from those symptoms. That might have been fine for the adults, but to us kids he was just weird. He and my mother's sister lived in a converted Greyhound bus on acreage outside of Sacramento that he had bought through the GI Bill after the war. It was always fun to visit them as kids because most of us had never known anyone who actually *lived* in something other than a house. Eventually they built what resembled a home and moved into it, but he never sold the bus. In fact, Maynard never sold anything. This led to another perk when we visited them: we got to stay in a motel because there was no room in the bus and Mom was afraid to stay in the house.

But there was a cool side to Maynard—especially for us kids.

For transportation, Maynard bought decommissioned police cars that he would fix up to be as close to real cop cars as possible. He even had a permit, or so we were told, to carry a shotgun in one of those cradles between the front seat and the dashboard just like real police cars have. I remember one time that he got in trouble with the law for repainting one of the cars to look too much like the real ones. I think they gave him a small fine and he promised never to do it again. We knew this had actually happened because Aunt Ann had said it was so and the next time we saw the car, half of it had the paint sanded off, although he never sanded the other half.

Like I said earlier, Mom's family had yearly reunions. They hadn't always been yearly, they told us (which seems kind of often), but became that way later on, when my brother and I were little. I asked my aunts and uncles about the frequency of these events. The consensus was that they were held yearly to make sure you had probably recently attended one before you died. At least that's what the old folks told me. Especially, Uncle Wilmer.

4

Uncle Wilmer, and Maynard, Too.

om's older sister, Rosie, who was older than Ann and was also a defector from Lutheran, married a man named Wilmer Dawson who thought all this religious stuff was a bunch of crap, but in a nice way. Along with Elsie's husband Uncle Olaf, Wilmer was one of my heroes. He was rough, gruff, tough, kind, generous, and a great father to my cousin Dan (the leader of the singing). Wilmer might have graduated from high school, but I'm not sure. He grew up around my mother's family there in the country where everyone knew each other. He was also German. Everyone was German. He was street-smart without the streets. Let's say "country-smart." He could fix anything, make anything. He once made me a perfect wooden replica of a 30-30 lever-action rifle, on a shop-smith lathe—perfectly painted and detailed, one of my prized possessions as a kid. (There's a painful end to the story of the rifle that has nothing to do with Wilmer, so we'll talk about it later.) Here's probably the best description I could give of the man: he lived to be ninety-five and, when he was ninety-three, Rosie and Dan took him to a specialist for some ailment. More of a nuisance, that's what Wilmer said, than a health problem. Not what Rosie and Dan said. In setting up the appointment, the nurse doing the scheduling asked for Wilmer's medical records to be sent over. The two of them weren't sure what to tell the nurse for, you see, Wilmer had never been to a doctor.

Then the time came for the yearly family reunion. This is where Maynard comes in again. Maynard wore dark-blue "Can't Bust'em" brand coveralls, with a dark-blue work shirt underneath and a matching coat jacket that zipped up the front. Wool-lined—whether in the heat of summer or the cold of winter—and thick, black, Wolverine work boots. I never once in my life saw him wear anything else. In addition to this attire he wore an "ear hat." Dark-blue, once again, and wool-lined with a drop-down-flap for each ear. Now, I would sit amongst the uncles at these reunions. Sometimes my brother would, and Rosie and Wilmer's boy Dan would, too. The women would sit over to one side, the kids would run around doing what kids do, and the teenagers would pop their pimples and stare at each other. The rest of my male cousins wouldn't sit with anyone. Well, except for themselves. Some got bored easily, some didn't care, and some sat with the women, a practice which was looked down upon by some of us in the "adult male" group—although we always took great pains to formally greet all of the aunts. But the girl cousins made us a little nervous. They weren't the most attractive lot and the one or two that were passable were, well, our girl cousins, for cryin' out loud! And we were sure they, too, were Pentecostals, children of Pentecostals. We sinned enough as it was.

There was an unwritten pecking order in this close-knit society for the male cousins. My brother, Dan, and me were in the elite group of cousins who sat with the adult uncles. It was never planned. It just was. I don't think the three of us even realized it as youngsters. But, as I got older, it made me uncomfortable as I'd hear mumbling from our other cousins about our real or perceived stature. Most of the time, the reunions were held in the massive Bidwell Park in the city of Chico, California, out by Five-Mile Dam. Ann, Mom's older sister, and Maynard, living down by Sacramento, had a longer drive to get to these affairs than most of us, so almost everyone was already there when they'd arrive. Now Wilmer, who had never seen a doctor, was a troublemaker when it came to Maynard. He didn't believe the jungle fever stuff like most of the adults did, and thought that Maynard was just full of shit. Now you couldn't say that in front of the Pentecostals—which meant almost everyone—but a chosen few would sit around in private and discuss Maynard with Wilmer.

There was a sort of unspoken sentinel system in place at these affairs that consisted of the kids who were out playing in the trees along the road. They would signal or shout out the arrival of so-and-so or so-and-so. "Here comes Ruby and Lester" or "Here's Leroy and Bobbi" and the like. It was especially exciting when whoever was announced as arriving had kids in the car—fresh meat for the other kids. But nothing compared to "Here comes Ann and Maynard!" Everything stopped. Maynard always whined and complained when he had to walk too far from his car to his appointed seat, prominently placed—through Wilmer's direction—amidst the brothers-in-law and selected older male cousins. And Maynard always carried a few extra pounds. So we always left a spot open for his car, real close to the gathering. Ann was very spry, and a warm and bubbly person and would get out first and walk through everyone giving and getting kisses and hugs.

It always took a little while for Maynard to get rolling, once they got there, to actually leave the car. First of all, he always carried a side-arm on his person. Many times during the trip from Sacramento the gun would become lodged under one of his butt cheeks (no one ever knew if it was loaded or not) and cause the corresponding leg to go numb. He'd struggle out as best as he could and stand by the car until the feeling came back. It was at this moment that Wilmer would cry out, "What ya' doin' up there, Maynard?" and crack himself up while slapping his leg. We all knew what Maynard was doing, but we'd laugh anyway. We'd hear some sort of "grumble, grumble" from Maynard's direction, and then resume our waiting. The next thing Maynard would do, once he got his feeling back, was to go around to each tire and check the pressure with a gauge. Many times we were lectured on the dangers of under-inflated tires, especially because in those days tires had tubes. Then, if things were satisfactory—and they always were—it was back to the driver's door for Maynard.

He would release the shotgun from its cradle in the dash, stand straight up, and briskly open the magazine to confirm that the weapon was not loaded. (Apparently his permit did not allow for a loaded gun.) Then he'd replace it. If all of this was taking too long, there'd be another yell from Wilmer, "You don't even have bullets for it, Maynard," another knee-slap, and more grumbling from the hill. Now we all know that an adult male doesn't wear a hat in a vehicle. ("It's not right," as Maynard would say to us. "What's gonna fall on your head in a car?") But sometimes Maynard would forget to put his hat on, the ear hat, before he got out and conducted his inspections, and Maynard never, ever failed to put his hat on. Well, most of the time he didn't. Wilmer never let it slide, and would holler "Get your hat on, Maynard!" Maynard would quickly—or as quickly as he could—grab his hat, put it on his head, and pretend that it had always been there. But this sudden, impulsive, movement created a great suspense which was what most of the uncles and adult cousins waited for, with great anticipation. The women never noticed, or if they did, they never got the significance of this ritual. In Maynard's haste to place the hat on his head, would he present himself to us with both flaps down, or just one?!!

5

We Had a Dog Named Lady

We **had a dog named Lady who was a** Springer Spaniel. Now, Springers are known to be good hunting dogs, but my brother and I had trained her—or not trained her—and she wasn't much good for hunting. But we thought she was good, and she was always a fixture at our Great Pheasant Hunts. Our uncles and cousins grumbled (after all, they had *good* hunting dogs) but we were able to use Lady because it was our farm after all! But Dan had the best dog: a Brittany Spaniel named Rusty. Brittanys can be temperamental and one-person dogs, which Rusty was, but we all put up with it because he could sniff out and retrieve any bird better than most dogs any of us had seen. "Bird" is the key word here.

Amidst the corn stubble and grass we hunted in, were jackrabbits. Crazy suckers the rabbits. Drove most dogs crazy, too, when the dogs detected them, and when the hairy beasts took off it was close to impossible for the dogs not to follow, but not Rusty. That's what made him special. Lady was a different matter. We hoped and prayed that we all would have "limited out"—which usually only took from the opening of the day's hunt at eight o'clock until eight-fifteen—before Lady kicked up a jackrabbit and took off. And, once she took off, it would take a while before we saw her again, exhausted, with her tongue hanging out. And, of course, the rabbits were never in danger, at least from her.

One time Dan, my brother, and I had limited out and were sitting on the tailgate of our pickup, Lady lying at our feet. A jackrabbit appeared, and she was off. We didn't waste our time trying to call her back, and shooting her was out of the question. (Of course!) We had several natural gas wells on the place (we thought we were gonna be rich) that were enclosed by chain-link fences, probably forty feet by forty feet square. The rabbit happened to take off toward one of these with Lady on the chase and losing ground by the second. Now, jackrabbits are about the dumbest creatures on earth, and this one was no different, and it didn't realize that there was no way Lady was ever going to catch it. When it approached the enclosure around the well, it began circling it. Who knows why. That's just what they do. Well, this gave Lady a chance to catch up and, with renewed vigor, she began to chase it around and around. But the rabbit was so much faster that, after a couple rounds, it had completely caught up with Lady and the scene had the appearance that the rabbit was actually chasing the dog. With its diminished intelligence it took the stupid thing a couple rounds to realize what it was doing, after which it darted off into the grass. Lady never knew it was behind her. Kinda funny for us to watch. Remember, the world is flat and the earth was made in six days.

Dan was a real hunter. My brother and I hunted, but Dan was a "hunter." One year, Dan had begun to do his own reloads and, on opening day, had brought a couple boxes for my brother and me. My birthday happened to be around that time and my parents had bought me a new Stevens double-barrel shotgun—the only new one I ever had. The three of us set out at eight o'clock and we were barely into a field when a pheasant rooster jumped up near me and I shot. I missed it, or so I thought—which wasn't unusual—and Dan shot and got it, as usual.

A few moments later, another one jumped and I shot again. The next thing I remembered was sitting on the ground with the barrel of my new gun wrapped around my left hand. On the previous shot, wadding had gotten stuck in the barrel and, when I fired the next time, the percussion blew the barrel open. I was lucky not to lose my hand. The exploding barrel had only missed it by a half-inch, or so. We sawed it off and it became a sawed-off shotgun, which, of course, is even more dangerous.

6
Puppy

One time we had gone into town to the feed store to purchase supplies for the animals. At the front of the store they typically had a cage, made available to people who had a puppy or two that they wanted to give away. They were always cute, but this time the puppy was *really* cute. And the cage always bothered us. We begged our father to let us take it home and he finally gave in. I don't remember what we named him, probably "Puppy," which we usually named our dogs—except for Lady, of course. It was a male, a mixture, probably golden retriever and something else. We got him home and had a great time with him. We didn't have Lady, yet. None of our dogs were ever kept on a leash or in a pen, which was usual for the country. If a dog didn't stay around, it simply didn't last long. As he got older, though, Puppy began to wander. He'd run along with us on bicycle rides to the country store for sweets and sodas. At first he would stay with us, but as he got older he would stray off and finally get home hours later. This never seemed to be a problem, but Dad warned us about Puppy getting in trouble when he wandered.

We had gotten him in the early summer and he had grown to be a big dog—probably seventy-five or eighty pounds—by the time he was a year old. Winter had come, and we would go down to a neighbor's pond and duck hunt. We'd sneak up behind an embankment adjacent to the pond and leap up. It would alarm the ducks—mallards and canvasbacks—and they would take flight, and we'd shoot them and Puppy would jump in to bring them back. He didn't have any training. It just came natural to him. This went on over the winter and was repeated many times. Now and then Puppy would wander down to the pond and Old Man Reiser, who owned it, would see him and shoot at him. He never hit our dog, but it scared Puppy home. The old man would get tame ducklings from the feed store and raise them in the tulles on the edge of the pond. Usually the muskrats got them before they grew up. My brother and I—and Puppy—always left them alone. But this was a bad combination with Puppy in the mix. He was a hunting dog, after all.

Sometimes Reiser would drive up in our yard in his beat-up old red Chevy pickup and stop over by the milk barn and get out and scream and yell at our dad in German. We'd ask Dad what he said, but Dad didn't speak German. Even if he had he wouldn't have been able to understand Reiser with the screaming. The tirade would end just as abruptly as it had begun and he'd just get in his pickup and drive away. But one time dad got through the German and the shouting and told us that Reiser had told him that he thought Puppy was eating his baby ducklings. We had never seen it, but that scared my brother and me, and we vehemently denied that our dog had anything to do with it.

But Dad warned us that he had enough to worry about without having to fret about Reiser and his ducks. About a week later, Reiser came tearing up the driveway in his pickup again, jumped out, and threw a half dozen dead ducklings at my dad's feet. The old man didn't say anything. He just got in his pickup and drove away. We were very quiet, my brother and I, as we did our chores that evening. Dad didn't say anything about it until the next morning.

The next afternoon, another neighbor we knew drove into the yard when we were doing our chores in the early evening and asked where our dad was. We indicated the milk barn, and he went to find him. My brother and I had a bad feeling. Our neighbor was someone who scared us. He was a raging drunk and mean as hell when on a binge. He seemed to be sober, this time, but we could smell the booze. He worked as a day laborer on farms in the area, but couldn't keep a job and Dad would give him work now and then. We had heard his bragging about "shooting things." We hoped it was a coincidence that he had come by, and not about Puppy and the ducks, but Dad must have called him. The neighbor reappeared and asked where Puppy was. Our hearts sank, but we didn't need to answer him because Puppy appeared from behind one of the calf pens near us and ran up to our neighbor to greet him. The man grabbed him by his collar and, pulling a length of rope from his coveralls, took Puppy over to a fence and tied him to it. We couldn't watch. But we couldn't, *not*. The neighbor went to his pickup and got a rifle and came back and shot Puppy between the eyes, while we watched. Then got back in his pickup and drove away. He never said another thing to us. Puppy slumped down, whimpered, and died. My brother and I cried and cried. We couldn't even bring ourselves to cut him loose and bury him until the next morning. My brother and I and my mother (our sister was too little) had a funeral for Puppy and then we buried him at the back of the ranch where nothing would bother him. It took us a long time to get over that. It was just so insensitive, we thought.

And the ducklings kept dying.

7
George's Grocery

A couple of miles from our farm, up by the new school, was an old country store. It was named Capay Grocery, but we called it "George's Store" or "George's." Beside it there was a repair shop and a funky gas station. A man by the name of Arlo Little owned these other two shops. We didn't like him and he had a mean son, a bully. But George was George Bambauer, another German like everyone else. He was a tall, stern man, but fair. After school in good weather, and when we had a little money, we would ride to George's on our bikes and buy a Coke and a candy bar. In those days almost all sodas were sold in glass bottles and the deposit on those bottles—I think three cents—was a very important source of revenue for us kids. We'd scour the roadsides and pester our parents and neighbors for their empties. But, as with most things, it was never enough. We needed a new source of revenue.

Behind George's store was a shed where he kept supplies, for restocking the shelves, and the empty Coke bottles that the delivery truck would pick up every week. Everything was a "Coke," same as "Kleenex" was the name for a tissue. We'd just say "Let's drop by for a 'Coke.'"

I don't remember who it was—maybe my brother or our friend, Richard (who was another story), or even angelic me—but one of us came up with the very intelligent idea of "borrowing" the empty bottles from George's shed, taking them back into the store and turning them in for the three cents. It wasn't stealing, after all. We pulled this off successfully for a couple weeks and were swimming in cash. We'd bought treats we had never imagined.

The day this ended was on a day that only Richard and I had gone to the store after school. The rest of our crowd must have had better things to do, or fate had stepped in. We'd dismounted our bikes in the typical manner in front of the store and headed for our cash machine out back. (I didn't mention earlier that the shed had a padlock on the door but that was only to keep out honest people. We were budding criminals, after all!) Doing the quick math, we grabbed enough empty bottles to cover the costs of our refreshments and marched back around to the front of the store. Immediately upon entering, when our eyes had adjusted to the light, we knew something was wrong, terribly wrong. It was in the air, and in George's eyes. I've mentioned that he was tall and stern, but fair. But, at that moment, I was sure about the tall and stern but not the fair.

While George had been looking at me, Richard had slowly set his bottles on the floor and had bolted for the door and was gone on his bike in a flash. Suddenly, it was just George and me. Although I was much younger, eleven or twelve years old (and quick on my feet like any kid), and he was probably sixty, he was a foot taller than me and probably outweighed me by a hundred pounds. Violence was out of the question, for two reasons: first, he'd kick my ass; and second, my parents, the Pentecostals, would find out and they'd pray for me at church and I'd be on the prayer request list for the Wednesday night service. I wouldn't be able to face my friends. (I'd get that slimy Richard!)

All this went through my head in a flash as George towered over me. "Steve, I'm surprised at you. You're from a good family that I've known all my life. Good Christians," he began. What was interesting, and probably helpful to my case, is that George had remained a Lutheran and not one of those judgmental Pentecostals. "What do you have to say for yourself?" he continued. What could I say? I had seriously considered blaming it all on my brother and friends, since they weren't there, but I realized that notion wouldn't fly because I was standing there holding the evidence. Further, George's next statement iced it.

"For the past couple weeks I've been watching you boys take the bottles out of the shed and turn them in again. I was suspicious about where all of you had suddenly gotten all the cash, and one day I just followed you around back. I slipped back into the store before you saw me." He was pretty stern. Then he said the worst thing: "What do you think I should do?" Oh, brother! Now I had to pick my method of execution!

"George," (remember, we always used first names.) "I'd pretty much do anything to keep this between you and me." George contemplated. I knew he had always liked me and that this had truly shocked and surprised him. I was hoping that that would carry some weight, as any kid would.

To give my parents credit, if they found out about this it wouldn't have been tar-and-feathers or anything physical. They weren't that way. But, to some extent, it would have been worse, because it would have been *sinning*, especially to my Mother. "I am so disappointed in you," she'd have said. "You've sinned to God." And she really believed that. I'm not condoning what we did, but our pranks—especially this one—did not qualify us for the gas chamber. But, to Mom, sinning was worse than that. Hell was nipping at our feet.

But my parents never found out.

After thinking about it, George answered me. "Steve, I'll tell you what. I'll let you pay the money back. I've kept track of it, and you can tell me how long it will take and that's what we'll do. And I won't tell Ruby and Lester. Does that seem fair?" He wouldn't tell my parents. That *was* being fair.

"Thanks, George," I said with my head down. "What about the others?" I asked, referring to my brother and our absent friends and the bastard, Richard.

"Steve, not just because you're the only one of the group that's here right now, but because I know I can trust you to live up to paying the money back..." (He did actually say that, it's not just coming from my selective memory or artistic license or ego.) "You know," he continued, "it's not just the money but the honesty. I'm going to hold you responsible. If you can get your brother and friends to pitch in, so be it. But that's up to you." I told him it would take six months or so, which he agreed to, and we shook hands and I left. I didn't feel very good about myself. As I rode past the school my brother and the other friends, criminals, and the bastard, Richard, were waiting for me.

"What happened? What'd he do?" They wanted to know. "I worked it out. I'll tell you later when I feel like it," I replied. And I rode off, all of them staring at me. They didn't bother me when I was like this. My brother caught up a ways down the road and asked if George was going to tell Mom and Dad. "He didn't say," I lied. We rode in silence the rest of the way. I eventually told him when we got home, but made him promise not to tell the others. "Make them sweat," I said.

I paid the money back in the agreed-upon time, with a few adjustments to the contract, and got some money from my friends to help out. Not what they owed, but some. My brother paid all of his. Extra chores never looked so good. Mom and Dad never found out and my self-respect rose in my eyes. And I could feel the respect in George's gaze when I went to the store and didn't have to sneak around. It was a good lesson. I was still a kid and human and screwed up in other ways, albeit not quite as creative, but it was a good step.

8

The Missionaries

Mom's brother and sister-in-law, who had been missionaries to Ceylon—the sister-in-law who became a lesbian—had several children, all sons. (This was before she announced she had figured out her sexual orientation and that it wasn't what it used to be.) The oldest son, Paul, was a year younger than I and the next, Tim, was a year younger than my brother. The rest of their children, my first cousins, I really didn't know because they were much younger than I—even younger than my sister.

Each summer after they returned to the States, they would visit us on the farm for a few days. I really liked my my uncle, Mom's older brother John, but my Aunt Bonnie who switched orientations was another matter. Big, red-headed and raw-boned she resembled a cartoon character. Her manner of speaking was something like that of Julia Child, but with a baritone or bass resonance. As a kid, you get used to the people you're around and your family members and don't really notice quirks or deviations. Everything is the norm. But, as I got older it became apparent that the Creator had paid a cruel joke on my aunt. Bonnie never really spoke to anyone, she preached. Not in the religious sense, but everything she said was dramatic. (Imagine Edward G. Robinson: "Now, see here, I say!") We never knew what to make of her, but John made up for it. When she came out of the closet it was really no surprise to us kids, and we realized that the marriage and kids were just a cover. We never were able to figure out the missionary thing. Seemed like a little overkill. We thought she had gone a little far.

The oldest kids of this union, Paul and Tim, were polar opposites. Paul was a momma's boy. That's quite a visual, given Bonnie's unusual looks being passed on to a male. Something was always wrong with him, sickness-wise. All of these maladies might have been completely legitimate, but my brother and I didn't think so and we gave him no slack, as kids will. Now, we weren't bullies or anything, but we were farm boys and used to doing heavy labor and, as we got older, we were pretty physically fit. On the other hand, Paul was afraid of everything, including every animal that was more that ten pounds. The rooster chickens scared him to death and would chase him all around the barnyard when we could get them going, and we had our ways. We put him in the pens with the bulls and they'd charge him, but we'd pull him out before they got too close. A couple of times we were a little slow on the trigger. (Oops.)

He thought the little lambs were so cute when we fed the bummers (baby lambs that had lost their mothers). We'd feed them by putting a big rubber nipple on thirty-two-ounce Coke bottles filled with milk and hold the bottles up for them to suckle on. He thought this was great until one of them bit his finger, thinking it was also a nipple. Then he was scared of the lambs.

We had a dairy on the farm and had a milking herd, and the milk was sold commercially as a source of income for the family. In the milk house, next to where the cows were actually milked, there was a large bulk tank where the milk was chilled and held for the trucks that took it to market. It was raw milk, rich in cream, fabulous to drink. Of course we helped ourselves to all we needed in the house, and would fill up large, emptied, gallon-sized mayonnaise jars with milk from the tank and keep a supply in the house refrigerators. It seemed that we would always run out of milk in the house at the most inopportune moments, like at night. Just before bed someone would have to take a jar and go across the yard in the dark—about a hundred and fifty feet—and fill it up for our before-bed snack.

This is where my cousin Paul comes in. It was on one of these milk-less occasions that he and his family happened to be visiting us. I was nominated to go get the milk. Actually, I was the only one in the family who wasn't afraid of the dark, except for my dad, of course. I asked Paul if he wanted to come along. He replied, "Isn't it dark?" (Well hell-yes it was dark, it was night time for cryin' out loud!) But I talked him into going anyway.

We headed out toward the barn and I pointed out the milk house and a yard light that illuminated the building and the door. I told him to go ahead with the bottle and I'd be right behind after I did something. He nervously agreed and went on. I quickly dashed ahead of him in the dark where he couldn't see me, and made my way into the milk house ahead of him. I heard him open the door and enter the building, where the outside light illuminated him somewhat. He was white as a sheet, scared to death. He turned the interior light on, which helped his courage somewhat, and moved toward where the ladle, used to scoop the milk into the bottle, was hanging. As he reached for it, a hand came out of the darkness and gripped his arm. My hand. I thought he was going to die.

He let out such a blood-curdling cry as I've never heard before or since, dropped the glass bottle on the cement floor—where it shattered into a million pieces—and was out the door and running toward the house before I could get out, "Paul, it's me, Steve." No human had ever moved so fast. He ran right through the screen door on the back porch on his way into the house. The wailing and blubbering from inside could be heard from a mile away. It was one of the funniest pranks ever pulled—and I really wasn't much of a prankster—but I knew there'd be hell to pay. Dad came out on the back porch and called my name. When I came out of the dark he couldn't hide a grin but he had to give me what-for to appease my uncle and, especially, the not-yet-converted lesbian. But it was worth every bit of the verbal punishment. And Cousin Paul actually had the last laugh, which I don't think he even planned. It just happened by chance.

I mentioned earlier about the rifle Wilmer had made for me which had become a prized possession of mine. Well, on the morning my aunt and uncle and the cousins were leaving we had been playing cowboys and indians up in the hay in one of the barns. My brother and I had provided all of the weapons, which included toy pistols and holsters, and my prized rifle. Paul had begged and begged me to let him use it in our playing, and I had relented and let him. He told me how neat he thought it was and that he wished he had one. "Yah," I said, "I really like it, too."

Soon we heard my mom and dad calling to let us know that our guests were loading their car to leave and that it was time for the boys to come down from the barn, so we all got down from the hay and headed for the house. Everyone was standing out by the car and saying goodbyes when Paul turned to Uncle John and told him how excited he was about the fact that I was giving him my prized rifle. I couldn't believe my ears! I was dumbfounded! Paul turned toward me and, with a smile, said, "Thank-you so much, Cousin Steve. I will always cherish this." And he patted the rifle and got into the back seat of the car and closed the door.

I wanted to kill him. I turned to my father to plead my case. I hadn't said anything of the sort to Paul, I told him. I had just let him use it while we played in the barn. I said, "You know how much I love that gun and Wilmer made it especially for me. How can you let him take it?" My dad shrugged his shoulders and muttered something about how me giving the gun to Paul made up for the way my brother and I had treated him. Treated him? We gave in to his every whim. We had no choice between my aunt and uncle's catering to my cousin and Mom and Dad knuckling under when they did. I began to object further, and my dad put his hand up to silence me while they drove off. I was livid. This was the last straw. My dad came to me, to console me, but it was no use. I never forgot that episode with my cousin and, to this day, have not ever spoken to him again. And he's been afraid to look at me when we've seen each other at family get-togethers. They lived far away, which helped us remain civil, but he was just a flat-out liar about everything. I should have known.

I know my behavior has been petty. That was years ago and we were only kids. I told Uncle John about it later and he had no idea, which I already knew. He felt terrible, but said Paul had had such a rough time of things over the years that it was probably best just to leave it alone. He was right, of course. But seemingly little things that are insignificant to adults mean so much to kids. It's important to remember that.

9

Preacher's Kids, PKs and Church Camp

Although **Pastor Maude and her husband Speedy didn't have** any children, most of the preachers who came before and after them did. I was pretty little during the ministry of the pastor before these two and don't remember if they had kids or not. But during the later part of the "Reign of Maude" I can remember that we heard rumors about these youngsters and became aware of their particular style and shenanigans. For these young people—these kids—were raised twenty-four-hours-a-day by parent disciples of the flat-earth, six-day-creation society (to these same adults God created the world in six days and then rested on the seventh).

It was hardest on the girls. For the preachers, the fathers were chauvinists and had been wild, hell raisers as kids. But they had been "saved" and there was no way they were going to let some smart-mouth, handsy boy take their girl possession away from them, like they themselves had done to the fathers of the girls they had plundered before they had "found God." They would prevent this no matter what and by whatever tactics it took. And they played with the souls of their children. And there's nothing more powerful than if you never allow the light to come in. We non-preacher's kids had enough trouble dealing with the teachings of the Pentecostal religion as it was, but these poor things couldn't get away from it, even for a minute. I'm sure, even in their sleep, they were tormented by the dreams and nightmares that came out of the incessant judging during their waking hours, much like I was. Restful sleep—very rare as I recall—was a welcome relief from this onslaught, but it was only temporary. And as these kids got older and developed hormones and facial hair and curves in the right places and all that stuff started to take them over, they became like caged lions.

These preachers and their wives—who were really indentured servants—almost became like zoo keepers, raising their children from afar as they grew older, becoming afraid of these youngsters. It's like raising a cute, baby pit bull that grows up to be a man-eating beast. The very ones they had put their version of a godly fence around were turning on them. The danger had gotten too great and for the most part—the inmates were running the prison. These preachers of their gospel had made every attempt to shelter their children from the world, and I quote from the New Testament, the Pentecostal's bible: "Be ye in the world, not of the world." But raging hormones and the devil were reaching closer and closer to their children's souls. Like a pack of wolves, they were becoming less and less afraid of the fire that guarded the prize. Taking closer and closer swipes at the rewards "out there," being more and more willing to suffer touches of pain as they edged ever closer.

The keeper of the fire would surely tire from this onslaught, they thought. It was only a matter of time. And for most of these Preacher's Kids (PKs), the prize was escape from the craziness of their unnatural lives. The preaching of abstinence from absolutely everything that other kids, good kids, were doing—for better or worse—made these things ever more enticing. Earthly punishment was having less effect as they grew older and even the eternal punishment that had been preached to them from birth was losing its sting. The silent prayer of "Just let me be *normal*, one time, Lord…" pounded in their heads. The crossing of the broken glass under their feet, a barrier between them and freedom in the form of Hell and damnation, was now worth it for just one taste.

We witnessed many of these escapes and the wailings of parents. Intercessory prayers were offered up by groups that gathered in the homes. Prayer requests were given at the Wednesday night meetings for these "lost lambs of God." We were asked to pray for them. Pray for everything. If you can't figure it out, pray for it. Even though all that most of these kids ever wanted to do was go to a movie, dance like Fred Astaire and Ginger Rogers, kiss on the lips, date someone they might not marry, and stay out past eleven. But nothing was quite as remarkable as the spectacle they created when the summer came around and they were allowed to go to "CHURCH CAMP."

You were eligible to attend church camp by the time you turned thirteen. I was born in late October and was always one of the youngest, if not the youngest, in my class. Therefore, I had to wait until I was almost fourteen the next summer to attend my first camp. I had lobbied mightily to my parents and church elders to make an exception for me, but to no avail. A year to a teenager who has just received a massive blast of hormones is like an eternity. But I was better for it, you see. (Yah! Sure!)

Camp took place over a two-week period in July of each year. There was the option of staying the full two weeks, or just for one. The first couple years we went (my brother and I always went together) we could only stay for one week as family finances were tight and Dad needed us on the ranch. But the summer before I turned sixteen we were able to attend the full two weeks. Miraculously, somehow we had earned and saved some extra money and Dad had found someone to help around the farm while we were gone. These affairs were held up in the Sierra Nevada mountains of northern California along Battle Creek. I can still see the sign at the turn-off from the highway: "ASSEMBLIES OF GOD BIBLE CAMP." In spite of the ominous name it was really a pretty area, with creeks and meadows; except for the dust, the red, powdery, choking mountain dust.

On the appointed day we'd load up the family car and head north and east. We'd climb and climb on crooked Highway 36, due east, and then north, ever higher and higher until a regular phenomenon would take place at almost the same spot on the road every year: the car would vapor-lock. But before the vapors took over, the car would begin to jerk wildly, like one of the Pentecostals back home.

("Slain under the power" is what they called it.) And this was very funny to my brother and me—as there was never much to do in the back seat and we were dying from the heat—but it wasn't funny to Dad. After a few eruptions from us there in the back, a giant paw would come at my brother and me, waving madly from the front seat. Followed by a loud, "The two of you knock it off!" This sequence would happen a couple times until the car would go no farther and Dad would lurch it off to the side of the road. And it was *only* a thousand feet from the edge of the road to the bottom of the canyon—a fact not lost on my brother who was terribly afraid of heights—but we never died.

Then came the sitting. We would just sit there. It wasn't always this way. The first time this had ever happened, on an older car a few years before, Dad had gotten all fired up and had gone to the trunk to get out his tools, such as they were: a pair of pliers, a crescent wrench, a screwdriver and some baling wire. That combination could fix anything, at least in his mind. "Grumble. Grumble. Can fix anything with these things," he'd announce. Not true. He'd gone to the front and opened the hood to expose the engine. The blast of heat that had come up at us was as though the flames of Hell were approaching. "It's hot as HELL in there!" he'd said. It was okay for a Pentecostal to say Hell in that instance because it was a reference to the place where the cause of all this resided: The Devil. (Hence, "I'm having a devil of a time," I guess.) Flip Wilson's "Geraldine" comes to mind: "the devil made me do it!" Or at least he made the car do it.

"Dear, do you think you can fix it?" my mother would ask.

"I'm trying, dear," Dad replied with mock sensitivity, for he was getting madder by the second. And it got worse from there. For there was nothing he could do but wait, along with all of us. We all got mad at each other and then no one spoke for the next hour. Not even a "Can we go now?" The cause of our problem was that the gas line had been run too close to the engine block and would heat the stuff to a boil, which would make the engine jerk. Dad had informed us that if we would just let the engine cool off he could get the car going again and make a run for it, to our waiting Paradise. It was hard just to sit there, but we had no choice. And after what seemed like an eternity to us kids, even to my parents, Dad got the beast fired up and we made our run for it.

We came around the last corner with the car rattling and spitting, the ASSEMBLIES OF GOD BIBLE CAMP sign came within view, and the devil had taken over again. But he had waited too long and we had been able to again lurch off the road and into the driveway to the camp. Then the car had died, like a trusty old mule that gets you home with its last, dying breath. You would just bury the old mule, but we needed the car to take us the half mile to the camp office. And we had the road blocked to about eight cars behind us that weren't suffering from the vapors—and they were filled with girls and PKs.

But the year I turned sixteen we had a newer car and the vapors didn't have quite the hold on it they had had before. It was a more reasonable wait and then we were able to make it the rest of the way with no incident and pulled up in front of the dusty camp office.

There were teenagers everywhere! Screaming and yelling and running. Most were between the ages of thirteen and sixteen—since most kids escaped the Pentecostal life as they got older—and were out from under their parents' thumbs. It was mostly the younger ones who were making the noise, as one might imagine. The older ones, upon arriving, took up the arduous task of choosing a potential mate, or mates, of the opposite sex to share in the generally unsupervised joys of sinning—at least unsupervised to the degree they were used to back home. And there was no way on earth that enough counselors who guarded this flock were available to keep the devil from entering their midst. And at least half of these wild things were PKs. Need I say more?

The competition was fierce, for it was about a two-to-one ratio of boys to girls. So you had to move fast. Build your plan quickly, and then implement it. But, believe it or not, I was painfully shy. I had not yet kissed a girl other than my mother, except for a painful incident I will explain later. Then I saw her.

We had just bid Mom and Dad farewell—and they had taken off down the driveway to the main highway—when the most beautiful creature I had ever seen in my life appeared before me. A dark-haired, unbelievably well-put-together girl (I should say woman) of about my age. I almost passed out, but didn't. She walked toward me, as if in a dream, and spoke.

"Excuse me. But can you help me? I can't seem to find my counselor and I don't know what to do." At that moment I got religion. Maybe there was a God after all! Now, I had no idea what to tell her or where to tell her to look but I wasn't going to let *her* know that.

I fought back the effects of dry mouth, got my composure together, and spoke. "I think I know where to find her. Come with me." She fell in beside me and we went on our way to I-didn't-know-where. I forgot about my brother. As good luck would have it—or bad depending on how you looked at it—we had no more than rounded the corner of the camp office when we almost ran into a counselor I knew from the year before. He was one of the few cool adults in the camp and we had hit it off. "Hey, Steve, good to see you're back. Who do you have here?" he asked, indicating my new friend while trying to put his tongue back in his mouth. I forgot I didn't know her name. I panicked and kind of mumbled out, "She's looking for her counselor." Now that was impressive on my part, I thought. Damn it. I probably blew it.

"Let me see what I can do, Steve," he said, and took her away from me. She waved back over her shoulder. "Thanks, Steve," she whispered as she was whisked away, by a Man-of-God, no less. I still didn't know her name. Just then my brother walked up.

"What happened?" he asked.

"I'm not sure," I answered.

What a shame. I had gone from the penthouse to the outhouse in a matter of about ninety seconds. Affairs of the heart were so fickle, I thought, so fleeting. Especially for someone like me who couldn't get his foot out of his mouth. Oh, well.

"We better find our cabin." My brother's voice brought me out of my fog.

"Yah, we better," I replied, and we set off through the pine trees.

The "cabins" were wood and canvas structures. The floors, and about four-feet up the walls, were wood planking, with canvas extending the rest of the way up and over the top. They were waterproof, but we fried during the day and froze at night. Even though we were up about four thousand feet, the temperature got into the nineties during the day and down to the low thirties at night. But there was one benefit to the heat during the day: each afternoon we were allowed to go down to Battle Creek and swim. And the girls could come, too, wearing bathing-suits. And bikinis had just been invented.

We unpacked and got our things arranged in the cabin, which we shared with two other guys, a good match, simply by chance. They would later become our valued partners-in-crime. We sat around for a while and talked and compared notes. Our roommates had noticed a few other female candidates beside the goddess, whose favor I was sure I'd lost, but really never did have. They had seen me talking with her.

"Is she your girl?" they had asked.

"Nah, I wish," I told them.

It was late afternoon and we had been told there was a camp meeting at five o'clock to go over the rules and things, and to get everyone acquainted with. There also was an obnoxious loud speaker that just then blurted out that the meeting would start in fifteen minutes. Show time! We sprayed Right Guard under our armpits and slathered Old Spice on our faces, whether we yet shaved or not, and headed for the Tabernacle, joining in with the others from our side of camp. We were all male, because it was boys on one side of camp and girls on the other, but that segregation wouldn't last for long.

There were about two hundred of us who assembled that afternoon. The tabernacle was made of giant logs that had been peeled and placed in the ground, vertically. Massive wooden trusses spanned between them with canvas covering it all and extending down the sides to the ground. It was pretty toasty during the middle of the day, but not bad in the evening. We filed in—much as how the animals would have entered the Ark (Don't get me going. I grew up on a farm. I know what animals eat, and poop!)—two-by-two, boys on one side and girls on the other. That, too, didn't last long. Up front was a stage, but the Pentecostals called it some other name, with a pulpit in the middle for preaching and singing and saving souls, or whatever. Right in front of the pulpit and whatever they called the stage was the altar. It might as well have been the fiery furnace mentioned in the Bible, since almost all of us would spend various lengths of time on our knees in front of it, repenting for real, or imagined, or yet-to-happen, sins—and doing this in alternating states of joy and inconsolable guilt. We were convinced that we'd be burned right there if we didn't confess. Or most were.

She was sitting one row in front of me on the girls' side, on the right side of the aisle about four seats in. I had immediately seen her when we had marched in. You couldn't miss her with that striking dark hair. She was even more beautiful than I remembered. It had only been about two hours since I had first set eyes on her, and our meeting had been so brief. I didn't think she had seen me walk in. But then, why would she? I was sure she had moved on. I stared at her the whole meeting, obscured from her view by a rather heavy girl seated in her line of sight to me.

The "grand jubbah" of the camp, Winston Culp, who ministered in some backwater town over by the Coast greeted the crowd and told us we were going to have a fabulous time over the next two weeks and bring glory to the Lord—we, the future of a God-fearing America. (We'd bring glory all right. Although maybe a little different version than he was referring to.) He went through the rules, the do's and don'ts, and preached a little—which Pentecostals can't resist because they're paid by the soul—and let us go after about an hour. It was time for dinner, which was at six o'clock sharp, each evening.

"Dinner," we called dinner "supper" where I come from. And "lunch" was "dinner," in country-speak. Whatever you called it, each meal in the mess hall became a beauty contest. And you had better have been sitting in the right place, with the right people, especially the first day when most kids didn't know each other. The first dinner time was taken up with, in addition to the eating, scoping—a pretty self-explanatory activity during which you made mental notes of the crowd. What guys you wanted to hang out with and likely female candidates. And what counselors you wanted to get next to, to cover your back, so to speak. And this was important because, for the duration of the camp, you needed a strong coalition with these adults to build a defense against any and all accusations that you had anything to do with the skullduggery that took place. For there were unspeakable shenanigans taking place under the cover of darkness in all corners of our retreat, the domicile known to all, far and wide as the ASSEMBLIES OF GOD BIBLE CAMP. (For cryin' out loud!) Bottom line, if you built a coalition you could get away with almost anything. And it didn't hurt things to have a cousin as your counselor.

Cousin Fred Muster, Minnie and Manuel's boy, was eight years older than I was. Even though he was a Pentecostal he was a real cool guy. Generally these two descriptions are mutually exclusive, but not with him. He was one of the hell raisers I mentioned earlier who had "found God," but he was a straight shooter. He made no bones about the fact that his finding religion had been a life-saver. But he wasn't a fence-rider like so many of the run-of-the-mill Pentecostals. He told you where he stood and you could agree or disagree, your choice. But he hadn't completely forgotten his past and would condone our hell raising as long as we kept it in perspective and didn't let it get out of hand. And to what degree we deviated from the norm was up to him, not us. But we did have a certain amount of influence with him, a certain amount of pull. And, of course, we used that to our advantage. The fact that he could have physically beaten the hell out of all of us didn't really come into play. It really didn't. Just the threat was enough. And he had enough self-confidence to know it.

I had noticed *her* when she made her way into the mess hall, with a couple wannabes following her, the kind that pick out someone they think will get them where they want to go the fastest and then grab-on—basically insecure losers. In this case, they knew there would be a lot of fallout from the "pretenders-to-the-throne." And they'd do just fine with the crumbs, thank you. They sat completely across the building. I didn't think she'd seen me. As dinner was winding down and kids started to move out of the building, I slowly made my way in her direction, trying not to seem too eager. Cool like. What a fraud I was, considering that, at that moment, I might have killed for her affections.

But one thing I'd learned over the years is that in order to be successful in these matters you must make friends with the hangers-on. They're like Secretaries to the Chairman of the Board or, in this case, the Chairwoman. They can make or break your career, or your audience with your real target. As I grew closer too her highness (that's really not a fair title for she was very sweet and unpretentious) the guards began to notice me and put up their defense. They crossed their arms as people will for a "Do Not Approach" signal and began to encircle her. But she noticed me before they finished. Her eyes lit up. My heart raced!

"Hi, Steve, I was hoping I'd see you," she said, and the guards backed off. But, as I said, I had some experience in these matters and, as hard as it was, first spoke to the Captains of the Guard. "Hi, girls, you look pretty tonight." And I gave them a big smile. That had taken everything I had, for these guards were pretty rough and I didn't want to make my real target think I wasn't interested. I've had this situation backfire on me before when I hadn't balanced my affections properly. I immediately turned my gaze toward her and said, "I was hoping to see you, too." She looked me right in the eye and smiled. That did it. The trailer was hooked to the star.

"Would you like to take a walk around and talk a little?" I asked.

"Sure," she answered. Thinking about that still gives me goosebumps.

Her name was Patsy. Patsy Small. She lived farther up in the mountains in an out-of-the-way milltown. Her dad ran the mill. She was of Indian descent, a Native American now, and not a Pentecostal, but curious. Her parents sure must be beautiful people to have a doll like her, I thought to myself. I told her I thought she was really pretty, which was moving pretty fast on my part. She thanked me. We just sat in silence there on a log we had found for quite a while. She had an older brother who was coming to the camp the next day to stay for a week. (Oh! Oh! Trouble!) But she said I'd like him and he'd like me "'cause, I was a nice guy." Well, I'd take that.

It was time for church and I had to change my clothes. It was seven-fifteen and the service started at seven-thirty. I told her I'd see her in a little bit, walked her back to the mess hall and took off running for my cabin. I was on cloud nine. It was hard to look at her, sitting between the guards, from across the tabernacle that night and to not be able to sit beside her. But we made eye contact whenever we could. I was smitten. Her brother came the next day. We got along fine once we had the time to talk privately and he laid down the ground rules for any romance we might contemplate while at camp. We shook on it. I was a farm boy and pretty strong, but his grip was impressive. In a nutshell, his rules were: "You mess with my sister and I'll kill you." Pretty straightforward, I got the point.

At the ASSEMBLIES OF GOD BIBLE CAMP there was a tradition: One boy and one girl were elected by the campers as "King and Queen" of the camp. This happened on the second full day, even though most people hadn't really gotten to know each other that well by then. But the powers-that-be wanted the royalty to have as long a reign as possible so it made sense. The vote was not very scientific, as the counselors didn't know everyone either but, as luck would have it (and I know what you're thinking), my beloved Patsy and I were elected to reign for the duration. Now, Patsy was a clear choice, without question. My selection was somewhat suspect as I was accused of having unduly influenced the voting, which might have had some basis in fact. A sense of urgency might have come over me when it became obvious that Patsy was going to be the choice for the girls. I'll admit I had advance notice of the decision through my inside sources. And I had been seen in the company of the future Queen. Okay, I'll admit it. I said to my Cousin, Fred, "I gotta be King!" and he was a king-maker. But I was a good king, by my own admission, and benevolent to my subjects, as long as they stayed away from my Queen.

But it wasn't long before an erosion to my power began. Even though we didn't walk around with crowns on our heads, everyone knew the Queen and I were an item. I could clearly see how my male subjects would envy me for my relationship with the Queen, but the imperceptible advances at first were becoming more overt. An incident took place that magnified how grave the situation was beginning to be. A couple days after ascending to the throne, my Queen, while sitting on our log with me during a break from the teaching on sinning, came right out and told me that Johnny So-and-So could really play the guitar and that she was very impressed with his musical talent. *And* that he had volunteered to give her lessons. (I bet he had. But in what?!) She wanted to know what I thought. You know what I wanted to say, but I rose above it and said, "I think that's great." She didn't need my permission, after all, but I wasn't benevolent enough to let this twit, whoever he was, make inroads with my Queen—no matter how innocent they were. I sprang into action.

I did have musical talent, and could carry a tune without a water bucket under it. I sang in a quartet back home and we were organizing one to perform for the camp (which never happened). But Patsy had specifically said that this guy's guitar playing had impressed her. So I had to play the guitar for her, but I needed to learn fast, especially since I didn't know how to play. I had plunked around a little on my cousin's instrument, but that's all. An opportunity to make the most out of this situation came when the date of the talent show was announced. Love does funny things to one's common sense. I quickly signed up for a guitar solo in the competition, and immediately told Patsy.

"I didn't know you played the guitar, Steve," she replied.

"Oh, yes," I boasted.

It wasn't but a few moments before I realized that my goose was cooked. I had two days to learn to play the guitar well enough to at least not embarrass myself in front of two hundred people and God and my Queen. Well, in this instance I probably should at least leave God out of this. By my bold actions I had stemmed the tide. The assault on my throne had been dealt with, at least for now.

I was a dead man!! I had jumped out of a plane without a parachute. It was only a matter of time before I hit the ground. But I was already dead.

I practiced on my cousin Dan's guitar, who was at camp with us. He had become a Pentecostal, but was a good guy. He was left-handed, but played a right-handed guitar, upside-down. (Now, *that's* talent.) I never told anyone that I had signed up for the show. That would have been too embarrassing. And they would have used logic to talk me out of it, like: "You must be out of your mind!" The Queen even noticed that I wasn't my old self. I made the excuse that I must have eaten something that didn't agree with me, but it was nice to see her concern. I felt guilty.

The day of the performance came. A summer storm had come through, which was pretty rare in the West, and had made things kinda muddy, but inside the tabernacle we were nice and toasty, and scared to death. At least I was. I didn't think anyone else would have been so stupid to even contemplate what I was about to do, let alone go through with it. But I had no choice. It was my Queen or death, that simple to a not-quite-sixteen-year-old.

The evening had cooled down a lot and a new front had moved in. There were raindrops on our heads as we entered the building, as I entered to await my execution. I wasn't dressed real warmly, but was sweating from head to toe. Boy, I sure hoped no one noticed, but that was the least of my problems. Brother Culp opened with prayer and we sang a couple hymns and he saved a couple souls and then he asked everyone performing that night to come up on stage. I had somehow been able to get Dan's guitar inside the building without him noticing—he wasn't in the show—and with a small detour grabbed it on my way to the stage, leaving my brother and Dan and my new friends with their mouths agape, muttering under their collective breaths, "What the hell is he doing?" You can imagine what it was like when I took my seat with the rest. I first picked my Queen out of the crowd, her face radiant with pride, but made every attempt to avert the gaze of the rest of my subjects, and I couldn't even venture a look at my brother and Dan or my cronies. It was pure hell. The clock was ticking toward the very-soon end of my life as I knew it.

After we were all seated up there and had gotten our things together, the brother introduced us one by one, mentioning the instrument we would be playing and the tune that would go with it. By the time he got to me, I had lost my mind. I didn't even know where I was. One by one, six other kids did their performances and there were two in front of me before it was my turn. That's when the heavens opened. Hail began to fall so heavily that within a couple minutes you couldn't hear anything. The roof had begun to sag under the weight and was in danger of collapsing, and all the counselors were trying to shout over the noise, trying to tell us to get out of the building. The thunder and lightning was incredible. Well, I'll tell you what: I got out of that building so fast it was unbelievable. I even forgot about my Queen. I don't think it was really dangerous, but the adults were taking no chances. I found her almost immediately as we ran for the mess hall, like everyone else. I grabbed her arm and held on as we ran.

It really wasn't that far, probably two hundred feet, but it seemed farther under those circumstances. Once inside, and after we had gotten our wet coats off, we finally spoke. Patsy spoke first.

"I am *so* disappointed that I didn't hear you play. I hope they reschedule things. I want to hear you play."

That wasn't exactly my feelings but I replied, "Yah, I hope so." They never resumed things that night and never rescheduled. Go figure that out. I know I certainly didn't deserve that reprieve, but I took it.

Johnny So-and-So was never heard from again. Especially after I hit the game-winning home run the next day in the annual contest against the guys from the Civilian Conservation Corps that had a camp four or five miles across the meadow from ours (I really did. You can ask my brother). "The Criminals" we called them.

As I rounded the bases, she was cheering at the top of her lungs. For a moment, I forgot about everything—the talent show debacle, everything—and just enjoyed what was happening, my gaze fixed on her. You can imagine the conversation among us boys in the tent that night as we gathered to discuss the day's events. "Hey, about the talent show last night, what were you thinking?!" God works in wondrous and mysterious ways.

Patsy had become the love of my life and for the rest of the time at camp we were inseparable. It was brutally painful to say goodbye, for I think deep down we knew we would never see each other again, some intuition. We were from different worlds and cultures. But for fourteen days it was bliss, even the bad times. I never attended church camp again. I was beginning to more strenuously question this religion and the maturing process had taken me away from that type of event. My Queen and I sincerely promised to write each other and we did a couple times, but then the letters eventually stopped from both ends.

The next summer my family took a vacation to my aunt and uncle's dairy in southern Oregon and, on the way home, I talked them into taking a detour to see her. I had tried to get hold of her by telephone before we left on the trip, but to no avail. And when we got to her place she wasn't home. Her mother said she didn't know where she was, as if she didn't live there anymore. She didn't know who I was and appeared to be reluctant to talk. That hurt a little. I couldn't believe Patsy hadn't told her about me. I sure had told my parents. There must have been something going on in her family that she never told me about. Looking back, I realized that I had felt it from her brother and, thinking about it now, there was a sadness about her at camp the year before. But for two glorious weeks we were royalty. And nothing on this earth could ever take that away from the two of us.

There's more about this camp I'd like to tell and maybe I can get to it later on, if you care to hear about it. Good and funny stuff. After all, I never did get around to the shenanigans the PKs pulled or the invasion by the hoodlums-in-a-car that we thwarted. But, for now,

I just want to sit and think about my short romance, like Patsy and I did on our favorite log back then, more than forty years ago, and shed a tear or two for my youth. I was lucky to have it.

10

Mrs. Roberts and Depression Cookies

When I was old enough, I was sent to the Capay Elementary School. It was located at the north end of the farming community we lived in, about five miles from our farm. I was not yet six years of age, since my birthday was in late October, as I've mentioned before. The age cutoff for first grade was December 1, which really didn't mean much. I don't think my parents really thought about my age. My birthday was before the cutoff, so I went. But, as I've mentioned earlier, I was always one of the youngest—if not the youngest—in my classes. That was pretty rough until I was twenty-one, which is the age that really matters after all. (It's kinda' fun that now, when I go to class reunions, I'm always younger than my former Classmates. Old farts!)

School for me, and for all of the kids in the community, started with the first grade. There was no kindergarten. I have an eleven-year-old daughter who started formal schooling at the age of four in pre-kindergarten. She's now in the fifth grade and is probably learning things I wasn't taught until the eighth or ninth grades—or later—or if at all. But that's the way it was for me in the country, and that's okay. I've somehow made it, and was able to buy the laptop I'm writing this with, so I guess I survived without kindergarten.

The first day of school was quite a scene, what with my mother's blubbering and my blubbering—and that was just over losing my pacifier under the bus. I think most mothers go through the same emotions when their kids go to school the first day. And I was the eldest, so Mom had never experienced it before. I cried some, I recall, but it was as much about the bus driver as anything else, Old Man Carpenter, who had a mean look. He had driven the bus for thirty-five years and had hauled every one of my Mom's siblings, including her, to school over the years, but he scared me. I hadn't been out much—maybe that's why he made me cry—but we finally got me on and the door closed and we were on our way. My mom couldn't leave my brother alone while she took me to school the first day—since my dad was milking the cows and she was too nervous to take him along—but she picked me up after school.

The school consisted of three classrooms with cloak closets where we put our coats and things, a cafeteria, and a dining room. A main office and restrooms made up the rest of the school. There were three grades: Mrs. Stanley taught the first, Mrs. Gardner the second, and Mrs. Roberts the third. The school grounds consisted of the main building I mentioned and a big dirt playground with a baseball diamond, which was surrounded by huge eucalyptus trees. It probably covered four acres. Most of the boys played in the trees and that's where we made our hideouts, with no girls allowed. Some of us played a little baseball on the diamond.

Mrs. Stanley was the first grade teacher. A tall, white-haired, regal-looking lady and very proper, she called her husband "Mr. Stanley," a practice which was new to us. Even when we heard her address him in person—which only happened a couple times when we kids were around—she would still call him, very formally, Mr. Stanley. But she was a good teacher.

There were fourteen of us. We all were a little scared of her because of her manner, but I think it helped with our studies. There wasn't any cutting-up in her classroom. She had taught my mom and all my aunts and uncles. It was the same with several of my other classmates. The curriculum was pretty straight forward with the "Three Rs" and all, nothing fancy, but this is where I did meet my first girl friend—but she didn't know she was. (She'll probably chuckle if she reads this.) Her name was Sharon. Sharon Ball and she had a brother named Pepper. Really. "Pepper Ball." His real name was Charles, like his father, but we called him Pepper. At Christmas, I wanted to give Sharon something as a token of my affection. It was an old rusty knife I had found out in the trees by our fort. She pretended to like it.

I saw her parents at an "Old Timers" get-together a couple years ago out at the new, old school on the county line where all the kids in my class attended beginning with sixth grade. Her dad looked surprised when he saw me. I hadn't seen him in thirty years. He said I was "all grown-up." I hadn't meant to grow up, I told him, and that I was as surprised as he was about it all. Her parents looked good. They said Sharon and her husband and two boys lived in a beautiful area down near Santa Barbara. One of her boys was in the Dodgers Triple-A Farm System. It would be fun to see her sometime and meet her husband. (It's okay with my wife. She's heard the story.)

There's one other thing about first grade. Shortly before the end of the school year, Mrs. Stanley very sternly told me that she wouldn't pass me on to second grade if I didn't learn to tie my shoelaces. Well now, that scared me. She had told me that on a Friday and when I came back on Monday I proudly showed her my new shoe-tying skills. I was the only kid who hadn't known how—or so I found out later—but you know how kids are.

Mrs. Gardner was my teacher for second grade, when we were seventeen strong. I remember the least about her. She was somewhat unremarkable, I suppose. As with Mrs. Stanley, she always referred to her husband as, "Mr. Gardner." Not "my husband" or anything, just "Mr. Gardner." But, unlike Mr. Stanley, we never met Mr. Gardner. At least I don't remember ever having done so. Maybe later I did, but I don't think so. She and her husband lived up at the north end of Fifth Avenue, just east of Sixth. Up by Ramo Alberico's place. He was one of the three Alberico brothers. There was Aldo, Beans, and then Ramo. Best farmers in the area. Italians. Maybe the reason I don't remember as much about Mrs. Gardner as I do about Mrs. Stanley is because you really learned a lot in the first grade. You came in with your head empty and that's where you began to fill it up with knowledge. And in this instance, second grade was more like a bridge from Mrs. Stanley to MRS. ROBERTS.

Mrs. Roberts was my third grade teacher. If you wanted to learn, she was your man! If not, you were left behind. That wouldn't work today, unfortunately, but it sure did then. Today she'd surely be Chairman of IBM or something. She was probably in her late fifties, trim and fit. Whatever you learned before you met her was but a precursor to what she was going to teach you. In my opinion, this was one of the most thorough educations anyone could have had during the five-year period that I was her student. She graduated each year I did, from the third through the seventh grade. And I was immensely better for it.

She was married to Mr. Roberts and used the same formal reference to her spouse as the other teachers did: "Mr. Roberts" this and "Mr. Roberts" that. We never met him, either. The two of them weren't able to have children and had adopted a boy about four years older than me whom they named Keith. We never really knew each other as kids but got more acquainted as adults. He was a good guy. Her first name was Nell—I guess short for Nellie—and all the adults called her that, but it was the first time in our short lives that we had heard one of our teachers called by their first name. Mrs. Stanley was always "Mrs. Stanley" to children and adults alike as was Mrs. Gardner, but not Mrs. Roberts. She was "Nell" to our parents, and we liked that for some reason. Her mother was still alive and she referred to her as "Mrs. Huvey," not "Mother" or "Mom." While studing with Mrs. Roberts, there were twenty-five students in the class.

The seats in the classroom were of the old type: a desk with a lid that opened, an inkwell, and an attached chair. We didn't use the inkwell, of course. The desks were arranged in five rows of five seats each. And, every Friday, we had our tests and the student with the best grades sat in the first seat in the first row to Mrs. Roberts's right and so on, all the way to the last seat in the fifth row. You didn't want to be in that last seat, but we didn't need to worry because of Darrell, whom we called "Grandpa." He had spent three years in the first grade and therefore was a lot older than the rest of us and about a foot taller. Graduating along each year with Nell and me and the rest of the class, he occupied that seat for five straight years—a record I don't believe has ever been broken. It became kind of like a home to him. He never flunked again. They just kept moving him along, but he never got out of that seat.

Mrs. Roberts taught us the names of all the wildflowers in the area, the native and imported trees, and the names of all the horse breeds found in North America. I don't know why the horses, but it was interesting.

There usually were the same four girls in the first three seats. Nicki always in the first, which I don't recall she ever relinquished, Carol in the second most of the time, and either Greta or Sharon in the third. Now and then some other girl would make a run at those three, but no one ever dislodged Nicki. She was the smartest girl I had ever known. So smart she intimidated most of us.

Of the twenty-five students in the class, nineteen of us graduated together from the eighth grade, and Nicki remained the smartest. I wasn't one to raise my hand in Mrs. Roberts's class, but if you waited long enough you could usually get the answer from something Nicki said or asked. Mrs. Roberts loved Nicki's intelligence. What's interesting is that for high school the eighth grade class was almost split in half by the county line that, ironically, ran almost right through the middle of the school grounds, with about half of the kids on the north side going to one high school and the ones on the south going to another. Or, maybe it had been planned by the adults to divide us!

Nicki and I were two who went to different high schools and I hadn't seen her in, maybe, fifteen years when one day I ran into her. We were building some houses in the town where she had gone to high school and I had dropped into a convenience store to get some sodas for the crew. I was standing in the checkout line when I noticed her at the cash register and realized who it was. When I got to the front of the line I introduced myself. She appeared embarrassed, but was very friendly. I guess she seemed embarrassed to have me see her working there. It was no affair of mine, but she said she had gotten pregnant right out of high school and couldn't go to college and was now divorced with three kids. "You poor thing," I thought. With all that intelligence I didn't expect to find her in this job, but we need cashiers, too. I said it was great to see her and went on my way. I've never seen her again.

By the time we were finished with Mrs. Roberts at the end of the seventh grade, we had learned Algebra, Spanish, and the poet authors of "The Classics." We had memorized all of the Presidents, knew each state and its capital, and knew all of the signers of the Declaration of Independence. We had read Ralph Waldo Emerson, "The Children's Hour" by Henry Wadsworth Longfellow, and Henry David Thoreau. We had studied the 1930s Dust Bowl in the Midwest that spawned such writers as John Steinbeck and F. Scott Fitzgerald, could name all of the Indian Tribes West of the Mississippi, and had taken a field trip to watch the counting of the upstream run of salmon at Shasta Dam. From the fifth grade we had read a book every two weeks that was completely unrelated to anything we were doing in class and had written and turned in a two-page summary of each, all of which she read, and much, much more. It was, literally, incredible. And I've thanked her a million times in my head for what she gave me. There's not a passing day when I don't use something, some piece of knowledge, that came from her teachings.

Periodically over the years I've run into former classmates and they all feel the same. What a legacy Mrs. Roberts has passed on. She lived into her mid-nineties and was lucid until the end. I had the good fortune to have seen her about ten years before she passed and told her what she meant to me. She was very pleased to be remembered after all those years.

*****

By the sixth grade, my interest in girls was moving along somewhat. But it still took a backseat to my love of sports. And, in the sixth grade, a new girl by the name of Mary enrolled in our class. She and her family had moved to our community and purchased a sheep ranch that her father ran. Maybe it was because she was new, but we kind of hit it off and I wrote her name on the inside of my baseball glove, in a place only I could see, unless I wanted to show it to someone. Sharon was still my main squeeze, but as I look back I don't think I ever made much of an indication of that. Even when I saw Sharon in her late-teens and early-twenties my heart rate would speed up a bit, but we just never made a connection.

Maybe one of the reasons why we never got together is that, as a teenager I invited her to our Pentecostal Church one Sunday morning. She attended the Friends Community Church, up past the school, which we were told was kind of like the Quakers. But we didn't notice that they were any different than regular people. There were no bonnets or old-style dresses that we could see. The service she attended with me, this pretty and sweet blonde girl that I proudly sat next to in the back pew, was especially violent. I don't know if it was because there was a newcomer in the crowd and they were showing off, or what, but it was in the top five most violent of all time. People were speaking in tongues, interrupting each other, jumping up and down with their hands in the air, wailing and screaming and falling down in the aisle—"slain under the power." It was total mayhem. The only thing we lacked was Brother Seamans. That would have shot it to number one. She never came back with me. No one ever did after sitting through one of those services, any service. It was embarrassing to see her later on. What could I say to her? It wasn't the Lord as far as I'm concerned. He's too good a guy in my book. I saw her from time to time after that, but she went to the other high school. She got married like I would, in her mid-twenties, and moved away. It wasn't meant to be.

In the sixth grade, we also moved into a new school. The one I mentioned earlier that was divided by the County Line. For the first three years we had attended the Capay Elementary School as I've said, and then moved four or five miles across the countryside to Macintosh School for grades four through eight. The area we lived in, which was about one hundred miles north of Sacramento, had originally been made up of Spanish Land Grants from the 1840s. The Capay Rancho and Macintosh Rancho were the ones that surrounded or made up our community. Over the years these lands had been divided up into working farms and ranches, especially after the war with Mexico, the Bear Flag Revolt, and California having declared its independence and becoming a state in 1850.

I attended Macintosh for two years, fourth and fifth grades. Mrs. Roberts followed me. My brother never did attend it, as he was two grades behind me and went right from the Capay School into the new one on the County Line. Of the three grammar schools I attended, Macintosh was the coolest. It resembled a Spanish Mission and was surrounded by even more massive eucalyptus trees, even better for our forts. My cousin, Fred (the eventual camp counselor), had attended the school several years before and had uncovered a Civil War-era revolver in the dirt under one of the trees and had cleaned it up by soaking it in solvents and diesel oil. We always thought that was pretty neat. We made up stories about it. He traded it later for an old shotgun. None of us had much of a concept for the value of old stuff.

Macintosh was about a mile and a half to the northeast of our farm. And I walked or rode my bike to school. But, by walking, I could shorten the distance about a half-mile by cutting across Old Man Reiser's place, past the pond. Reiser didn't take very good care of his fences and his cows were always getting out on the road or into our place. Everyone complained about it, so he'd put up an electric fence system to encircle his property. This worked out okay for a while, but the big animals would lean against the wires to graze on the other side of the fence and the low voltage current wasn't enough to deter them. So they'd start getting out again, and there were more complaints. So he put up a direct current, one-hundred-ten-volt system, like you would have coming to the outlets in your house. It would shock the hell out of you if you happened to touch it, which we did before we realized what he had done. And if the grass or soil beneath your feet was wet, it really got you. But we worked out a system of getting over or under the wires. The single wire was attached by glass insulators to either wooden or metal posts, and ran along the inside of the regular fencing. We found places adjacent to our property where the grade allowed us to get a running start and then jump over. In other places, the grade under the wire was such that we could crawl through.

In the fields that it was necessary to cross to get to school, Reiser kept his bulls—dairy bulls. To the uninitiated, there are mean bulls and there are tame bulls. Dairy bulls are mean as hell for some reason. These are breeds like Holstein, Guernsey, and Jersey. In my experience the Jersey bulls were the worst. And we had some. The tame bulls are mostly all of the beef bulls, like Angus, Hereford, and Charolais. I don't know why the distinction. Reiser's bulls were Jerseys, so to cross this pasture to get to school the short way, you needed a plan.

The first thing I did when approaching the fence from our side was to look to see where the bulls were. There were four or five and the field covered about forty acres. That determined where I jumped across. Once that was determined, I plotted my course to avoid the animals, until they noticed me. Then I was off, over or under the fence and running like hell, my lunch pail banging against my thigh, and checking out of the corner of my eye to see if the bulls had noticed me. It was about a fifty-fifty proposition. But, even if they saw me, I usually made it safely across, as long as I hit the right spot in the fence on the other side so I could slide through under the wire without getting shocked. Well, of course I made it across without getting killed or something, or you wouldn't be reading this, but "safely" was a two-part proposition: avoiding the bulls and avoiding the wire. You could make it safely through the field and then get shocked all to hell from the combination of the wet grass and scraping your back on the electric wire.

Once I was shocked badly enough that it brought my teeth together so violently—with my tongue in the way—that I almost bit the thing off, but I didn't die. Ignorance is bliss. I couldn't imagine kids doing that—or being allowed to do that—today. These episodes hastened the repairing of my bicycle to allow me to ride on the paved roads, and on a more permanent basis, for obvious reasons. The problem with the bike is that there were "puncture vines" that had unbelievably nasty thorns on them which could penetrate anything, especially bike tires. And if you got off the pavement in the late spring, summer, or early fall when they had really dried out it was a disaster. And if you ever stepped on one barefooted—which is what most of us always were when not in school—it was almost unbearable pain, resulting in hopping around and screaming, typically. Thank God someone finally invented the stuff you could put in bicycle tubes to stop the leaks; that changed my life. No more bulls.

We finally put an end to Reiser's direct current electric fences. We took a pair of bolt cutters with handles about two feet long—so we wouldn't have to get close to the wires—and attached heavy rubber covers to these handles which completely encased them so that no metal was exposed. And then we could cut his electric wire without getting shocked, which we did. He'd fix the breaks, and we'd do it again. He'd come up in our barnyard like before and scream and yell. We'd do it again, and he'd do it again. But finally he tired of the exercise. He sold his cattle and moved to town. We showed him. (Yah, right!)

*****

At Macintosh school I always brought my lunch from home. I don't remember much about the school kitchen or cafeteria, but I was happy with my lunch box and my Buck Rogers decal, and hot chocolate at recess out under the giant trees in our fort. But that all began to change when, at the beginning of the sixth grade, we moved into the new school. It was all bright and shiny, as you could imagine, with all the newest bells and whistles. It had a real gymnasium with basketball hoops at each end, which was turned into a cafeteria for lunch by folding down long tables and benches that were stored in receptacles in the walls.

I even remember the name of the contractor that built the school: Jake Funk. We thought it was a funny name, but we were told he was the best builder of schools. "Old Jake Funk," that's what Dad called him. Dad didn't like him. Dad was on the school board, along with

Sharon and Pepper's dad, Charley, among others, and he said that Old Jake Funk was a cheat. That he had tried to get more money out of the school district when he was done, blaming "change orders." In my later career, I learned about change orders from the other side. I never did hear Old Jake's version. But, back then, I was just a kid.

The new school had a spic-and-span kitchen, and two full-time cooks. (Man-o-man, that was neat.) And they made all the dishes and cakes and pies we never had at home, due to our limited resources and the lack of a commercial kitchen, like most people. And every kid wanted to eat "hot lunch" as they called it, but my brother and I couldn't, because it cost twenty-five cents. The upper-crust kids could, but not us. We brought our lunches in brown paper bags, not the lunch pails like fifth grade—which was a bit more cool—but it still wasn't hot lunch. And our bags weren't the "right ones" that the upper-crust kids might have brought, for they had bags that were specifically made for lunches. Ours were old grocery bags from Purity Grocers, Safeway and others. But I want to give my Mother credit. She did pack a mean lunch, as if it was a "Day of Pentecost" Lunch, much in demand and coveted, but only for the "chosen" (sic).

A typical packed lunch went like this: For the sandwich, we'd have a fried beef patty which she would wrap in wax paper and then foil. Then she'd take a slice of tomato, sliced dill pickle, and lettuce, and wrap it up the same way. She'd take two empty glass baby food bottles and fill one with mayonnaise and one with catsup, and sometimes a third one with French's mustard, if we were flush. She'd put two slices of white Wonder Bread in wax paper, and we'd have the makings of our sandwich that we'd put together at lunch. This method kept it from getting soggy by the time we ate it. We'd usually have a banana or an orange and, if we were really lucky, some sort of chips, admittedly, not bad so far. Then, for dessert, we'd have two "Depression Cookies."

These treats were what their name implies, having been discovered in a cave during the Great Depression, like the Dead Sea Scrolls. They were actually powdered sugar and water mixed together to form a paste, which was slathered on one graham cracker and then again on another, which was pressed onto the first one to form a sandwich. They actually were pretty good. We didn't have store-bought pastries and cookies very often. My mother wasn't much of a cook, which she'd admit, but she was a mean baker, she made cakes from scratch in those days, and she made the most of what she had to work with.

I heard rumors that there were those within my class that had taken a fancy to the Depression Cookies. I had shared them from time to time, and it appeared that it had whetted some of their appetites for them. A few names of those rumored to be coveting my cookies had been mentioned, but nothing I could prove.

One lunchtime, during the fall of sixth grade, we were all in the cafeteria doing our thing—the snooty ones with their hot meals—when I finished the main courses of my meal and was going for the dessert in my brown bag. It was at this time that Carol, one of my classmates who was seated directly across the table from me asked, "Steve, do you have any of *those* cookies in there? I'll trade you my dessert for one." She had been one of those mentioned in the gossip. (Just to set this up a little, sitting next to Carol were Mary, the new girl whose name was now on the inside of my glove; Nicki, of the high-intelligence; and Sharon, my never-told main squeeze. I would have given everything I had to any one of those three, in varying degrees of course, but now I was being asked to share by the least likely candidate of all, for Carol was not an attractive gal, but she tried really hard. And, as a result, was really pushy.) Before I could answer, she grabbed my lunch bag and reached in and pulled out one of the cookies. Then she shoved her tray across the table with her uneaten dessert in plain site. It was chocolate pudding—which I really liked so it wasn't going to be a bad trade—but I still wished it would have been one of the others who had offered. "Oh, thank you, Steve," said Carol in appreciation, but what she said next froze me in my tracks!

"This makes me want to just kiss you!" Oh my God, I thought to myself. Why couldn't this just be one of the others? For them I would have puckered up immediately, even though I was still pretty shy.

"Not now, Carol," I responded authoritatively and whispered to Richard, the bastard, who was sitting next to me, "We've got to get out of here! Meet me outside."

"I need to use the restroom before noon recess," I told Carol and started to get up.

"Just let me kiss you before we go out." Boy, she was persistent.

"No, Carol, I've gotta go!" And, with that, I was able to slip out of my seat and walk briskly to the restrooms. On my way, I nodded to Richard and mouthed, "Wait outside and guard the door." When I came out of the bathroom and started heading for the doors to the outside, Richard was standing there and told me not to worry, that Carol had taken off to the other side of the playground with her friends, seemingly having forgotten about the kissing. What a relief. The two of us walked out the door to the playground, but I hadn't moved more than ten feet away onto our playground when Carol and her minions came out of nowhere with her, screeching, "Now, I can kiss you!!" and a thousand hands grabbed me and tried to pin me down.

I was stronger and quicker than they estimated and I broke free, heading for the backstop of the baseball field that was on the far side of the playground. If I could just make it around the back of the field I might be able to get to the trees and up into the safety of the fort. I was running as fast as I could. (Imagine the movie *Chariots of Fire*.) Carol was right on my fanny, and gaining. At that age, girls are still more developed than boys and she was faster than I remembered. And, right behind her, were all my *former* friends who had double-crossed me, and the good-looking girls, too. The rest of the kids on the playground didn't even notice. Kids always were running after each other.

The backstop was looming up ahead. I was gonna make it. I was directly even with it and turning for the trees. But I cut my angle too sharply and my feet went out from under me. Carol was on me like a cheap suit, and the others were there, too. There were just too many of them and they kept me pinned to the ground. It was pure hell, and Carol loomed over me with the most insidious look on her face that

I had ever seen in someone.

"Now I'm gonna kiss you," she said, very quietly, very self-assured. She could be that way with a hundred arms pinning me down. I squirmed, but it was no use. I was a goner. She put her hands on her hips. She wasn't a big girl, but staring down at me she looked like it as she briefly stood over me, taking in her prize. Then slowly, ever so slowly, she squatted down and began to lean over me, her hands on my immobile chest. All the while she was pursing and licking her lips, making them ready for the kill. My poor little life began to pass before me. I wondered if my parents or my brother and sister would miss me. They surely would, I hoped. I wondered if I could get a message to them, but it was too late.

As I had gotten older I had daydreamed about my first kiss, as most youngsters do. But in those dreams it was always one of my pretty classmates or someone like that doing the kissing. Now I was merely seconds away from having my virgin lips violated by Carol Chandler, the least likely of candidates. No sooner had it started, than it was all over, but it took me a long time to get over that. I headed to the fort up in the trees to lick my wounds, my friends in tow.

Oh, I wanted to be mad at them, and I was, but it didn't last. They had just been used, like most of us, in a sad attempt to gain favor with the women, a pursuit that lasts a lifetime for most of us.

II

The Fort

I just referred to "the fort" in my last, sad tale. Every kid out in the country had one, of some sort or another. We were no exception, but what was neat about this one is that it was on the school grounds. We had other forts at home, but we could play in this one at recess.

It was an elite group who were allowed to be members of the club that occupied the fort. Our sixth grade class was now twenty. Let's say half were girls, so that left ten of us boys. Two of our classmates were automatically eliminated. Darrell (Grandpa) was eliminated because he was so goofy and clumsy and tall that he really couldn't fit and would probably fall out. And Lawrence. Lawrence Self. You can imagine his nicknames. We'd crack ourselves up. He was a little, mealy-mouthed runt with no teeth who tattled on everyone. He made such a stink about not being included that we made him our "Sentry on the Ground," but he was never allowed up into the fort. He kept a lookout for the girls. The adults never bothered us. I mentioned that the earlier schools had eucalyptus trees, and our new school was no exception. Although these trees were younger and had suffered from a severe frost several years before, they had been cut down to their stumps and had grown back bushier, with several trunks growing out of the same old stumps. This made an excellent base for our tree houses—our forts.

We would nail two-by-fours on edge into the trunks and build a rough rectangular base between them and cover it with old plywood that we got from wherever. We did this in three trees, which we then hooked together with a sort of cat walk. Then we built some walls out of two-by-fours, again, and put a makeshift roof over things. We found some clear plastic somewhere and enclosed things for the winter, which made it pretty toasty. Since most of the school year was in cooler weather we didn't need air conditioning. Then we made a rope ladder that we could pull up once all of us were inside, so it was pretty secure. The only thing that was really troublesome to us was the Black Widow spiders. The first year they didn't bother us because we built the fort in the fall when it was cooler and they weren't out and about. But, over the summer before our second year, they had taken over the place. Most of us had grown up around them and we'd learned how to deal with the critters, after all, our dry, hot weather suited them to a tee. I know it sounds sick, but I like spiders. I surely didn't want to get bitten by one—which I was, later on as an adult when I had let my guard down—but if you took the proper precautions you were alright. So, by default, I was elected to rid the place of the Widows.

I had a secret weapon. It worked very well if you weren't up in the hay barns or in dry grass, but our fort and the trees were okay. I would "borrow" a can of hair spray from my mother's stash and get a book of matches from somewhere and make a crude, but effective, torch. I'd open up a couple of the clear plastic flaps and aim my machine at a nest of Widows, push my finger down on the nozzle, put a match in front of the spray and let-her-rip. Fire would bolt across the inside of the place and zap the critters. It literally worked every time—over and over until all the Black Widows I had found were gone. A few burn marks were left behind, but the inside was no worse for wear. That exercise usually happened a couple days before school started, while my other club members would wait on the ground. It was a ritual that couldn't be missed under fear of expulsion, and once I gave the all-clear signal they would climb the rope to join me. Let the games begin!

12

Speedy's Funeral

I've discussed **Maude and Speedy in my story. Once** I graduated from High School and got on with my higher education I completely lost contact with them. Not that I had ever had much—even while they tended to our flock—but they had pretty much left my memory. The long tentacles of the Pentecostals would reach out to me from time to time, but I was moving further and further, almost completely away from them—as far as anyone with my childhood ever does.

So it was with definite surprise that I received a call from my mother in the early 1980s informing me that Speedy had died and the family had asked me to be one of the pallbearers. That he had died wasn't what was surprising, since I thought he was old when I first met him. It wouldn't have surprised me if I had been told that he had died many years before, because he and Maude were so completely out of my life. During the phone conversation with my mom I asked about Maude, and she told me that our former pastor had indeed died several years before. I wasn't asked to be one of her pallbearers. And we had teased Speedy so, both overtly and covertly, that I would have placed myself near the bottom of any list that would have had me part of this solemn occasion. But I said "Yes, I'd be glad to."

The funeral was in the town of Red Bluff at the north end of the Sacramento Valley, along the Sacramento River. My dad had also been asked to be a pallbearer, which was much more logical. We sat through the service and—once it was over—made our way outside. As one might imagine, I saw many people from my old Pentecostal days and the conversations with them were generally light-hearted and pleasant in nature, which relaxed my fears somewhat. Once the mourners had left the building and gathered outside in front of the chapel we, the pallbearers, were instructed to return to the sanctuary and bring Speedy outside and place him and his casket in the hearse. The family members were placed in a limousine that would follow the hearse and the pallbearers would follow in a third limo. I was standing fairly close to the funeral director while this was going on, and after the family's limo had moved away from the curb he turned to me and asked if I would drive the limousine that would carry us to the cemetery since, apparently, the appropriate driver was not available. I said that I would.

So there we were. I was the limo driver carrying Gaylord Enns, Tom Kalb, Milton Ollenberger, my dad, and some guy I didn't know, to bury Speedy. I was in the company of four Pentecostals from my past, and a guy I didn't know—who I found out later also was a Pentecostal. So, once again, I was in the company of these people, my dad not withstanding. But it would be safe to say that all of those who had gathered were of the same mind. It was in the air. At the obligatory gathering after the internment to eat and talk, it was assumed—because of my being there and having been given such an important task in driving the pallbearers—that I was one of *them*. I quickly dispelled that notion and got the hell out of there. Whoever runs life certainly appears to have a sense of humor.

13

Grandpa Gottschalk

I've mentioned my grandpa (Papa)—my mother's father— previously, the hard-headed German who was married to Grandma—my mother's mother who was a saint, as I've also mentioned before.

Grandpa, Phillip Gottschalk, of German descent, was born in 1880 in what is now modern-day Albania. In the early 1890s, Czar Alexander III of Russia was offering free land to German farmers, who were thought of as being very productive people. He specifically offered it to those willing to emigrate and settle in the Western Steppes Region of the Ukraine, on this potentially very productive farmland. The Russian people were suffering from a lack of food due to poor farming practices, and the Czar was becoming more and more preoccupied with civil unrest within his country.

The Russian leader was subscripting the young men into the military, leaving fewer and fewer to work the fields. This unrest was being exacerbated by the lack of food and this offer, in part, was an attempt to mitigate that situation. My great-grandfather, Frederick, accepted the offer and moved his family to the Western Steppes Region, south of the capital city of Kiev, traveling through Macedonia, Bulgaria, and Romania on the way. The information that I have is about my grandfather and his older brother, Frederick II—"Uncle Fred." There are other siblings who appear in old photographs of my grandfather's family and which my wife and I have on the walls of our home, but Uncle Fred and my grandfather are the only ones who touched our lives.

By 1903, Czar Nicholas II, having ascended to the throne after his father, Alexander III's death in 1894, and now facing the mounting challenge of the Bolsheviks, continued the subscription of young men into the armies as his father had done years before. My grandfather's family had been notified by other neighboring farmers of the approaching military and that the military were actually taking youngsters of no more than thirteen or fourteen years of age. The family took no chances, and—packing everything they could carry on their backs and on two small wagons—left their farm in the middle of the night and started the trek south to Odessa on the Black Sea. Hence the town in Washington State named in its honor by the Russian/German emigrants. Grandpa told us the cows were still in the milking barn when they left because the sounds of the soldiers had gotten so close that they couldn't wait any longer to leave.

From Odessa, the family was able to book passage on a ship to England, where my grandfather and my great-uncle Fred worked in London for a year as blacksmiths to earn the money necessary to take the family on to the United States. They entered this country through Ellis Island and originally settled in a German community in North Dakota. After a few years, the whole family moved again to central Washington State, and to another German community in a small village by the name of Hicksville, which is shown on my grandfather's naturalization papers, near what is now Odessa, Washington.

My grandmother's family had also made the same sojourn from the Ukraine through London and on to America. The two families did not know each other in the old country and my grandfather and grandmother did not meet until their families settled in North Dakota. The two of them were married in 1905—my grandmother at age seventeen and grandfather at age twenty-five—and shortly thereafter they moved to the Odessa, Washington, area with other family members as I've mentioned but really never knew.

Several of my mother's older siblings were then born in

Washington and moved with the family to northern California in 1920, or thereabouts. My grandfather took a job as a ranch manager on one of the large Spanish Land Grant operations in the area, and the family lived on the ranch. A few years later, they were able to purchase a farm of their own on which they built a home and lived with my mother and her siblings who had not yet left to make their own lives. After my mother and father were married, they bought the original farm from my mother's family and that's where my brother, sister, and I were raised. It was also at that time that my dad and my mother's brothers got together and built a home for my grandparents across the farm from our main house, where they resided until it was necessary to place them in an assisted living center.

*****

Dan's Journey

In the mid-1970s my Cousin Dan, son of Rosie and Wilmer, made plans to visit Europe. As part of those plans, his itinerary included a tour of the Balkan countries of Eastern Europe—which included Albania, our grandfather's native country. He was a motorcycle enthusiast at the time, and rented one in Italy and used this vehicle to undertake his tour into our grandfather's native land. His route took him from northern Italy down around through the former Yugoslavia and into northern Albania. Before undertaking his trip he had contacted the American Embassy in San Francisco who, in turn, put him in touch with the Albanian Mission to the United States for assistance in entering that country and attempting to find our grandfather's place of origin. As most people know, Albania was—and has remained—one of the most backward countries in Europe and very resistive of outside intervention. This has made it difficult for westerners in particular to enter and visit the country, but Dan was able to get through most of the red tape and set up his visit.

It had been virtually impossible to arrange for accommodations in Albania and so Dan had brought along with him a sleeping bag, tent, and such utensils as were necessary to spend the nights out in the open countryside. He had entered the country from the north and was making his way south toward the capital city of Tirana. It was not far from this city that he had been told our grandfather had been born. One morning, having arisen from his encampment, he packed up his things, loaded them on his motorcycle, and resumed his southern trek. After traveling a few miles, he rounded a bend in the road and suddenly came upon a horse-drawn wagon, loaded with hay and carrying a peasant woman and her two children. It appeared that the wagon had broken an axle. He laid his bike down on the pavement so he could slow his speed by using the safety bars and gently slid into the wagon, making almost imperceptible contact.

Just at that instant, and as if on cue, the woman began wailing at the top of her lungs, her children began crying and carrying on and a police car appeared. Two policemen leaped from the vehicle while speaking excitedly in their native tongue, handcuffed my cousin and put him in the back seat of the car. One of them went to Dan's motorcycle that was still lying on the pavement, righted it and, firing it up, took off down the highway. The remaining cop jumped in the car and took off down the road after the bike, with Dan in the back seat.

After three or four miles, they entered a small village where the policeman on Dan's bike was pulling up in front of a building that appeared to be a police station. The cop in the car with Dan pulled up beside Dan's motorcycle, parked, opened the rear passenger door, and let him out. They took him inside the building, past some desks and a lady who seemed to be a clerk, and into a crude cell. They closed and locked the door to the cell, and went out to the front of the building where the woman they had passed on the way in was sitting at her desk. She appeared to be the one in charge. Dan peered out at them through a small, barred window in the door. The two policemen and the woman spoke excitedly in a mixture of what seemed to be German and their native tongue. Dan is fairly fluent in German but he couldn't understand the conversation. While they spoke, they would turn and look at the cell door while gesturing and then go back to their discussion. After a bit, the two cops left, leaving the woman out in the entry area seated at the desk. Periodically, she would come back to the cell and peer through the window at Dan, and then go back to her desk. All this had happened so fast that Dan hadn't had much time to figure out what was going on, but he did know that whatever it was, it wasn't good.

It had been a couple of hours and Dan had been lounging on a primitive cot when he heard new voices out front and hurried to the cell door. Two new people had entered the room and were talking with the woman. They were gesturing and carrying on a very animated conversation, when one of the new arrivals suddenly turned on his heel and came back to the cell door. Peering in, the man produced a key from his coat pocket and unlocked the door. He entered the cell and, locking the door behind him, motioned for Dan to sit down on the cot. The man was not dressed in a uniform, but was in a type of business suit. He rattled off—in the same tongue the other men had used—a barrage of words directed at Dan, not seeming threatening, but conversational. But it was obvious by the expression on Dan's face that he wasn't understanding what was being said, so the man then paused and began again in broken English and German.

The man wanted to impress on my cousin the severity of the offense he had committed and that he had interceded on Dan's behalf. That he had made "arrangements" to have him let out of jail so that he could continue on with his journey. Then he paused while looking sternly down at Dan. The man repeated the story several times, until he was sure Dan understood, which he confirmed by a nod of his head. Telling the story later, Dan said he expected the man to give him some sort of extraordinary requirement in exchange for being set free, but the man took out a piece of paper and a pencil and wrote something on the paper and handed it too Dan. In English, in crude handwriting that was very difficult to make out, was what Dan thought was written: "How much will you pay?" Dan had about a thousand dollars in cash, but didn't want to imply that he had much money. He was still less than halfway through his trip. Trying to suppress his anxiety, he looked up at the man and shrugged his shoulders and extended his hands face-up as if to indicate that he had no money. The man smiled a bit and shrugged, then took the paper back. He began writing something again and handed it back to Dan: "For $20 you have freedom."

They had taken Dan's backpack when they had put him in the cell, but he still had his wallet in his back pocket. Dan said he had never been so glad to give someone twenty bucks in his life and, trying to hide his pleasure, quickly got the money out and gave it to the man. He hesitated for a moment, looked at Dan's wallet, then at Dan, shrugged his shoulders and turned and walked toward the cell door, indicating for Dan to follow. The man unlocked the door and let Dan pass while motioning toward his backpack that was sitting where he had left it when he had entered the cell, and then directed him toward the front door of the building. Dan said his heart was in his throat and—trying to conceal his nervousness—he thanked the man, shook his hand and briskly walked out the door to freedom. His bike was sitting where the cop had left it. He jumped on it, fired it up, and sped away—not looking back.

When thinking about the episode while he rode along, it was obvious to Dan that everything had been a setup: the Albanian version of a speed-trap. Gypsies, which the woman most surely was, were still very prevalent at that time and, as thieves, were looked down upon by their society. Obviously the police and this woman had struck a bargain to make a little money off these foreigners passing through. Mulling over the twenty dollars, Dan marveled at the small amount they had asked for; but, when you think about it, the average Albanian worker made the equivalent of about thirty dollars a month. What he gave them was almost a month's pay, and it was in dollars which would purchase even more, especially on the black market—quite a sum to them and not enough to kill the golden geese that were the rare tourists. Dan spent about another week in the country and never ran into the trap again, although he did talk with other westerners who had the same thing happen to them. It was all part of the experience of traveling there, he guessed.

Dan found the village where we're pretty sure our grandfather was born, and an old man there remembered the Gottschalk family. The embassy in San Francisco had prepared him a document in the Albanian language which basically said that Dan was a United States citizen in good standing and was tracing his lineage back through Albanian culture. Other than recognizing the name "Gottschalk," there was a complete language barrier with the old guy. However, after reading the communiqué, Dan said his eyes lit up and he took him to a building in the center of the village that served as a sort of makeshift "hall of records." The old fellow—who he said was probably close to a hundred—began rummaging through piles of dusty record books. Dan helped him with the task and, after an hour or so. he had obviously found what he was looking for; birth records from the 1880s. Among others, these records contained references to the births of my grandfather and great-uncle Fred. It can't be completely documented—because all the man would say that Dan could understand was, "Gottschalk! Gottschalk! Gottschalk!" as he excitedly pointed at writing and dates in the old volumes—but it appears that it probably was records of our grandfather's family. The dates were correct as far as Dan could tell. We can't be sure, but it makes good fodder for stories at family gatherings.

14

Grandma Gottschalk

Grandma Gottschalk was born Rosalia Knecht in 1888, somewhere in Prussia—which is now Germany—and emigrated with her family through Poland to the general region of the Western Steppes of the Ukraine that my grandfather's family had settled in. As I've mentioned, she and my grandfather didn't meet until they had settled in North Dakota.

When my father purchased my grandparent's farm in 1949 and we moved into the old farmhouse, my dad and my mom's brothers built a small home across the farm where Grandma and Grandpa lived. My brother and sister and I were very lucky to live so close to our grandparents and we spent many hours listening to them talk about their lives and eating the great food Grandma prepared.

Now I'm not crazy about German food as a rule, but everything Grandma made had a special taste. There were "küchen," German pies with various fruit and cheese fillings; "kechla," sweet-rolls with powdered sugar frosting and various jams spread over them; and "kartoffel" soup, which was boiled potatoes with dill, garlic, and dried, minced onions from her garden, sometimes with ground pork in it. Grandma and Grandpa didn't eat beef, but I'm not sure why. I can remember the times Grandma would call over the old World War II battery phone—the lines connecting the phone from our house to theirs' having been strung on poles across the field— and announce that various pastries were ready to take out of the oven. "Darlinks," she'd say, "Da *küchen* is finished." My brother and I, and later our sister, would run like mad across the field to their house. The aroma of that great food still comes back to me. We'd sit in the kitchen with Grandma—sometimes with Grandpa if he wasn't in a foul mood—and she would serve us these wonderful treats. Maybe the "knoephle" soup if we were lucky. If we had gone to the "putcher" shop there might be pork to grind. We loved turning the crank on the grinder that was attached to the kitchen table and turning out the lean, ground meat.

Grandma never learned to drive a car. When we were too young to drive, we'd ride in the car with our mother to town to do her shopping. Mom would give each of us several items to select from the shelves in the grocery store, and then we'd take everything back to Grandma's house. But every couple days grandma would need a few things from "the store"—which meant the old country store about two miles from our ranch that I've talked about—and my brother or I would ride our bicycles to her house and get the list, and then go to the store for her.

Lard, bratwurscht, tea and other odds and ends. When she'd give us the list there would usually be some change or, now and then, a dollar bill underneath—hidden by her handkerchief. That was for us. We never asked for it, and she never made anything of it. We didn't need money to pay for things at George's Store, because everyone had a charge account. The only thing she ever said about giving us a little something was that we should never forget to do the same for others. She meant not just money, but kindness.

Grandma was one of the Lutherans who became a Pentecostal. But she was so completely different than the others in the Assembly of God Church I grew up in that it's almost impossible for me to describe her relationship with her God. Capital letters: G-O-D.

If you took every tenet set forth in both the Old and New Testaments that described how a person should live her life, it was Grandma who actually lived them. Not interpretation, to her benefit, but absolute simplistic faith—and it worked because it was so pure. She was non-judgmental—which is the hardest for most

Pentecostals to refrain from, always had time for someone else, and she listened. When my grandfather would be unreasonable to us and others she would only say, "I pray for Papa." Each evening one of us in the family would call across the fields on the old phone to her house and say goodnight. She went to bed around 8 o'clock each evening, summer or winter. To us kids that was remarkable, because we wanted to stay up to all hours. When we'd ask her, "What are you doing, Grandma?" She'd say, "I'm just talkink to da Lord." Most people saying that to me would make me uncomfortable, but not Grandma. She had a direct line.

Since I have the opportunity (by self-proclaimed artistic license) to pontificate on things, I have categorized those Pentecostals who are—or have been—in my life, in two ways. The first are those whom I would *not* want to spend Eternity in Heaven with. I make no bones about the fact that I have absolutely no concept of either, but to follow that thought—and to my way of thinking—it would be eternal damnation for them and me. The second group are those whom I would *gladly* spend this real or perceived Eternity with, knowing that each of those on this journey was there for the pure merits of their earthly performance. That for them there was no right or wrong, just human beings on a spiritual train, reaping the rewards of kindness and caring. In football, you can hit a running back on an end sweep, stopping him just short of the goal line, and then pick him up so the two of you can do it all over again. You each might be on different teams, but the mutual respect is there. I doubt if there will be sissies in heaven. My grandma, now living there—to my way of thinking—and my cousin Fred who has "walked the walk" with those giant hands clutching his flock—both Pentecostals—can be on my team any day. They lived it. And *do* live it. I would hope to be so fortunate. I should have told them so when I had the chance.

15

Living Across the Field from Grandpa and Grandma

I've categorized **Grandpa Gottschalk as a hard-headed German, which** by all accounts he was. But, when we kids would sit at his table for a meal, he would lead us in a prayer of thanksgiving, tears running down his cheeks. Then he would whack us with his cane afterwards if we were eating too many of the boysenberries in his garden—a complete contradiction in our young minds. We'd ask Grandma why he acted so mean. Once again, she would not judge, but simply tell us Grandpa carried a great burden that began with his move from the old country. If that was good enough for Grandma, it was good enough for us.

Grandpa had a 1939, two-door Chevy Sedan that he drove until he was in his late 70s. Down along the Sacramento River, where the soil is fertile, a man raised watermelons and, for a couple years we took an old trailer—that we had put makeshift sides on about a foot high—from the farm, towed it down there, and bought some of those melons. Then we brought them back to the farm for others to buy, or just gave them away. This wasn't out of open generosity to the community, but typically what everyone did. Someone did this, and someone did that, and it all came around in sort of a circle. Each helping out the other with no strings attached. When the neighbors would come to our dairy on the farm and buy the raw milk, they would—in turn—buy melons from us. I think we sold them for six cents a pound. It had become a sort of summer ritual. Many times we would just sit out by the irrigation well and break the melons open and gorge ourselves.

Sometimes, old Cinto Alberico, father of the brothers I mentioned earlier, would come by in his Willys Jeep pickup—a converted military vehicle—and sit under the cottonwood trees by the irrigation well near our ranch-house with his good friend, his Scottish terrier Luigi Basco, and smoke his pipe and tell us stories in his native Italian. He knew we didn't understand a thing, but Luigi did.

I don't recall the specific year and whether we had hauled melons on the trailer or not but, for whatever reason, Grandpa had decided to take his car and go buy some watermelons from the guy down by the river. And on the way home, he stopped by the little grocery store in the village of Hamilton City to buy some Cokes for all of us to wash the melon down with. That was quite a display of largess for Grandpa. He invited me to go along, one of but a few occasions that I can recall having ridden in the car with him. I was only nine or ten and had to sit on a wooden packing box to be up high enough to see out the side or front window.

So, there we were. We'd visited the melon patch and Grandpa had picked out six of them, two of which I held on my lap and four that were down on the floor boards under my feet. Grandpa had impressed on me that it was my responsibility that the melons got home safely. I didn't go into the store on the way home when he stopped to buy the Cokes, but stayed in the car guarding the melons—not moving a stitch. In a few minutes, he returned and—after putting the sodas in the rear of the car—he opened the driver's door and prepared to get us underway.

Something I have to say about Grandpa is that he had never mastered the intricacies of operating a motor vehicle, and he always used anger to deal with the situation. The old sedan he drove had a button on the floor that he needed to depress to activate the starter, and the car needed to be in neutral to successfully start the engine while not running over—or into—something. But he would inevitably push the clutch in and then step down on the starter button and—just when the engine would fire-up—let his foot off the clutch, forgetting the transmission was in gear. This would make the car lurch forward and the engine would die. *"Gott im Himmel!"* he would mutter under his breath.

This reference to "God in Heaven" was one of the accepted forms of swearing to a Lutheran-cum-Pentecostal. The former which he used to be, and the latter which none of us were sure of. This was accepted, as was the phrase, "Heaven's on Earth," in German. I asked my grandma and mother many times why they or Grandpa would use these phrases in an angry manner when it would appear that if they said, "Heaven's on Earth" it would mean things are so good it's as if "Heaven is on Earth," which is where they believed they were all headed, this perfect place. Why use it in anger, for it contradicted their philosophy? The same for "God in Heaven." It was nteresting stuff for a wannabe normal kid who wasn't yet dry behind the ears.

The next thing that Grandpa would do after the car had died (*Gott im Himmel!*) was to push the clutch in and put the gearshift lever in neutral. But he had to be careful with this maneuver if the car was on any sort of slope because, if it was, the thing would start to roll away. (*Gott im Himmel!*) That's what happened on this occasion. The car started to roll and, noticing this, he jammed his foot down toward the brake-pedal, but he missed. So we were rolling out toward the main road and Grandpa was using the German language in ways it wasn't intended to be used. Then he found the brake pedal and the car lurched to a stop a few feet from the highway. All the while I was sitting on this wooden fruit box trying for dear life not to let go of the two melons on my lap and keeping an eye on the four on the floor. (*Gott im Himmel!!*)

So we were at a stop, next to the road, on a relatively flat surface and Grandpa still needed to start the engine. The next maneuver is one I learned later on in my driving career, but had not yet been mastered by my mother's father. What you must do to safely start the engine is to put the gearbox in neutral, put your left foot on the brake pedal, and then depress the starter button on the floor. If all of this led to successfully starting the engine, the next thing you had to do is quickly pull your right foot off the starter button and, while moving your left foot to the clutch, place your right foot on the brake pedal. And all this needed to be accomplished in the blink of an eye.

The maneuver did work, and so Grandpa and I were sitting there next to the highway with the engine running, but we still need to get the damn thing in gear. That's where it got dicey. As I've mentioned, Grandpa would try to slam the shift lever into gear without the clutch. Sometimes his foot missed the pedal, other times he just ignored the thing. Well, this time he did a combination of the two and was successfully able to get the car in gear and we lurched onto the highway, made a hard right turn, and headed down the Canal Road toward the farm, "going like sixty."

"Going like sixty" is a phrase from my grandma. From time to time, Mom would take Grandma to Chico for a doctor's appointment or something. My earliest recollection of these events is in the mid-to-late-1950s. And it was around that time that Grandma coined the phrase. The speed limit was forty-five miles-per-hour and—on the straight stretch of Highway Thirty-two between Pine Creek and Meridian Road—Mom could really get the old 1950, pea green Plymouth rolling and, with a head start, could pass the occasional slow-moving car. It was at this time that Grandma would announce that we were "going like sixty."

So now Grandpa and I were hurtling down the Canal Road "going like sixty" and, looming up ahead, was the Southern Pacific railroad crossing that leads to the Holly Sugar plant. In those days, because the speed that cars traveled on public roads was considerably less than today—and railroads having been there before cars—the grade on the approaches to either side of railroad crossings was somewhat severe. As we grew closer and closer to the crossing, I periodically stole a glance at Grandpa. Any thoughts of suggesting it might be prudent to slow down a bit were dashed by my view of the death grip he had on the steering wheel and the German muttering under his breath. He looked like a man *possessed*.

We hit the approach, went airborne, landed perfectly, and

continued our journey, Grandpa, the watermelons and myself no worse for wear, but it was a brief respite for up ahead was the big-one: THE BRIDGE ACROSS THE CANAL. To negotiate this crossing required about an eighty-five-degree left turn onto the bridge that took you over the canal onto Wyo Road. This time, as we were approaching the bridge, I summoned up the courage and said to Grandpa, "The bridge is coming up." Never looking at me, he replied, "*Was ist los?*" ("What's the matter?") At this speed, we're not going to make the bridge, I thought to myself. Apparently agreeing with my assessment of the situation he began the downshift—another maneuver he hadn't mastered.

In cars of the era of the old Chevy Sedan, shifting down to lower gears was accomplished in one of three ways. The vehicle moving only a few miles-per-hour when the downshift was attempted; double or triple-clutching (pressing the clutch-pedal down to the floor numerous times) to allow for the gears in the transmission to properly align; or jamming the shift lever into the lower gear, eliciting a loud grinding sound from below the floor boards. Grandpa did a combination of the last two. With "*Gott im Himmel's*" and "*Meine gute's*" ("My goodness") being uttered by Grandpa in rapid fire, he got the thing into a lower gear and we slowed down enough to make the turn onto the bridge. But we were going too fast to stay on the roadway and—a couple hundred feet past the bridge and onto Wyo Road—we gently drove into an empty drainage ditch that was about six feet deep. The car rolled over on its right side. Grandpa was now sitting on top of me and the watermelons.

It was a complete mess. Grandpa, a disciple of the "when a problem arises get angry and kick things" way of thinking, was once again creating new German words of anger and disgust. He was trying to get the driver's door open, but each time he managed to push it up gravity took over and it would slam down again. "*Gott im Himmel!!*" And, right in the middle of all this mayhem and in one of his most awesome displays of anger, Grandpa managed to blurt out the most incredible question, in a combination of English and German, "Why did you let the watermelons get broken?" For cryin' out loud! I almost get killed and all he cares about is his three-dollar-and-sixty-cents-worth of melons? But that was Grandpa.

In between our efforts to get the driver's door open and get out of the damned car we would lay on top of each other, Grandpa, the watermelons, and me, until we would regain our strength and then try again. During these struggles a passing motorist stopped, actually a neighboring farmer, and helped with getting us out. Then he turned his car around and made his way to our farm where Dad, upon hearing of our debacle, fired up one of the tractors and came to pull us out. We were quite a sight while waiting for him to show up, sitting there on one of the fenders of the old car that was now at road level in the ditch.

Passing cars would stop and offer to help—it was different in those days—but I'd tell them we were okay and that my father was coming to get us out. Grandpa didn't say much. After we got the car out of the ditch and surveyed the damage, we found that there were only a couple new dents on the passenger side to go along with those that Grandpa had inflicted in the past.

As an aside to this story, years later, my brother, my sister, and I inherited the old '39 Chevy. Thinking it needed a new coat of paint—forget the dents and scrapes—we talked our father into buying a couple gallons of automotive paint at the Farm-all Dealer in town (the predecessor to International Harvester) and, with brushes, we painted that sucker Farm-all-Red! In our excitement to show off our car around the community, we all jumped inside and took it out for a little spin: our two Australian Shepherd dogs; two cats with no names; our Springer, Lady; and my brother and sister and I on board, with me driving. Just one little problem: the paint wasn't dry and as we cruised the countryside every imaginable bug, bird, weed, tree limb and piece of roadside grass did its business on our new car. It didn't matter that none of us had a driver's license, but that was the way it was in the country.

The old '39 Chevy was never quite the same.

16

Pentecostalism as I See It

One can argue that my version of the Pentecostals is "sour grapes" or whatever, and that's fine. As the Lord told me, we're all entitled to our own opinions. But I was born into the very womb of the movement—the very core—into the absolute judging of those who didn't subscribe to the Pentecostals' particular interpretation of the Bible. Those who attended our little church were mostly the outcasts of accepted society. Not that they were bad people, but they weren't "fancy" as they liked to describe it. They would talk about the *fancy* churches in town and how these congregations had their elitist ideals and looked down on us, the true, enlightened, Children of God. For some reason, this unfailing belief that those of our faith worshiped in the only true manner raises more questions than it answers. Even to this day, my parents—who are in their mid-to-late-80s—firmly believe and espouse the belief that if you don't follow the tenets of the Pentecostals in the literal interpretation of the Bible, you are lost. Heaven and Hell are absolute, and govern every breathing moment of their lives.

One of the first things you learn as a Pentecostal, once you've been "saved," is that there is a list of things that the Church believes. "This is what we believe," they'd say. In my experience these "beliefs" adhere or deviate from the Bible in a convenient manner. Most of the beliefs we were taught are those that tended to separate Pentecostals from other Christians—the very elitism that they railed against. In most cases the "don'ts" were completely out of the norm of society. Not just "Though Shalt Not Kill" or "Though Shalt Not Covet Thy Neighbor's Wife"—although that was fairly prevalent in the Assemblies of God—but more to the "no dancing," "no going to the movies," "no roller skating" (which was popular in my day, but was eliminated because the music that was played was much the same as that which was danced to), no nothing. I remember for Christmas in 1962, when I was fourteen, Dad bought us a black-and-white Packard-Bell television/hi-fi console set from Al Hinz Appliance. Mom had asked for it so she could watch the New Year's Day Rose Parade. I remember going with her after she'd finished her shift one day at the Sprouse Ritz Five-and-Dime in town to look at and dream about it, black-and-white and beautiful. (As for the Rose Parade, flowers mustn't have been in color, yet.)

But more to the point, we would watch *Rawhide, Have Gun Will Travel, Johnny Yuma*, and other fluffy Westerns and the *Red Skelton Show* (although we couldn't watch the June Taylor Dancers because their skirts were too short and they showed too much thigh in my parents' opinion), but when my brother or I would ask to go to a movie with friends the answer was a firm "NO." And these movies might have been starring the very actors from these shows I've mentioned, or maybe a Rory Calhoun or even John Wayne in a Horse Opera, as they were sometimes called, so the "NO" was completely contradictory. But it was the "This is What We Believe" that set the Pentecostals apart, and made our sect as elitist in the Pentecostal's minds as we thought the Methodists, Presbyterians, and Catholics were in their *fancy* churches. We were taught that we were children of a special dispensation. That, somehow, the word that had been written by spiritually-inspired Men of God, and found in the form of the Dead Sea Scrolls, was absolutely interpreted as referring to us: the chosen Sons and Daughters of God. Even though, if you want to add a touch of scholarly thought which was looked down upon as a "work of the devil," the scrolls had been written in the ancient form of Hebrew, difficult or mostly impossible to literally translate into English. But we were told that God had given us a special understanding, we, the disenfranchised, the outsiders that couldn't belong to the *fancy* club.

And those in the Church always asked God for something. "Please, God, give Mary-Sue a new dress for Easter." "Help Johnny's little league team win the championship." "Help us buy a new house." You see it today on TV when a newly-saved athlete gets all fired up about how God will help the team win. And, all the while, another new convert in the opponent's clubhouse is quoting God's will for why his team will be victorious. God might give us humans the talent to excel at something, but it's up to man to accomplish it. I have asked my parents over the years why they would always ask and not thank. At dinner it was always asking God to *bless* this and *bless* that. Never thanks to God for what we have. The only events I can unequivocally recall that were used as thankfulness to God were the celebrations of Thanksgiving, exactly as its name implies. All of us who were gathered would join hands and Cousin Dan would start the Doxology: "Praise God from who all blessings flow! Praise Him all creatures here below!"

The very basis of the Pentecostal religion is: "My life on earth is made up of misery and grief, but there's a better place I'm going. When you come back, Lord, you'll whisk me away to Heaven where the streets are paved with gold. No more sorrow, no more pain." The overriding thrust of this belief was that it wasn't necessary to accomplish something in the community here on earth, for the reward lay in Heaven, unless you were the televangelists that came later. (I wonder what street they'll live on in Heaven?)

I have this dream that when I die, and I'm in line outside the Pearly Gates and, as we inch ever closer, I finally come face to face with St. Peter. He asks me my name and I give it to him with some fear and trepidation but, miraculously, he finds my name written in the "Book of Life" and announces that I can now enter. Being the inquisitive sort that I am, I pause and ask Peter, "Are the Pentecostals here?" Peter gives me a brief smile and then says, "We don't really know where they are, Steve."

But you know how dreams are. They can't be trusted—unless you're one of the Prophets who wrote the Bible—or so I've heard.

17

As a Teenager

I **know that kids in general have one hell** of a time during their teenage years. Physical and emotional changes are mostly out of control. It's like someone turned the light on in a dark room and, like cockroaches, we all scurried for cover. We weren't sure that we were doing something wrong but weren't sure that we *weren't*, either. In the blink of an eye we had gone from pure innocence: "Look at little Stevie, he's so cute," (and this might have been when I was pulling the wings off a grasshopper) to…"You gotta' watch 'em, they're teenagers now, you know." What the hell happened? To my way of thinking, no one who has ever lived—from cave people to the most enlightened—had any real prior knowledge of what it was like to become a teenager. One day you're the toast of society and the next you're "One of Them!" Later in life, I recalled discussions with friends and family about how my little Johnny was such a wonderful child and the joy of my life. But then these well-meaning people would blurt out, "But you just wait until he's a *teenager*!" A very cold chill would come over me as I contemplated what I had just heard. Not *my* Johnny. Not him. I'll admit that more than once I snuck into both of my boys' rooms to see if they were still "my boys." Seeds of doubt only germinate if watered by the tears of denial. Our fears only grow legs if we let them.

And, with the rest of the evils of teenager-hood, if you mix in Hell and damnation, the do's and the don'ts (and all the other stuff that the Pentecostals throw at you) into a teenager's twisted, pathetic existence, you can come out the other end with a really screwed-up kid. One day you're sitting next to Betty-Sue and she's just a girl, with zits, and the next day you're wondering what color her panties are, or if she's wearing any. It happens so fast. And kids are just not prepared for this stuff.

But, you see, I think it was all a setup, and that's how they got us. The biggest push, the all-out war against the devil, was waged during the time we all were teenagers. There's not a better time to go after us. We didn't know what the hell was happening, anyway, so it makes sense for them, the adults in the Church, to get us while we're weak and confused, for cryin' out loud! They would hammer and hammer on our minds with the idea that even if we thought about something but didn't act on it, the thought amounted to sinning. Well, for Pete's sake, we were sinning all the time anyway as teenagers and, suddenly, I notice Betty-Sue next to me in a different light and even my thoughts are going to send me to hell. Her panties be damned!! There was just no hope for my soul. The cards were stacked against me—but the Pentecostals had their own way out.

We feared the Catholics, for some reason. I'll never forget how, on that second Tuesday night after the first Monday in November, 1960, sitting in the kitchen of the old farmhouse, my dad and I were listening to our Philco radio. We were up much later than usual, but this was a very special occasion, for it was Election Day and all of America was waiting with baited breath to hear the final results. Nixon and Kennedy ran the closest Presidential race in United States history. Then Howard K. Smith came on and announced that John F. Kennedy was the winner. My dad reached over to the radio, angrily switched off the power and said, "We're all doomed now, there's a *Catholic* in the White House!"

The problem Pentecostals always had with the Catholics is that they could go to confession on Saturday night and be forgiven. That just wasn't right in the Pentecostals' minds. These Catholics could sin like the dickens all week and ask the priest for forgiveness on Saturday night and the sins would be wiped away. That belief subverted everything that the Pentecostals held sacred, because the forgiveness of sin was a very serious matter and one that couldn't just happen in a confessional on Saturday night. You had to carry the sin with you, as a burden. And, as Pentecostals, we knew exactly what specifically amounted to sin. It was kind of like "the sin that keeps on giving." It was just too easy for these Catholics. They told their sins to priests, and not the right sins, according to us. We had the correct list. But they trusted this man to talk to God and confirm their forgiveness—kind-hearted, caring people that they were. But the Pentecostals came up with something even better: the Altar Call.

At the end of every service, the minister or evangelist or whoever was giving the sermon would slow down his delivery and begin an incantation. In a voice only above a whisper it would begin, "Are there those here amongst us that are not right with the Lord, that if you should die this night before you wake, God would not welcome you into Paradise? Those whose sins are not forgiven, those that haven't let God into their hearts? Are you saved, Brothers and Sisters?" And in our church Erma Kalb would begin playing the organ to the tune of "Just as I am without one plea, but that thy blood was shed for me." Of course, this was mostly aimed at the teenagers whom everyone knew were the biggest sinners of all.

Well, that did it. The girls would break down first. They'd begin crying and wailing and they'd virtually run to the altar in front of the church, where Brother Seamans had held forth not so long ago. Adults in the congregation would make their way up and lay hands on these poor sisters and ask for God's intercession. The organ music would continue and the low, quiet voice of the minister. "Is there anyone else that isn't right with the Lord? If you died tonight would you know where you're going?" Even the most hardened teenage soul couldn't resist this admonition and so the young males would join our female counterparts at the altar and cry and wail with them, not exactly sure why (peer pressure is so powerful to a teen), but it seemed like the thing to do. If you didn't participate in this whole ritual it went without saying that you were definitely lost for eternity since—once again—everyone knows how teenagers sin. And when you were alone with your parents afterward and you hadn't displayed the proper contrition, it was the worst. It just wasn't natural. (Leave the kids alone, for Christ's sake!) This ritual happened every last time we went to church, over and over and over again, this preoccupation with sinning and dying tonight. It's not hard to understand why I didn't sleep well in those days.

18

The End of the World

If a group of people were so preoccupied with their state of affairs on Earth—about how awful their plight was and how wonderful it was going to be in Heaven—then, of course, the end of the world would probably take up a large part of their cognitive thought. And it did. And these people would come up with all kinds of "signs" about this real or perceived eventual outcome. They still do it today. We've all read about and heard the stories of Jim Jones and David Koresh, and of the Mayan calendar that ends with 2012. But to a kid who is only just beginning the sinning part of his life and the joys and terror that come with it—and by pure human nature believes that there's a lot more to come—this "end of the world" stuff is hard to take, for a couple reasons. First, if the end came too soon, you might be short-changed on your sinning; and, second, the forgiveness that it took to actually survive the end and gain entry into Heaven was so jumbled-up in your mind that each second of your life was spent in either regret or fear. I think that's why we despised the Catholics so. For them, if you could at least make it to Saturday night your sins were forgiven. No ifs, ands, or buts. So they had something to shoot for. But, even with the Altar Call we kids didn't know if we qualified for Heaven or not. The fear of the unknown is what completely gripped us during our waking hours—and that's what the adults used against us.

The Book of Revelation

At the Wednesday night prayer meetings—and I should add Bible study—the minister would take a book of the New Testament and verbally break it down like a science lab project in school, typically starting with the book of Matthew and, over the next five or six months, ending with the book of Revelation. My brother and I were scared to death of the book of Revelation and mysterious afflictions would take us over—requiring bed-rest during these particular lab sessions—whenever we could pull them off. The Church didn't typically study the Old Testament, much, because it was believed that it was just a story of the Jews, but there was no anti-Semitic feeling or anything. In fact, amongst the Assemblies of God movement there was an activist group called "Jews for Jesus" which was overseen by a short little fellow by the name of Homer Specter. He, of Jewish faith himself, had been recruited to leave that discipline and come over to our side and, in turn, recruit other Jews.

Basically, their mantra was that Jesus, Son of Mary and Joseph, was the actual Messiah mentioned in the Old Testament, which was— and is—the antithesis of the Jewish religion. Our people were so literally uneducated in world history and anything outside of biblical writings, especially their absolute adherence to the New Testament, that they didn't understand what agony they were putting most of these people through. The Bible clearly states in both the Old and New Testaments that the Jews are the chosen Children of God, and their belief that the Messiah has not yet made his appearance on Earth is at the very heart of their sacraments. It nowhere mentions in the Bible that those who adhere to the Assemblies of God interpretation have it all figured out, but they certainly thought they did. And they once again preyed upon the weak and disenfranchised of the Jewish faith. The number of lives of these poor people that were completely ruined or damaged is incredible. For, after this "conversion," they were neither fish nor fowl.

My view of all this may be, once again, somewhat distorted—as I've mentioned before—by the fact that I questioned everything as a youngster and, later, as a teenager in the Church. Not overtly, though, for I was a good kid. People patted me on the head and went their way. "You know, Steve's a good kid," they'd say. But, to me, things just didn't add up. And they didn't add up for my brother, either. As a child, you are taught to obey your parents and adhere to their philosophies. My parents were very kind people and meant well. They just didn't aspire to great knowledge of things non-biblical.

And, in the Church, everything was extremely literal. One very dedicated follower of Jesus, John the Baptist, who is mentioned in the New Testament, ran around in the desert, half-naked, preaching his version of the gospel that he embraced. Admonishing no one and asking everyone to give away all their earthly possessions and follow him. And he couldn't understand why people found it difficult to accept his message. He was a lunatic, for cryin' out loud! You can't expect people with real lives—responsible people—to throw away everything they've worked for. I believe religion is intended to supplement man's normal pursuits or it becomes a sideshow, just as with the manifestation that I experienced in the Assemblies of God. But the Church and my parents were of the opinion that we're tormented by the devil.

Yah, that's another thing: the devil was always the scapegoat for the unexplainable. Are we so weak that we can't tell right from wrong? Good from evil? Don't we all have that "little man" sitting on our shoulder who whispers in our ear? Do we need the sledgehammer of sin and damnation to make us walk the straight and narrow? Give God, if you believe in him, the credit for instilling some common sense in our brains. But when you play with someone's eternal soul, be he young or old, it's very powerful medicine.

But the book of Revelation was the scariest threat. We were told by the very enlightened of our Brethren, the epistle had been written by Men of Faith who were given the words by God in dreams, and then got up in the morning and wrote it down. One of these dreamer/ writers is thought to be Matthew, the tax collector who was credited with being the author of the first book of the New Testament, who was one of the twelve disciples gathered at the Last Supper. Ole Matt had quite an imagination for one who worked for a precursor to the modern day IRS. Revelation had scary descriptions of visions these writers described that spoke of bloody ram's heads and all sorts of gory detail, and these writings were thought to be the result of all these divinely-inspired dreams.

Have you ever been able to get up in the morning and write down in exact detail what you had just dreamed? And, furthermore, have it then translated into a completely different language and have its story be exactly the same as when you dreamed it? Which no one would know but you, anyway. Armageddon, the battle at the very end of the world where the blood of those involved "flows as deep as a horse's belly," was the epitome of the terror of these dreams. Not that these prophesied inevitabilities were completely unreasonable to contemplate, but that there was evidence all around us that these things were beginning to happen *right now!* That's what we were told, every last minute, every breathing moment. It was as if anything you did could trigger these things. Stepping on a cockroach could start the end of the world. (*Gott im Himmel!!*)

So everyone in our Church was completely preoccupied with the end of the world and what had been prophesied. A good example of how this can happen is the current fascination with Nostradamus. It's incredible to me that persons of spiritual persuasions find the predicting of the future by these "anointed ones" so accurate, but they themselves can't even remember where they ate lunch yesterday. This blind acceptance of the thoughts and opinions of others is one of the things that made it so scary as a kid: that if you even dared question something on an intellectual basis of any kind, you were labeled a heretic. After all, God looked into your mind! There was no place to hide! It's not that I wanted to refute all of these things, but I just wanted to have some evidence on a tangible basis. I remember many times yelling out in frustration to God, "Just help me know something for sure, please!" But because, as a kid, you are controlled by your parents and if you question anything that was written in the New Testament and is interpreted by our Men of God as "The Truth" and is professed by the adults around you, you are doomed to hell. At some point in every church service there would be a reference to "the things that have happened since we last met," in their minds only confirming the hastening of the end of the world.

But I still had so much sinning to do: my first kiss; sex with a woman. And, all around me, was this preoccupation with The End! (Damn it!)

19

The "Talent"

In our church it was emphasized that anyone with a "talent" should announce the fact and ask to perform this gift in front of the congregation. As I recall, there was some sort of biblical foundation in this exercise. Something like, "If you have a talent, don't hide it under a bushel." Or maybe you should. This edification typically took place during the Sunday evening services. As you might imagine, it was a Barnum & Bailey type of retinue which would line up adjacent to the pulpit during these affairs. Most people gave it one shot and—having experienced their brief brushes with stardom—politely returned to their seats in the pews, but not Mrs. Ollenberger. She was the wife of Henry and the mother of Milton, Kenneth, and Louise. She just couldn't leave it alone. And she had three performances under her belt. And she wanted so desperately to fit in.

Mrs. Ollenberger—her name was Emma as I recall—was not an attractive woman. Standing barely five feet tall, and equally as wide, with hair in various stages of disarray, she would sit in her pew— second row, third seat, left side—and hum under her breath the tune and words to the hymns. Then, suddenly, very loudly, vibrato and volume in equal doses. She sang some in German and some in a mixture of German and English. I do believe—and please forgive me all that I might offend—that Mrs. Ollenberger was the catalyst for Yogi Berra coining the phrase, "It ain't over 'til the fat lady sings."

So, one day, a well-meaning member of the congregation—during the convivial greetings and conversations that typically took place after the services—suggested to Emma, "Why don't you honor us with a piano solo next Sunday?" (Emma also played the piano with the same zest.) It was as if the heavens had opened, and Mrs. Ollenberger loudly announced that she would be glad to. Now here was this woman—mother of Milton, Kenneth and Louise—being regarded as one of the most privileged of the congregation.

She was dressed in her finest that next Sunday evening, and even Henry had accompanied her to church that night to witness her "coming out." Henry was a bit taller than his wife, but she outweighed him by a hundred pounds. And, since this was such a special occasion, he had put on a freshly-washed pair of overalls with a nicely starched white shirt beneath.

Now, my brother and I typically dreaded these Sunday night services, because *Bonanza* was on at seven o'clock. And, every Monday morning when we got to school all of the "normal" kids were talking about what they had seen on television the night before. We didn't have a TV until I was fourteen. But this Sunday evening was an exception, for we couldn't wait to witness Mrs. Ollenberger's spectacle—and we had every reason to believe there would be one.

The service began rather uneventfully as I recall—beginning prayer, the welcome and such. But, after the third hymn sung by the congregation and led by the music director Erma Kalb, Mrs. Ollenberger's warbling had gotten to a fever pitch. It appeared she might not last until after the prayer requests and the announcement of the church-related events of the coming week—when the stage would be hers. But—even though she couldn't completely contain her warbling—she made it. And, with some excitement, the Minister announced the next segment and introduced our special musical entertainment for the evening. Of course we all knew her, but it lent an air of class—which the dear sister sorely longed for. The stage was hers.

Getting out of the pew for a woman of Emma's girth was no small task and we all waited politely while this effort played out. Well, almost all of us. We kids in the back row had a difficult time controlling our giggles. Glances from the adults only tended to exacerbate the situation—especially when their glares were followed by brief, knowing grins.

She was off! She was moving, her shawl dragging on the floor behind her, stuck to the high heel of her right shoe. Very alertly, Tom Kalb quickly darted out from his seat in the pew behind her and managed to get the crocheted thing out from under her heel. (Tom had been quite an athlete in high school.) Emma didn't miss a beat, with her head high and ample chest out. But then came the next hurdle: the three steps up onto the stage. Most of us had witnessed her attempts to negotiate this impediment in the past and it hadn't been a pretty sight. But, once again, help came from the audience, this time in the form of her son, Milton, who rushed up and—taking her by the elbow—gently said, "Let me help you up, Mom." Well, she did and he did, and he even went so far as to help her across the stage to the piano, pulled the bench out, and assisted her in seating herself. This exercise was somewhat briefer than that of the rising from the pew, but was accomplished with no less pomp and circumstance. She pushed and pulled, twisted and turned her enormity and eventually appeared to be comfortable. I recall glancing over at my dad in the pew in front of me and noting that he was just entering the first stages of REM sleep. It appeared he might miss the whole thing.

But, just when it appeared our soloist was getting things together two problems became apparent. The first was that—due to Mrs. Ollenberger's shortness of stature—her feet couldn't reach the pedals on the piano; and, secondly, she had gotten herself too close to the keyboard. Not being able to plant her feet on the floor to move the bench away from the piano, she was stuck. Noticing this dilemma Tom once again came to the rescue and bounded up the stairs and asked dear Emma, "May I assist you?" She let him and, with a clear demonstration of his athletic prowess, he was able to move her a sufficient distance from the keyboard.

But the first problem still hadn't been solved. It was causing her much consternation that she wouldn't be able to properly play and sing her solo while not being able to activate the pedals, which were typically used by the pianist to produce the proper accentuation in concert with the plunging of the keys. (If you know what I mean?!)

This time, Erma came to the rescue. Erma was not quite as quick as Tom but what she lacked in speed she made up for in tenacity. She had been seated at the organ watching the whole thing and wasn't more than a few feet from the piano. She quickly stood up, stepped behind a curtain and, producing a small padded stool of less height than the piano bench, raced to where Emma was seated, feet dangling, and said in the sweetest voice, "Dear, why don't you try sitting on this?"

That seemed to satisfy Mrs. Ollenberger. But we still had to get her off the bench and onto the stool. Once again, our athlete to the rescue. Tom bolted upright, made the stage in a single bound and between him and Erma they were able to get Emma off the bench and onto the stool. But now her chin was barely above the keyboard. The three of them huddled briefly and disbanded, leaving our soloist there on the stool, one of her chins almost resting on the keyboard. (Imagine the visual.) It was obvious that Emma had taken charge and the show would go on.

Without much further fanfare, she broke into the most incredible barrage of loosely-described piano playing and singing—neither exercise coming near endangering, by any stretch of the imagination, a key known to man. For Emma played and sang in her own imaginary key—but what she lacked in quality she made up for in quantity. Maybe I can better describe the sound by comparing it to the howl I could elicit from my Springer Spaniel, Freddie, when I cued him with brief operatic intonations. Or better yet, it sounded like the piano was trying to kill poor Mrs. Ollenberger. Those of us in the back row were out of control with laughter and in relatively safe territory this time because, for a change, we couldn't be heard over her howl.

20

More Missionaries

Aman by the name of **Bernard Johnson was** planning to become a missionary to Ecuador in South America. He had a wife and two small children whom he planned to take with him to one of the most isolated of primeval forests at the Rio Shiripuno. Once there he was to minister to—and attempt to convert—the tribesmen of the Auca Indians, who were among the last, if not *the* last, cannibals on earth. Mr. Johnson was being sponsored by the Assemblies of God Church and was making the rounds of these churches in the United States to raise money for this venture. His roots were in the same region of northern California where our church was located. Brother Johnson had been a missionary in other parts of the world but had been "called by God" to minister to these lost savages.

I was only seven or eight years old at the time but I still remember—from that young age—this man was one of the most virulent advocates of the end of the world. It's my earliest recollection of this phenomenon, and it was—and is—the very basis of the missionary movement of western religions.

We have to "save" or "convert" these poor souls before the world ends so that they, too, may join us in Heaven (the "last one to leave, turn out the lights" syndrome). That premise was one of the most difficult of the beliefs I had to deal with as a child and teenager in the Pentecostal church. How in the world were we Pentecostals given the task of running around the world—ignoring cultures and civilizations that had been around and survived or flourished for centuries—and convincing these "unenlightened" people that they were doing it all wrong and that we could show them the "true way"? I know many other western religions send out missionaries, but this overt attempt to change the whole culture of civilizations, I believe, was particularly prevalent with the Pentecostals. It's as if we had to put a McDonald's in every village of the world—and in the Vatican—if we could. Over the past one hundred years or so, we have introduced western culture to peoples that weren't able to—or couldn't—adapt and have caused such mayhem as the world has never seen. And, yet, we wonder why they economically and socially cannibalize each other today. It's just a different method of cannibalization. Now, I'm not condoning eating your cousin or friend for dinner like Hannibal Lector in the movie, but we've taken away complete civilizations by destroying their value systems and attempting to install ours. I love the benefits of our western cultures, but to indigenous people of the world it has been a death sentence. Westerners come on late night television and plead with us to send them money so they can save a child, but that's missing the point. We've taken away the ability of these children's parents to provide for them.

As a result, we have so diminished the value of human life in the minds of these people that they have lost the ability—and the will—to continue the societies that have served them since time immemorial. And then we're being asked by these misguided souls to reverse the effect, these poor children notwithstanding. Children grow up to be adults, one way or another, but we've abandoned the adults of these societies, because they're hard to market. And, when children grow up, they're not like cute little puppies anymore.

As I've said, this was—and has always been—done with the philosophy that the end of the world is so imminent we must grab these people *now* by whatever means, so that they, too, can get out of here alive! They didn't have flat screens and satellite television. We had to tell them, because we've got it all figured out—for cryin' out loud! Bernard Johnson, as he was preaching before going away told us that the world was going to end on Monday, October 13, 1956. In the fifty-three years since, I wonder how much good we've done. I'm one of the biggest capitalists and proponents of western civilization you'll ever meet, but let's just be honest about things. Get religion out of the equation, the Lord notwithstanding. It's been too convenient. And now everyone has flat-screens and satellites.

A couple months after Brother Johnson visited our church and had met his goal of raising adequate dollars-per-soul, he and his family had gathered their possessions and were making their way to Ecuador. They were in Rio de Janeiro when the news came out that members of the very tribe that the Brother was going to "save" had killed 5 missionaries who had been trying to do the same thing Brother Johnson was going to do. The religious community called these men martyrs and I have no doubt that their intentions were honorable, but maybe the Auca Indians were just protecting their way of life. (That's what we all do, isn't it?) I don't know whatever happened to Brother Johnson and his family. They probably went on to greener pastures.

21

More Church-Camp

Something I forgot to mention earlier—and that probably **had** a good deal to do with my rise to royalty within the camp society—was an event that forever etched my brother and me into Assemblies of God Church Camp lore; as well as our Cousins Fred, Dave, Dan and, to some extent, other lesser players. (At least in our minds.)

The year before my ascension to the throne at Church Camp a group of scoundrels—older kids—were encamped across the meadow from our camp, probably two miles away, and they wanted our women! On foot, they would make forays to our encampment in the dark of night—cowards that they were—in an attempt to intimidate and confuse us. It worked on some, but there was a core of hearty souls that were up to the task of fending off these attacks.

My brother and I were proud members of this group of hearty souls, as were the others I've mentioned. This core group held numerous strategy sessions at the ice cream stand—up by the camp offices—during which we plotted how to deal with this threat. It was shortly after one of these sessions that, through good solid reconnaissance, we discovered the "enemy" had access to—or owned—a 1948 Studebaker two-door coupe, capable of transporting from six to eight personnel. They were now mobile. This changed everything. It was very somber at the next strategy meeting, for we were now facing almost insurmountable odds in our attempt to save our community and our women.

But an event took place that same evening about an hour after sundown—say nine-thirty—that I believe changed Assemblies of God Church Camp history and gave us the will and resolve to meet this challenge.

Church had been dismissed and the core group and our women were finishing our treats and socializing with the general population up at the ice cream stand when one of our advanced scouts sent a message to us that a motor vehicle had been observed heading toward our camp. Follow-up reconnaissance confirmed that it was, indeed, the Studebaker loaded to the gills with the enemy. But, before we could man our battle stations, the car came roaring through the camp in a cloud of dust, spun a donut on our baseball field, and tore out of there to the main highway. Well, that did it! The gloves were off!

There's biblical support for our next move in response to this cowardly attack. We raced to retrieve our weapons, mostly old bed rails, galvanized pipes and such, then took up our battle stations. Our advanced scouts had gotten word back to us that those in the Studebaker were preparing for another assault, and we were ready. We had stretched a heavy chain across the dirt road between two large trees and lay waiting in the shadows. Sure enough, they came back. As the car approached the chain stretching across the road, those in the vehicle noticed it and the driver attempted to stop the car to avoid hitting the thing, but they were going too fast. They barreled into it and the car stopped dead in its tracks. The hood was torn from its hinges and thrown back over the roof. And then I and the others leaped out of the shadows armed with our bed rails and pipes to begin a world-class assault on the car. We didn't care about the occupants. You've never seen eight nineteen-year-olds get out of a two-door coupe as fast as these did and take off running across the meadow.

The biblical backing for our attack was this: First Samuel 26:8. "Then said Abishai to David, God hath delivered thine enemy into thine hand this day: now therefore let me smite him, I pray thee, with the spear even to the earth at once, and I will not smite him the second time." And we didn't smite them, but we sure beat the hell out of their car. The County Sheriff didn't think it was so funny the next morning, but we prevailed. We never saw the scoundrels or the Sheriff again. Abishai was to King David as we were to Cousin Fred, our Counselor: loyal soldiers. And our legend was born.

22

The High School Years

O ne of the most powerful tenets of the Pentecostals was that a teenager should never date someone he or she wouldn't marry. So dating is like playing in the Super Bowl and having never experienced the regular season. You have no frame of reference and you aren't allowed to screw up. (Wow!) I suppose this premise was based on the philosophy that new blood—and the accompanying rational thoughts—should never be allowed to enter the group. That reduced our options considerably. So much so that, at the Sunday night Youth for Christ meetings, it was a sort of feeding frenzy. Some peripheral non-Pentecostal kids were allowed to join this crowd, but those kids were mostly children of quasi-Pentecostals who had married a "normal" spouse.

On one Sunday evening each month, we would all meet at the church at five-thirty (my brother and I had to really hustle with our chores those evenings). The four or five teenagers in our church would pile into one of the adult chaperone's cars and we'd take off bound for the monthly Youth for Christ hoe-down at whatever little church was on the agenda. Most of these trips took about an hour or so. If you were fortunate enough (remember, we had to consider the "date/marry" test) to meet someone at one of these functions who met your criteria, any courting would have to take place at a distance, for you would only see each other once a month at these functions. And the devil could send many "pretenders to the throne" to subvert your relationship. You could have a budding romance one month and be left out in the cold the next. It was pretty rough duty.

During one of these forays into teenage courting, I had met a sweet young thing by the name of Euless Willis. I'm not kidding about her name—and we actually had a cow in the dairy herd named Euless, but I knew the cow before the girl. Euless, the girl, was from up north about fifty miles. We were both fifteen. I should really say I was fifteen going on ten. After realizing at our first meeting that we were *made for each other* we had rendezvous-ed three or four times at the Sunday night affairs and it was now apparent that we should have a "real" date, which meant something without either of our parents in attendance.

It so happened that Euless had an aunt she was planning to visit who lived in a town not far from our ranch, and she wondered if it would be possible for us to meet and have our first real date while she was there. "Well sure!" I said. "Let's do it!" So we made the arrangements and, on the appointed Saturday night, I fired up the 1962, lime green, two-door Chevy Impala, piled my parents in the back seat (yes, my parents) and headed out for Chico. I must say I wasn't pleased to have Mom and Dad in the back seat, but at least I could call it a "date" to my buddies. Not only could I not drive alone because I wasn't yet sixteen, but even after I *did* turn sixteen and got my driver's license my parents wouldn't let me go on dates un-chaperoned for the first six months I had my license. That was especially hard to take for a teenage boy, and when I was finally able to take a date out alone I had to be home by 11 p.m.—even through the end of my senior year.

We found my date's house and I pulled up to the curb and, announcing to my parents that I could handle this, I marched up to the front door and rang the bell. Then I rang it again. Finally, a very scary-looking woman with an unfiltered Camel dangling from her lips answered the door. "Yah, wad'ya you want?" she inquired. Not very impressive, I thought to myself. I snuck a nervous glance back at my parents in the car, then nervously shuffled my feet and—summoning up what courage I could muster—replied, "I'm here for Euless."

"I bet you are," was her reply. She left me on the front porch and went back into the house and, yelling out in a voice loud enough to wake the dead—or be heard over the commotion that was going on inside—announced, "Someone here to see lover girl." I snuck another glance back at Mom and Dad.

In a minute or so, Euless appeared at the front door, apologizing for her aunt, the commotion going on inside, and the fact that her aunt hadn't asked me to come in. I assured her that everything was fine.

But, *Euless*!

In front of me was not the sweet, innocent and pretty young girl whom I had grown to know and covet, but a fire-eating vixen dressed as if her rate was two hundred dollars an hour. Breasts I didn't realize she had were spilling out of a blouse about two sizes too small, a skin-tight leather skirt at least eight inches above her knees, heels so high that they could have given her a nose bleed, and very red lips. And there I was with Mom and Dad in our '62 Chevy. I almost passed out.

So, I was standing on the front porch with this *woman*, and was at a complete loss to know what to do next. It seemed like forever, but I gathered my composure and held out my hand to help her down the steps, which was no easy feat in that skirt. I could hardly breathe as she neared me and planted a teasing kiss on my cheek. "It's soooo good to see you, Steve." (Holy cow!) Her perfume almost pushed me over the cliff. I somewhat gained my composure and firmly clasped her hand in mine as we began to make our way down the sidewalk to my lime green Chevy.

We were about ten feet from the car when she came to a dead stop, noticing my mom and dad nestled in the back seat. "Who's that in the car, Steve?" she asked. I had a lump in my throat.

"That's my parents," I told her.

"What are they doing here?"

I was in a bind because I had told her that I had my driver's license. I had to think fast.

"Oh, they just wanted to come along and meet you," was the best I could do, but it sounded lame even to me. I was standing there with this exquisite *animal* who had my heart thumping, and I saw both of my parents staring at her, mouths agape. Then she faked me out and briskly walked to the open back window of the car and—reaching out her hand as she introduced herself—said, "It's so nice to meet you, Mr. and Mrs. Morgan. It'll be nice to get to know you on the ride back to your home." (Damn! What do I do now?) And then my Mother replied in her inimitable way, "Oh, Dearie, were coming along with you." I could have crawled in a hole. My dad never said anything during the whole encounter. I don't think he could have with the bad case of dry mouth he must have had—never taking his eyes off my date, sitting there in the back seat with Mom—as if in a trance. Euless turned to look at me with a less-than-pleasant expression on her face, and it was obvious that she now was uncomfortable with the way she was dressed. My parents had obviously changed the equation, and even though she was good to look at, I had to admit that her garb was a bit outrageous.

For a moment I thought she was going to back out and have me walk her back to the house, but we walked a ways away from the car—out of earshot—and she gave me a small piece of her mind which I surely deserved. Then I explained the situation to her and she went along with me—us—anyway. I'm not really sure I could have handled what she had in mind, but it was fairly obvious what her intentions were. Even though I might not have been up to the task, it sure would have been fun trying—but that came much later. At least my parents let her sit in the front seat with me. It was pretty quiet as we drove several blocks to the A & W Drive-In and had our hamburgers and root beer floats. In those days I wasn't much of a conversationalist, and even if I would have been there was no way to have any sort of private talk. Almost every time we would chat a bit my mom would add something which made it even more uncomfortable. My dad never said anything. He was still in a trance—his open mouth probably caught several flies that warm summer night.

We were at the drive-in for no more than an hour, at most, and there was really nothing else to do. Normally, on a real date, we'd have cruised the Esplanade to see and be seen with the other kids. But there was no way in the world I was going to take the chance that anyone I knew would see me on a date with my parents in the back seat, so I just took her home. I apologized for the evening and she said, "That's ok. I kind of feel silly the way I dressed."

"Nah," I said. "You look great. Maybe we can have a *real* date sometime."

"Maybe we can, Steve."

She really did seem very nice. I walked her to the front door, gave her a light hug, told her goodnight and walked back to the car. Music blared from inside the house as she opened and closed the door. My mother started to say something when I got in the car, but I raised my hand and said it was okay—I probably wouldn't see her again anyway. After all there was that "only date someone you would marry" philosophy, and I must admit that I was somewhat confused by the change in her.

I found out later that she lived with her single mom and a brother. If her aunt was any indication of what her mother was like, it probably wouldn't have been a good fit anyway. I also found out that her mother was only sending her to the youth get-togethers where I had met her in an attempt to "straighten her out." I guess she was having problems in school and was a wild-child. I think all she needed was someone to really care for her, but that probably wasn't going to be me. I saw her periodically after that at youth functions, but it was uncomfortable. We talked a little but the bloom was off, which was too bad, because there was a sweet girl in there somewhere. I don't think she ever mentioned our "date" to anyone, or I would have heard about it. She was probably as embarrassed about the situation as I was. You can be sure I never said anything to anyone.

Dating was a dicey proposition in my family even without the Pentecostal overtones. We lived way out in the country and had chores and things to do. Without a driver's license I was land-locked. Although Dad would have me drive the truck to town to pick up cattle feed or other supplies before I had my license, I'd take the back roads and it was never a problem. Everyone knew everyone else and even if a cop would have seen me it wouldn't have been a problem. Everyone did it. That's just the way it was in the country. But I could never take a car to town on a pleasure trip without a license—and it was tough even with a license, until I got my own car just before my senior year. But, even with my own car, it was very difficult to lead a normal teenage dating existence, because of the sinning and "end of the world" thing.

I had many opportunities to date in high school. I wasn't bad looking, was reasonably intelligent, and was into athletics—and athletics were a magnet for babes. Between my shyness and this Pentecostal thing, though, it was like I had two left feet. I can't blame it all on our particular religion, but it typically brought a quick end to any budding romance.

It wasn't that I wanted to date a bunch of "heathens" but the severe guidelines of the Church and the do's and don'ts blew most of these opportunities out of the water. The fact that I was into athletics masked my religious background enough so that I could lead a relatively normal life at school, which is what occupies most teenager's lives. But, if and when I would announce to my parents that I had a date for Friday night the grilling would begin. This was not in a Gestapo manner, it was more sinister. My parents played with my soul.

"Stephen, you know what we believe," they'd say (especially my mother). Then they'd quote from scripture, the passage "Be ye not unequally yoked." (It was the "date/marry" thing, again.) Hell, I couldn't even get out of the starting gate, let alone run the race. Theirs was an absolute attempt to keep a youngster from finding out about anything that hadn't originated in the Church. It was the same with higher education. If, after high school, you were fortunate enough to be contemplating college—and unless you were going to attend a Christian school affiliated with the Assemblies of God—you were thought be a heretic, for, in their minds, the liberal arts colleges were a bastion of anti-Christian philosophy. "They'll ruin your mind," we were told. "Put bad thoughts in your head." "Make you question things." Any group that is so closed-minded I believe has something to hide. And the Church did.

The Church would lament the fact that there was a lack of "young people." "We need to get more young people involved," the adults in the Church would say. And it was this dichotomy and the resulting fear that drove them. After all, if we were allowed to know too much about the outside we'd cross over, so they attempted to create a bubble existence and keep us involved in teenage things within this bubble. And that was hard to do. It didn't work. Take a good look at the audience in a fundamentalist telecast and you won't find anyone under forty.

I've always been a voracious reader. That really never came from my parents for all they ever read when I was a youngster—other than the local newspaper—were the religious publications that were affiliated with the Church. Most prominent among these was *The Pentecostal Evangel*, which only served to solidify their belief that the Church's philosophy was the correct and only one. Later on in high school we would get *Reader's Digest* and that was a breath of fresh air, but we were warned to not put too much importance on what we read in the stories, for they were just made up. (Thank God!)

About three or four miles from our ranch was a little public library. Just a little house on a ranch that someone provided and which was filled with books stocked by a county librarian. There was no one on duty and it was a complete honor system, which we didn't fiddle with because of the priceless treasure that the books were. This was especially true since we had no television until I was fourteen, and the library had an almost complete set of every book that Louis L'Amour had written to that time.

You could create anything in your mind that you wanted while you read these books and dream whatever dreams you cared to. I remember, as a kid, telling people that all I really wanted out of life was a horse, saddle, bedroll, rifle, and canteen. And I could become the lead character in any book I was reading and act out many of the scenarios because of living on a ranch and being around horses and cattle. We weren't far from the Sacramento River whose riparian habitat provided a wealth of places to camp and hide and play. I also developed a fondness for A. B. Guthrie and his chronicling of "the Way West." But this love of reading created another crossroads in my life, for it introduced opinions and thoughts that—at the very least—opened my mind to other opinions and thoughts, and they begat other thoughts and *knowledge*.

In a normal, non-Pentecostal youngster, this acquisition of knowledge would be relished and cherished. And for me it was no different. But with the Pentecostal overlay this newly-gained thirst for knowledge was at odds with "this is what we believe." Even if what they/we believed wasn't at odds with whatever particular book or thought I was disseminating, it caused a stir in my family and in my mind. (I must say that I may be overstating this conflict but it remains a very real part of my memory.) But, notwithstanding what took place in my childhood, the impetus for me to write this book has never been to indict my Pentecostal roots and teachings but to expose them for what they are, right or wrong. Good or bad. And the Church's paranoia as a result of the possibility of young people gaining knowledge from an alternate source, did nothing if not fuel my intellectual fire.

I wasn't trying to figuratively "kick the door in" while addressing this whole issue but just trying to rid myself of the "just because" spectacle. You know the old saying, "*just because* doesn't mean it's so." That's all I was doing, and am doing. And, to my parents' credit, on this one issue, after awhile they pretty much left me alone. Maybe they did this because they were so busy making a living on the ranch or *just because*. Whatever the reason, reading served to fuel my curiosity and give me some respite from the drubbing my brain was enduring as a result of the Pentecostals.

The thing about western religions is that they're not a seven-day-a-week pursuit, like the eastern or mid-eastern religions. Those religions and their beliefs guide their daily lives. We westerners may not agree with their philosophies but you know where they stand. And for those others it's not just "we believe." They *live* it. Good or bad. We have our little *sins* that we approve of and, like the Pentecostals, sing in our churches and worship our God on Sunday and then do whatever we want the rest of the week. It seems like our God is only in a church.

I remember in my childhood when earrings, make-up of any kind, lipstick, and all baubles and bangles were thought to be sinful. "Not for the glory of God but for man," the Pentecostals said. But now you watch one of their broadcasts on television or see them in some tabloid and they look like Twelfth Street Hookers. What's happened to "Be ye in the world, not of the world"? I guess that's not convenient any more. It's not that it matters to me but it's an example of the manipulation of the "written word." When you develop rules for a club, there's a keeper-of-the-rules and the rules govern behavior within the group, pretty simple. But when you add a human being's eternal soul to the equation it gets dicey. The Pentecostals had their club and rules, and told you that these rules came from God, but reserved the right to interpret them in any manner they saw fit. (Or you're going to hell!)

That's my biggest rub. So, after all this fabulous newfound experience with knowledge that was separate from what we were spoon-fed, I still had to deal with my parents' "just because." That's what confounded me. I had newfound knowledge and literary experience but when push came to shove I still wasn't sure of my eternal soul. In a Pentecostal, that doubt becomes so embedded that it can overshadow reasonable thought. A non-believer, such as Mother Teresa, could do great things, and help the disenfranchised and the homeless of the world but be "lost" in the Pentecostal's way of thinking. As long as a member of the Church attended and participated in the services as prescribed they could get away with almost anything. But, as the Bible says, "He, who hath not love, is but a sounding gong and a tinkling cymbal." (Man-o-Man! It's hard to love while you're judging.)

As long as you live under your parent's roof you must subscribe to their way of thought—or at least it was that way in my teenage years. If you don't follow their rules it's "rebellion." ("Let's pray for him. He's rebelling, you know.") I have tried—and am trying— to provide an environment to allow for my children to develop their own thoughts and philosophies. I trust that some of what I've experienced and learned is taken into consideration by their thought processes. But I believe that the more important aspect of growing up is the development of the ability to think for one's self.

One example of testing the waters stands out in my mind. I was a junior in high school and had been *dating* a girl who was a senior— pretty heady stuff for a Magna-Cum-Pentecostal. But there were two strikes against this relationship: the first was that she was Asian and the second was that she was from a family of non-believers. "Now, Dearie," my mother would say, "You know that's not what we believe." She'd get a very sincerely pained expression on her face and continue, "You can't marry her, can you, darling." It wasn't a question. She really believed that.

Graduation time had come and I had been honored by my Asian girlfriend with an invitation to be her date at the graduation party. It doesn't get much better than that: a senior heartthrob asking a junior knucklehead to the graduation party. But there was a problem: I had to get this past my parents. My brother knew of this invite, and I solicited his council. His advice was, "Hell, Steve, just do it," which was a bit dicey for me at the time. Although I did value his "damn the torpedoes" approach.

It was literally two hours before the graduation ceremony and I hadn't approached either of my parents with my dilemma. I didn't have the guts. Out of desperation, I approached my mother first. She was somewhat receptive and gave me her typical "date/marry" speech and then sent me off with "ask your father." Dad usually wasn't consulted in these matters, due to the fact that—if pressed— he would just say "no." But, this time, I felt that I had a reasonable chance of success due to the fact that I had a mid-level approval from Mom.

It wasn't to be.

Dad was in the midst of the process of milking our dairy herd when I approached him. There were a couple hired hands with him, but they didn't speak English. This probably wasn't the best timing, but I had waited too long. I had rehearsed several speeches before I approached him and had made sure that all my chores were done. It was now or never.

"Dad, Tina has invited me to her senior party and I want to go," I said—already dressed to go.

"No, you're not," he answered, not looking at me.

"Why, Dad?"

"Because we don't believe in that."

"Believe in what, Dad?" I asked, following him as he ushered in another string of Holsteins.

"There'll be dancing. And it'll be late. No, you're not going!" A little anger was coming into the conversation.

"I'm going, Dad," I said. And, with that, I turned and headed out of the barn toward our lime green Chevy.

Dad was right on my tail and rushed past me, opened the driver's door and took the keys out of the ignition. Well, at that point, I was worked up. I had quite a temper in those days but had maintained my cool pretty well during our conversation. However, the unreasonableness of the whole thing pushed me over. It scared my dad when I got angry, and this time was no different. I wasn't a yeller and a screamer—never have been—instead, when I was really angry as a kid—and now, for that matter—I spoke in a very quiet voice. And that's what I did this time.

Quietly, I said "Give me the keys, Dad." And he did.

I went to the party with Tina and we had a wonderful time. However, one thing I did agree to was that I would be home by eleven o'clock. I was, and I missed most of the party. But I had won the battle—if not the war. The world didn't end and the Lord didn't come back and find me sinning and leave me here, but I felt guilty all night, and for no acceptable reason.

The excuse I made for having to be home by eleven o'clock was that I was handling the irrigation on one of the neighboring ranches and I had to change the water at that time. (I was responsible, after all!) Later on, my Dad became good friends with Tina's father, a relationship that remains to this day. Tina married and moved away. I haven't seen her in forty years.

*****

That's the other thing. I had to lie to my parents about where I was going with my friends on weekends and other social occasions in an effort to fit in with the "normal" kids and I had to lie to my friends and acquaintances about why I couldn't do certain things to appear to be *normal* and fit in. What a terrible burden I brought on myself. I guess I could have just given in, but that wasn't and isn't my nature. "Just because" isn't in my vocabulary.

*****

I hurt my leg really badly during a church basketball game in February of 1965. I had gone up for a rebound and one of the players on the other team ran into my legs and took them out from underneath me. As a result, I came down squarely on my right knee. The floor of the gym was concrete with tiles laid over it. Needless to say, there wasn't much give to the surface and I chipped the femur and smashed the kneecap. As young as I was, I had never suffered an injury nearly as bad as this during a sporting event—or any other time for that matter—and this incident was hard to take. Immediately after the accident my teammates picked me up and carried me off the floor.

They called my parents and my mother came to get me. When she saw the extent of my injury she almost passed out. My knee had swollen to twice its size in less than a half hour.

My mom was able to get hold of Doc Ely and we drove the eight miles into town, with me laid out on the backseat. It was about eleven o'clock in the evening when we got there. The doc took one look at my knee and said he needed to get the fluid out so he could get a good X-ray. He had me lie down on a table, propped my knee up with a pillow and stuck a needle, which was about six-inches long, into my knee. He took out about 300cc of liquid, which brought my knee back to a more normal size and then the three of us all pitched in and got me to the X-ray table. Once on the table, I lay back and he took a picture of my knee. He developed the X-ray and that's when he determined the extent of the damage. Then the three of us kind of dragged/walked me back to the original patient room and got me laid down on the table again. He'd decided that the best thing to do was to go ahead and put a plaster cast on my leg. He really didn't pay much attention to the fractured kneecap. He said that it would heal in time. So, with the cast on my leg, the doc, my mother, and I managed to get me to and into the car. I lay on the backseat once again for the ride home.

As you might imagine, the cast on my leg severely limited my ability to move around. But, in a day or so, I could do pretty well. The doc had put a rubber bumper on the heal portion of the cast so I could kind of hobble-walk. I had crutches, but didn't use them much—only when Mom or Dad was looking. I now couldn't do my chores, which really didn't make my brother very happy.

*****

Backtracking I should say that, in my sophomore year of high school I was fortunate enough to be selected for the varsity baseball team. That wasn't complete B.S. as our school had a student body of about five hundred, which is pretty good for a country school. Mr. Morris was our coach. Bill Morris. He had an assistant by the name of Mario Seraphin who, we were told, had been a catcher in the Reds Minor League system. There was probably one instance that won me a place on the team. Art Susee, the best pitcher on the team—and a senior to boot—was pitching in a simulated practice game. He didn't throw unusually hard, and wasn't a dominant pitcher, but he threw a lot of off-speed stuff, which made him hard to hit. He had been the Westside League Player of the Year the season before.

I came up to bat and dug in and awaited the first pitch. Art threw me his typical flat slider-curve and I bailed out and took a called strike. Morris yelled from the dugout, "Stay in there, Morgan! You can't hit a curve on your ass!" (Which was true.) Determined to not "bail out" the next time I dug in and awaited his next pitch. Art grooved a fastball belt-high and I hit it off the "404'" sign in dead center field. There were two runners on, and they both scored, and we won the simulated game. I had made the team. (As an aside, we played our high school ball in a former minor league park that was really kind of neat. All the old advertising on the outfield walls that was still there made us feel like major leaguers. The team had moved on, but it was fun to envision what it must have been like when even our little, three thousand population town had a minor league team.)

Around the second week of the season that year—which was about a month after I had struck my blow—we were practicing for a game with the Gridley High School team the following Friday. Gridley had a hard-throwing right-hander who had been mowing down the opposition. And much like Hall of Fame Pitcher Nolan Ryan in later years—who pitched for the Mets, Angels, Astros, and Rangers—he would snap off a hard slider after he had thrown you two blazing fastballs. So your weight was on the backs of your feet when you'd bat against him.

We had a kid named Fred Rudd—a senior and a tough kid—who threw hard and could break off one of those sliders. He was inconsistent, but Mr. Morris had him throwing batting practice to get us ready for Gridley. It was my turn in the batting cage, and I had dug in and waited for Rudd's first pitch. He started with the hard-slider and I bailed. Once again, from Morris, "Get off your ass, Morgan." Well, there was no way I was going to bail on the next pitch. And I dug in again. Fred wound up and let her rip. The ball was coming right at my head but I wasn't going to flinch. Coming, coming, coming, coming, splat!! It was either a hard slider that didn't break or a fastball that he lost control of. The ball hit the brim of my batting helmet and ricochet off the bone above my left eye. I came to with my head resting on home plate and with another of our country doctors, Doc Poulsen, finishing eighteen stitches over my eye.

That pretty much finished my sophomore baseball season—and my ability to hang in on a curveball. But, during my rehabilitation, I played catch in the outfield with another teammate and as a result realized that I had a pretty good breaking ball to go along with my natural fastball. I traded my bat in for the pitching mound.

Due to age restrictions, the summer after my junior year was the last year I could qualify for the Babe Ruth League. I had honed my pitching skills and prepared for the summer season. I met with a good deal of success, pitching a no-hitter in the process, and was looked upon by Coach Morris as the number one starting pitcher on our high school team for the upcoming season the next spring: my senior year.

Then I played in the church basketball game and ruined my knee.

*****

With my leg in its cast, I could operate the lime green Chevy with my left leg while my right leg was resting on the passenger seat. So I could get around. It had been about a week since the injury and our basketball team was playing the team from Paradise—up in the hills east of Chico. A couple of the cheerleaders whom I knew had asked me if I would like to ride along on the Rooter's Bus and I had accepted. This was a group that I typically didn't associate with because I was an *athlete* but, in light of my wounded condition, I accepted.

So we were at the basketball game in the gymnasium and I was wearing a sweater over a long-sleeved shirt and I was feeling rather warm. Naturally, I took off the sweater, which served to reduce my body temperature somewhat. After a while I became flushed again and wasn't really feeling all that well. but I concentrated on the game and when it was finished we all got back on the bus and headed back to Orland. I was burning up. It was about an hour's drive back and, once we arrived, we all disbanded and headed our separate ways. I had downplayed my fever. I managed to get home and safely into bed. And I fell asleep—probably around midnight.

I awoke about an hour later, overcome with sweat and feeling very poorly. I had soaked the sheets on my bed and was in real trouble. I was hallucinating. I was able to get my wits about me and called out to my mother who, bless her heart, had always managed to stay awake until my brother and I were safely home and asleep, and she was still awake this time. She came into my room and found me in a bad way. The pain in my right leg was excruciating and we needed to do something fast. She was able to get Doc Ely on the phone and, somehow, we got me to the car and made our way into town and to his office.

Once we arrived, the doc and my mother were able to maneuver me onto a table and get my leg elevated, which was hard to do with the plaster cast and the pain. Doc decided that he should get the cast off as soon as possible and used one of those vibrating, toothless saws to cut down the back side to release the cast. About three-fourths of the way through this exercise, the pressure from my swollen knee caused the cast to break the rest of the way, exposing this terrible black and green thing that was my right knee. During this maneuver— and not intentionally—the Doc had cut a swath in the back of my leg that was leaking blood rather aggressively. So we had my infected knee and blood running down my leg at three o'clock in the morning, just Doc Ely, my mother, and me. Dad was home herding the cows in for the morning milking.

I don't think I was in danger of bleeding to death—I coagulate well—but the combination of all this was very disconcerting. So the doc decided that he had to get the liquid poison out of my leg. He took a mammoth needle and jabbed it into the back of my leg, opposite the kneecap, and started pumping. He must have gotten three 100cc vials of liquid out of there. And all this time I was dealing with this stone-cold awake with no sedatives of any kind. Ole Doc Ely was so worried about my leg—and with good reason— that he forgot about the guy connected to the other end. Eventually he was able to get things under control and wrapped my leg in ace bandages and Mom and I went back to the ranch. Dad helped Mom get me back into my bed. It was six o'clock in the morning. We'd been at the doctor's office for three hours, and so had Doc Ely, a country doctor and a dedicated physician. He had done the best he could, and I had survived.

By ten o'clock that morning I was back in Doc Ely's office. It appears that I had contracted a rather aggressive form of staph infection that was generating large quantities of liquid and I was running a fever of between 103 and 104 degrees. And for the next forty-five days I ran a temperature of at least 102 degrees every day and every other day had at least 100cc of liquid drawn from my knee. I was lucky I didn't lose my leg. It had been only recently that an antibiotic had been approved by the FDA that could be taken orally to combat the ravages of this infection.

Needless to say, all of this kept me from attending school. As I've mentioned, it certainly curtailed the spring baseball season for me which—to a kid hooked on sports—was a bitter pill. Especially since I had had such a great season the previous summer and my prospects were looking good.

I was taking an advanced Biology class (we were probably dissecting six-legged frogs) when I suffered my church basketball accident. The teacher of the class was a fellow by the name of Igor Valov. As the name implies, he was a Russian émigré and had been in this country for fifteen years, or so. We thought he was a Communist. None of us had the brains of an ice cube and our parents had told us that anyone from that part of the world *must* be a Communist. (And that was *before* Fox News.) An extremely bright man, he taught the class with a vengeance, very tough when grading. As a result of his heritage and his rather large, unkempt appearance he was something of an outcast. My mother had gone into town to my high school to discuss with the administration the fact that I wouldn't be able to attend school for the next month and a half, and that I would need some tutoring to complete my required classes. In those days, the school wasn't equipped to provide a tutoring service, but provided the daily lessons—which my mother picked up from school every so often.

I hadn't been particularly close to Mr. Valov. I wasn't part of the nerdy group which hung around him, but wasn't one of the smart-asses either. When he heard that I was laid up and wouldn't be able to attend school for an extended period of time he volunteered to come to our ranch and tutor me in Biology and Calculus. So, three times a week, this fat, sweaty Russian would drive the eight miles to our farm and spend an hour and a half with me, while I was propped up in a rented hospital bed in the living room of our old farmhouse. Through his efforts, I was able to complete the required—and extended—lessons for my junior year. I'm sure I never thanked him properly since I was just a kid. I trust my parents did. He never asked for anything—and my parents wouldn't have offered—maybe he got some of Grandma's küchen. I don't know whatever happened to him but he sure had an impact on my life.

Through several mini-crises—with the infection coming and going—we managed to make it through to the end of my junior year, and for me to be able to take Tina to her senior party. That summer I was able to buy a 1957 Ford Fairlane two-door hardtop at the exorbitant price of $400. These were the days of the street rods so I felt compelled to beef up the engine and drivetrain of the car. There was an old guy at the Texaco station in the little town where Grandpa and I had bought the Cokes after our watermelon foray who was pretty handy with these things. I parked the car in his shop for most of the summer before my senior year while he did his thing. I won't go into the details but he soup-ed it up *real good*. And I spent most of what I made that summer working on the farm buying parts and paying the old guy. Finally I was ready to race, stop-light to stop-light, on the Esplanade in Chico. (Coooool.)

The injury to my knee severely hampered my ability to play sports my senior year. I had come on pretty strong at the end of my junior year on the football team and was slated to be a starting halfback that next fall, but it wasn't meant to be. In pre-season practice, my knee would swell up and cause severe pain, mostly immobilizing me. Sports medicine was non-existent, and my parents were simple farm people who did the best they could. I still held out the hope of being able to play baseball that coming spring but, being a right-handed pitcher and pushing off on my bad right knee, it caused my injury to act up and made it virtually impossible to continue. So much for my high school sports career. That was a rough time for me since, as with most aspiring athletes, I had had visions of grandeur.

23

The Army. Vietnam?

The fall after my senior year I was drafted into the Army. I turned eighteen in October and—almost a month to the day after my birthday—I got my draft notice. I wasn't either for or against the war in Vietnam at the time, and my father had served in World War II, but it wasn't a good time to be in the military with all the unknowns. The day came for me to show up at the induction center in Oakland. I and several others who had also gotten their draft notices met at the Greyhound Bus depot in Willows, about twenty miles from our ranch, and got on board and headed to the big city. That's the one and only time I've ridden on a Greyhound.

The induction center in Oakland—across the bay from San Francisco—was located on San Pablo Avenue, in one of the most filthy, maggot-infested, hooker-ridden parts of town. When we were getting off the bus we literally had to fight off the drug addicts and hookers to get into the induction building. Once inside, we were separated into groups alphabetically and sent to a sort of "locker room" where we were instructed to remove all of our clothing except for our underwear and shoes. Boy that was a scene. Other than the locker room in high school I hadn't been around so many partially-naked men. It wasn't a pretty sight, as you might imagine. Once we were properly disrobed, we then were instructed to meet up again in a fairly large room with a series of yellow lines on the floor, parallel to each other. There were probably two hundred and fifty people in the room. Several soldiers dressed in military fatigues addressed us and gave us orders on what to do next as we stood in line. About twenty of us at a time were instructed to move forward to a yellow line that was perpendicular to the one we were lined up on. We were then instructed to bend over and "spread our cheeks." Well, even I knew what that meant, so I dutifully bent over and grabbed my ass and pulled sideways with each hand. But several of my potential comrades were somewhat confused by the order and, having bent over, placed the index finger of each hand in their mouths and pulled sideways, which caused quite a stir and set a benchmark for what was to come.

Once our posteriors were properly inspected (What the hell was that all about?) we were then instructed to get back in our lines and proceed forward to another yellow line and wait until we were called. Since I had been through quite a severe medical trauma the year before, my family had prevailed upon the various doctors who had treated me to write letters to the draft board explaining their opinions that the damage to my knee would preclude my serving in the military. It seemed that everyone had a letter, so it slowed things down to a crawl. For five or six hours all of us, all two-hundred-fifty strong—naked except for underwear and shoes—in various states of cleanliness, loitered about in this massive hall waiting for our names to be called. My name was finally called and I did my thing with one of the Army doctors and, having read my paperwork, he classified me "1-Y: Non-Combat-Support." (Thank God.) That meant I probably wouldn't get shot at. They didn't actually take me and I got a letter from the Army announcing that I was to report for another physical a year from then on my nineteenth birthday. I took Greyhound back home. (That was actually my second ride, even though earlier I said I had only taken one.)

*****

In August of the following year—about three months before I was to take my second Army physical—I attended the County Fair with a friend of mine. I haven't mentioned, but I attended a small high school my freshman year in Hamilton City where my Grandfather had bought the Cokes to wash down the melons. The high school in this town was the one designated to be my assigned school, based on the districting set forth by the county school department. It probably had an enrollment of about a hundred and fifty kids. During that freshman year I had played football and baseball and done what freshmen do. But there was a friction that had built up between a rather large Hispanic population in the school and several of my classmates and me. I don't think it was a racial thing. That may be naïve, but that's just the way it was. These days we all have families and I've seen them from time to time over the years. We outgrew our aggression.

Because of this conflict—and also because I had shown some athletic prowess—my parents transferred me across the valley to Orland High School, because Orland had a strong athletic program. But through my remaining high school years the conflict with my former classmates had taken on a new life to the point that—when my friend and I attended the County Fair—the conflict was at a boil. Even though most of us had graduated from high school by then, the antagonism was very alive and well.

Mid-day of the Saturday when my friend and I planned to attend the fair we were crossing a bridge over the Sacramento River on Highway thirty-two when a carload of the classmates I've mentioned from my freshman year passed us. Being the cocky bastard I was in those days I saluted them with the middle finger of my right hand as our cars passed, which was not a good idea.

In the countryside where I grew up, the County Fair was a big deal—a place to take your best girl, to show her off, and to generally see and be seen. There was no way that the boys from my freshman days weren't going to be there. But, due to the events earlier in the day, it wouldn't be wise for any of us to bring female companions, so this time it was just my buddy and I that were attending. I smelled trouble.

My friend, Al, and I got there about eight o'clock and made the rounds of the various exhibits. Now and then we'd see some of our acquaintances and they'd give us an update on who had seen whom. Like, "We just saw them over by the cattle-barns." Things like that. About nine o'clock or so we began to get information that the boys from across the valley had been seen in the carnival area. About ten or twelve of them we were told, which was typical because they tended to band together. It was a forgone conclusion that we were going to run into them, and we wandered around the various buildings and exhibits until about ten o'clock when we came face-to-face with them in an aisle in the carnival area.

We saw them and they saw us—a bunch of testosterone-filled nineteen-year-olds. I've mentioned before that I had quite a temper as a youngster, but I had never really been in a fist fight, as such. The fact that I was pretty well put-together—and the resolve in my personality that came across as toughness—had always kept me from getting my ass kicked. But I wasn't so sure it would work this time. It was going to be hard to get around this thing. And, by "saluting" these boys earlier in the day I had—to some degree— thrown the first punch.

As we approached the group I said to Al under my breath, "You can take off now. I'm the one that got this started." "No way. I'm in this, too," he came back. We were now face-to-face with the group and the leader, a guy named Rick, stepped forward and basically said there was going to be hell to pay for what I had done earlier in the day. My response was that whatever he wanted to do, he'd better get started. He indicated that whatever was going to happen shouldn't happen there in the fairgrounds, because there were too many people around, and suggested that we go out into the parking lot to settle things. Al and I foolishly accepted. As we were all walking out of the carnival area toward the parking lot a couple of guys we knew volunteered to go with us and help with things. I thanked them and suggested that they come along, but stay back a little just in case.

We now were almost to where my car was parked and the Hamilton City boys were beginning to fan out around us. Noticing this, I told the leader, Rick, that this should just be between me and him. He was standing by my car and, mumbling something, half turned away as if to lean up against it. I relaxed a little and he wheeled around and brought his cowboy-boot-clad-foot up to the inside of my right knee—my bad knee—and dislocated my knee cap. It's hard to describe the pain, but in my moment of anguish I was able to take him out before collapsing to the ground. But there were too many of them and they overwhelmed Al and the two other guys who had followed us to help and pretty much beat the crap out of them. Then they were gone. After I had taken out Rick, for some reason the others left me alone. The whole thing probably didn't take more than a minute, but the local newspaper made a big deal out of it.

So, on August 10, 1967, I had another surgery on my right knee. In addition to the boot striking and dislocating my kneecap, it had chipped my femur again. That chip needed to come out, so the doctors opened my knee up with about a six-inch incision and went exploring. I had some damaged cartilage from the previous injury, so they took both the bone chip and the cartilage out and sewed me up. If someone had the same surgery today, there would probably be a barely discernable arthroscopic incision. The doctor said my kneecap would realign itself in time. Forty-two years later it still hasn't, but things have been fine.

But I needed to have my knee rehabilitated again, and it caused me to miss the fall semester at the junior college I was attending. I was able to live at home on the ranch during this time, but I had to pay my bills since my parents weren't able to help me much. Within a month or so after the surgery, I got a job at the local Shell gas station out by the freeway. Well, my leg wasn't in very good shape, yet, and walking on the concrete didn't help things. And the old guy I worked for, Clarence Schad, was not the nicest of people. Although it wasn't his fault I had a bum leg. I really shouldn't have been doing that kind of work in the first place, but I had no choice—and Clarence gave me no slack.

The station was located on an exit off Interstate five and was the last stop for gas on the freeway for about thirty or forty miles. In those days, when someone pulled into the station we did everything for them: pumped the gas, washed the windshield, checked the oil, checked the air pressure in the tires, checked the belts and hoses, and anything else that looked "iffy." I was running around like a chicken with his head cut off. As part of our duties we were instructed by Clarence—in fact he demanded—that we sell each customer something in addition to the gas: a belt, a hose, windshield wipers or whatever. We weren't supposed to let customers get away without them spending extra money whether the situation warranted it or not. We always had to find something wrong, and it made me uncomfortable to have to discover phantom problems most of the time. It was dishonest, but that was our job description and people were vulnerable so far from another station.

I had been working under these conditions for about a month and a half when I got my second draft notice and was instructed to leave everything home but a toothbrush and several changes of underwear. This was not good news. I was to report to the same induction center in Oakland for my follow-up physical in late October. It was going to be necessary to quit my job to allow for the time off, since Clarence would have never given it to me, but I really was ready to move on anyway. The job wasn't right. So I went by the station to announce that I would be quitting in a week due to my draft notice and he gave me the classic "You can't quit, I'm firing you," speech, and that was that.

*****

This time, my parents drove me to Oakland—since it appeared that I was really going to be inducted into the Army. Before we left, I had seen the doctor again and he had written a letter that basically stated there was no way on Earth I would be able to conduct my duties in the military due to the condition of my knee. Mom and Dad dropped me off after a tearful farewell and headed back to the farm to milk the cows, while I headed off for my induction physical, letter in hand.

During the processing period, we went through much the same

routine as we had the year before. The main difference this time is that they addressed each of us on more of an individual basis—not like a bunch of cattle as they had before. After they poked and prodded, each person was assigned a doctor for an interview. There were about twenty people per doctor, so it was quite a wait. After a couple hours, they finally got to me and I handed the doctor my papers. He shrugged his shoulders and said, "Everyone has papers," and handed them back to me. That was unnerving—I wasn't sure what he meant, but I had a pretty good idea. It wasn't a popular war, and people were already going to great lengths to avoid serving. Not that I wasn't willing to go, but the condition of my knee was so much worse than the year before I was really doubtful of even being able to complete basic training. Even though my dad had been in World War II and it just followed that if you were asked, you went, the war in Vietnam was really beginning to heat up and the public outcry was beginning to reach its fever pitch.

So the doctor sent me on with my papers to another area where they updated all my information and took another look at my papers. This time a young doctor—or maybe he was a medic—actually looked at them and wrote something down on a form and gave it to me along with my papers. Then instructed me to, "go down the hall to the room on the right," so I did. (By the way, we were fully-clothed this time.) When I got to the next room they asked me for the form I had been given and told me that I was among a group that was going to be bused across the bay to Letterman Hospital at the Presidio Army Base in San Francisco. They said it was at this hospital that they would make the final determination and told me I might be there a week or so. I asked them if this was standard protocol and they said "no." I was being sent because of the letter describing the condition of my knee. Well, at least someone was paying attention.

There were about fifteen of us on the bus—all with some sort of malady or another—real or imagined. We got to the hospital and piled off the bus and into the reception area where they issued us "khakis" to wear around the place. The uniforms had insignias that basically told everyone that we were possible pretenders. Not *real* soldiers, after all—at least that's what most people thought of us. (Oh, well.) If you haven't been to the Presidio area of San Francisco, you're really missing something. It is one of the most beautiful places you can imagine. It's located just south of the Golden Gate Bridge and is heavily wooded with magnificent views. If you're going to be stuck somewhere for a while, that's the place to be.

The next morning we started the process over again but this time they didn't poke and prod. For eight or ten of us, those of us with leg problems, they issued wheelchairs to get about. I guess they weren't taking any chances. That was kind of neat, because those of us who were mobile could zip around the halls to kill time and the boredom. And bored we were. No doctor even took a look at me for a couple of days, so I had absolutely nothing to do, and the television in those days was pretty pathetic. They did let us roam around the grounds to some degree, but when they saw our insignias they didn't let us go far, which was kind of spooky.

When they finally took a look at my knee and the papers they scheduled tests and then I sat for another day or two. In their defense, the hospital was very busy since it was a main receiving depot for the wounded coming back from Vietnam. That wasn't very pleasant and gave me a first-hand view of things—young guys my age with missing arms and legs—it was pretty rough.

When they got back to me, again, I was scheduled to see an orthopedic surgeon. He put my knee through all kinds of maneuvers, which made it sore as hell and then—after making notations in the medical record—said he'd see me again the next day. Two days later, I was scheduled to see another doctor. I found out that they were trying to determine if some of us with bad legs could be fit for clerical or supply duty. The Army didn't want to use able-bodied soldiers for non-combat if they didn't have to, and I guess that's why they took so long.

This latest guy was a young doctor who was full of enthusiasm. The others were "lifers," seemingly burned-out by their profession. He sat me down on the examination table and began investigating the condition of my knee. After a couple prods, he moved up against the table and—leaning against the upper portion of my leg—pulled the lower part at an angle. It bent almost ninety degrees. You could just flap my leg around, the ligaments were so loose. He did the maneuver a second time with the same result. Then he turned and looked at me and said, "What the hell are you doing here?" I responded with, "That's what I'd like to know." I explained that I'd been telling—and showing—anyone who would pay attention, the condition of my knee, but no one seemed to care. His response was, "That's the Army for you." He quickly signed my papers and whatever forms there were and announced that I would be going home. I called my parents and they drove down the next day and took me back to the farm.

Ironically, I have to thank Rick and the Hamilton City boys for saving me from Vietnam and that awful conflict, unlike many of my classmates.

24

College

Coming on the heels of all that had happened in my life the previous six months or so was lobbying by my parents for the next few months. It was their position (especially my father's) that continuing on with my education was just a waste of time, and that my obligation was to the family and that I should stay home and help on the ranch. They prayed about it and were convinced that their position was the correct one.

I don't know if my motivation was completely about achieving a higher education or just wanting to get out of there, but I held my ground and—in spite of my parents—enrolled again at the junior college I had previously attended in northern California. But I had no money and it was out of the question for my parents to help me, even if they could have, but my grandmother—Mom's mother—stepped in. You've heard me talk about her—she was an incredible lady. Even though she and my grandfather were on a very meager income, she found the money for my enrollment fees, books and other things. Over the years, when any kind of hard times befell my parents they always turned to her. As I matured and began to think about these kinds of things I was always fascinated with my grandma's ability to find the resources while my parents were never able to. This is painful to say but I believe my parents were "poor in spirit." I don't really know what I mean by that but they've never—to this day—been able to completely take care of themselves. A condition that my brother has washed his hands of, my sister has become resigned to, and I've done the best I could with.

I headed out to Shasta Junior College in late January of 1968, Grandma's money in my pocket. I have to say that my mom and dad did help in the only way they were able to by sending me off after every visit to the farm with meat, poultry, milk, and other farm staples that were produced on our ranch. I was very popular with my roommates and friends for the first few days after I would come back from a visit with my parents—until the food ran out, that is. But we were all starving college students, so I didn't mind.

My old assistant baseball coach from high school, Mario Serafin, had migrated to the college, and was now the baseball coach. My leg was coming around to some degree—and I still had a great arm—and we talked about my attempting to make a comeback and trying out for the college team. I gave it a shot, but my knee would act up so much after every pitch that it seemed like I would take one step forward and two backward. But one thing he did that was very positive was put me on a strenuous rehab program which worked my leg religiously, and started to rebuild the muscles which had atrophied dramatically after the second surgery.

It was near the end of that school year, after the assassination of Bobby Kennedy and Martin Luther King, that I talked with Mario about the fact that my girlfriend from high school was going to be attending college in the Bay Area at San Jose State, that I was considering heading down in that direction myself, and that I was looking for another junior college to continue my general education. And I hoped to, maybe, reinvigorate my baseball career. His therapy had done wonders for my leg. Mario mentioned that a friend of his was the baseball coach at Foothill College in Los Altos—right adjacent to Palo Alto and Stanford, which I didn't have a prayer of getting into (my grades barely got me out of high school)—and that he'd give him a call to see if he had an opening on his squad. Mario called his friend and was told that if I could come down for the summer and play in a quasi-pro and amateur league to find out what my talents were or weren't, he'd give me a shot. I accepted.

But this caused a problem in my family. I had no money, and the pressure by my father to join him on the ranch was pretty severe, so I needed a job. And I got one at the Sears on San Antonio Road in Palo Alto, in the stockroom, forty hours a week.

My mother had put out "feelers" for me to find a Pentecostal church to attend while I was establishing myself in Palo Alto. I had attended a couple youth meetings, but hadn't made any connections. My girlfriend from high school was preparing to move down and start her college years, and so I was pretty well covered. A former roommate from the junior college in Redding had also moved down. He was from Livermore in the East Bay and had a girlfriend in Palo Alto, and we got an apartment together. "Five-o-Five" Central Expressway, Apartment P. My roommate, Jim, paid his half of the rent but didn't spend much time at the place. He hung his hat at his girlfriend Paula's place.

As you might imagine, my first day on the job at Sears was taken up with instruction and learning the ropes. Since I was going to be taking classes at Foothill during the day, the management at Sears was very accommodating and allowed me to work a hybrid schedule: from four o'clock in the afternoon to midnight. My classes started at ten o'clock in the morning so that gave me time to sleep and do my homework.

It was nearing the end of that first day and I had been left on my own to stock some shelves in the particular part of the stockroom that supplied the cosmetics department. Carrying a load of stuff destined for the sales floor on an electric cart, I had just turned a corner before going through the doors to the sales area when I came face-to-face with Donna DiMarci. (Wow!) About five-foot-six and put together better than anyone I had ever seen. (Damn!) I found out later that she was the same age as I.

I apologized for having almost run her over and continued through the swinging doors out onto the sales floor. I delivered the supplies to an older woman at the cosmetics sales counter and was on my way back to the stockroom when Donna appeared again. She introduced herself and said it was good to have someone new working in the stockroom. We exchanged pleasantries and both of us went on our way. A while later I was moving stuff around in the stockroom and was over by the time clock when I saw her again— she was punching her time card in preparation to leave work—and I made a detour that took me past her. I said "hi" and she said it had been nice to meet me and that she'd see me the next day. I was able to blurt out a friendly response despite my dry mouth and went about my work.

The next day I got to work at my scheduled four o'clock, punched my time card to check in, and went over to where the stockroom boss had posted our work orders: another load for cosmetics. I located an electric cart and made my way to the cosmetics storage area. As I approached the enclosure I detected the faint smell of a very appealing perfume. Before I could react, a sweet, female voice said, "Steve, could you please help me get these boxes down?" I looked up and came "face-to-face" with Donna's legs. She was standing on one of the rungs of a ladder about six feet above the floor. (For cryin' out loud!)

Nineteen sixty-eight was an interesting time for women's skirt styles. Most relatively-young women wore them six inches above the knee—or so—much like Euless had previously done on our "date." The view of Donna stopped me dead in my tracks, and she knew it—and enjoyed it. I just stood there and stared. It seemed as if time stood still, but I was able to regain my composure and told her that I'd be happy to help her. After pausing a moment on the ladder to give me one more show, she climbed down and I climbed up and got the box she was looking for and brought it down to her.

Donna's father was an engineer with Lockheed and they lived up in the ritzy section of Los Altos Hills. As we got to know each other better we would have lunch together in the commissary at the store and make small talk and flirt (at least as much as I was able to given my shyness). One day, she asked me if I would like to go to her parents' house for dinner and meet them. Well, sure I would, I told her. Even though I was dating my high school sweetheart at the time, it seemed innocent enough to accept her invitation, and

I'll have to admit that she was driving me crazy with lust. I didn't know what to do about it. I was almost twenty going on twelve, so to speak. She was a very articulate, well-mannered and elegant lady but she had a raw sexiness that was very appealing. And what was kind of neat is that she didn't show it to the other guys in the stockroom, but reserved it for me. At least that's how it appeared.

The evening came for me to have dinner at her parents' house and I put on my best shirt and slacks and made my way to their house. She still lived with her parents in a quasi-guest-house on the acre or so of land that the compound was situated on. I don't quite recall how I was able to miss work, but I arrived at her parents' house about six-thirty and Donna and I had sodas while her parents drank wine and had a nice conversation. They were very interested in my rural upbringing, and I spun several yarns about my childhood and life on the farm. We finished up about ten o'clock, and I bid them farewell and Donna walked me to my car. I thanked her for the evening and she gave me a peck on the cheek.

I was floating and confused. Floating as a result of the nice evening I had experienced, but confused about my feelings for Donna. I was dating a wonderful girl whom I had met in high school and whom my parents loved, but I was having thoughts of romance about Donna. My high school sweetheart was the only girl I had allowed myself to be serious about, but now I was faced with a dilemma. I was beginning to have feelings for this new girl. And, even though I was almost twenty years old, the Church's—and my parents'—influence was still very strong.

One of my objectives in moving to the Bay Area—other than the baseball and college—was an attempt to physically remove myself from the Pentecostal influence. My mother would check in on me and would talk to her acquaintance at the church she had referred me to, and find that I hadn't been attending the services—especially the youth functions—and I'd give in and start going again. My girlfriend from high school wasn't a particularly religious person, but she went along with my religious background and my parents really liked her, which was a big deal. Developing a relationship with someone new would be difficult enough as it was—but gaining acceptance and approval from my parents made it even harder. What made it even more embarrassing in my relationship with Donna is that my parents came down over a weekend one time to visit me, and I introduced them to her. Bad move. They absolutely treated her like dirt and grilled her with all sorts of insulting questions. It was very uncomfortable and Donna's eventual response was, "What's up with your parents?" I just told her they were from the "old school," and left it at that. It's hard to describe what motivated my parents' behavior in those days in any situation—the Pentecostal thing notwithstanding. They're very unusual people. Their social skills are very immature. That's about all I can say.

As for my baseball career at Foothill, I was able to make a connection with my former coach's friend and tried out for the team in the early part of July of that year, but my knee just couldn't stand up to the abuse of pushing off the mound while I pitched and I reluctantly had to give up my career.

The school year started at Foothill the first of September of that year and, coincidentally, Donna also enrolled. I had signed up before I knew she was going to attend. It was her second year at the school and, after obtaining her Associate's Degree, she was planning to go on to Menlo College nearby to get her Bachelor's.

My girlfriend from high school also arrived at the end of August to begin her studies at San Jose State. She was two years younger than I and had just graduated the previous June. She moved into a dorm on campus and I had my apartment in Mountain View adjacent to Palo Alto. I had been dating her since her sophomore year in high school, when we had met in Miss Shumway's Spanish class. As a senior, I needed to get serious about my studies if I wanted to have any chance of getting into a decent college. Our romance began when she volunteered to help me with the class since I needed one more semester to make up my college prep classes.

We dated pretty steadily through her senior year, but had hit a bump in the road when I moved to the Bay Area. My parents' dependence on me was taking a toll on our relationship, for she saw it as it was, but I tended to view it through somewhat rose-colored glasses. They were my parents, after all. From as early as I can remember my mom and dad put me on a pedestal and made it rough on my brother. My being the oldest probably had the most to do with it. I know it sounds self-serving but from the age of fourteen or fifteen—to a large extent—I had almost become the parent in the family. Of course, this was really a dichotomy since I had all sorts of responsibility but my parents ruled the roost from the "Pentecostal angle." Needless to say, it was very confusing at times.

So I started the Fall Semester at Foothill College and worked my forty hours per week at Sears. One of the reasons I was always so strapped for cash is that I had foolishly bought a brand new 1967 Chevy Camaro, canary yellow with a black vinyl top, in the fall of 1966—the first year they came out. I had never had anything that was new and shiny and I had made some pretty decent money the summer after high school graduation by working at the Campbell's Soup plant in Modesto—where my uncle ran the place. The car cost me twenty-nine hundred dollars and my payment was one hundred and thirteen dollars per month and I made a whopping three hundred and twenty bucks a month working at Sears. Between the car, my half of the rent on the apartment, and regular living expenses there wasn't much left over. In fact, that fall, money was so tight—and I got no help from my parents—that Donna gave me a hundred bucks or so to buy books. No strings attached. My grandma, a lady with no formal education, had given me the tuition money again. A month or so after school had started I began to have problems with a wax build-up in my ears that was causing me considerable discomfort and interrupting my sleep. Donna gave me the twenty dollars to go to the doctor and have my ears drained.

What's interesting about my relationship with Donna—and what's always intrigued me about it—is that she could have had any guy she wanted. She was smart, drop-dead gorgeous, and with a personality to match, but she reached out to me. She would come by my apartment and cook meals now and then and just hang-out with me. One time she brought a new *Playboy* magazine with her and we looked at the pictures together, sitting side-by-side on my couch. I wish I had some juicy story to tell about that episode but, the whole time I knew Donna, I never once even kissed her. Like I've said before, I wasn't bad looking but I was this enigma wrapped up in an inexperienced country boy—with Pentecostals breathing down my neck. During that whole fall semester I carried on two romantic lives: one with my high school sweetheart and one with Donna. And, in addition to that, for a month and a half before I went home for the Christmas holidays I was leaving late on Friday nights and driving up to the ranch near Chico and catching a couple hours of sleep and then working all day on the farm. Then I would leave after church on Sunday and drive back down to be at school the next morning—and then to Sears at four o'clock that afternoon—over and over. It certainly cut into my social life, and only exacerbated my relationship with my family, but they needed my help and I couldn't say no. The die had been cast.

The Christmas holidays came and I needed to make a decision. My dad was putting severe pressure on me, as only he could do. He wanted me to leave college and come back to the farm and go into a loosely-formed partnership with him. I did like the farm life—as it was all I had known—and there was some up-side potential from a financial perspective. I talked to my high school sweetheart about things and she cautioned me against it, and so did Donna. But I went against their counsel and packed up my things and moved back to the ranch just before Christmas. I didn't even say anything to Donna. I didn't have the guts. When I got home, I wrote her a letter thanking her for her friendship and all her help. She wrote back and expressed her sadness with the whole situation and wished me well. She was a good gal, way more than I deserved.

25
Back Home Again

So I was back at home on the ranch, working with my dad and trying to figure out what I wanted to do long-term. I realized that I probably wouldn't be able to finish my education with all the things I was dealing with. I continued to farm with my father through the spring and summer of the next year (1969). Late in that summer I had gone into the local bank in town inquiring about a loan to buy some dairy cattle of my own and the banker, Jerry Gilstrap, told me about a government program—one designed to help young people get into the agriculture business. It was the Farmers Home Administration, or the FHA. The headquarters of this federal program in our area was down at the county seat in Willows, so I drove down the next day and walked in and told them my story. They, in turn, told me that I was a good candidate for the program and gave me a bunch of papers to fill out. Over the next couple of months of going back and forth to Willows—and all the red tape involved with the government—they submitted my application and I was approved for a forty-thousand-dollar, low-interest loan.

Following the business plan I had put together and submitted, these monies were to be used to purchase fifty milk cows, which I would run along with my dad's milking herd of about two hundred. In addition to the cows, the remainder of the money was to be used to purchase various and sundry farm equipment. I had made all the arrangements and had everything lined up and was ready to get rolling. All I needed was to reach the age of twenty-one, which was about a month away. But something happened on the eve of that birthday, which forever changed my life.

My birthday was on a Monday and my parents and I were in church with the others on Sunday evening. My cousin, Fred, was our minister and we had just finished the singing part of the service. Grandma was sitting in the pew in front of us. Suddenly she stood-up, raised her hands to the heavens and, slumping back down into her seat, asked to no one in particular, "Am I going home to Jesus?" She was suffering a massive stroke. We all rushed to her aid, but there was nothing we could do. She lived through the ordeal, but it made her virtually an invalid. Her whole left side was paralyzed. I remember looking down at her—her eyes meeting mine—and telling her that, "It's okay, Grandma." I took her good right hand in mine and squeezed it. She squeezed back. She never spoke again. That's the last communication I ever had with her. I know there were a lot of people who lost their rock, their anchor that day. I know I surely did. She was eighty-one years old and lived for another six years, but the lights were off. My mother, to her credit, would visit Grandma every single day in the assisted living center where we had placed her, and was convinced that she would recover. That's what children believe about parents who are so God-like.

I had located fifty, first-calf Holstein heifers that were for sale at a dairy about two miles away from our farm. The government cut the check a couple days after my birthday, I finalized the deal, and my dad and I herded my new cows down the road to our dairy. I was in business.

Grandma would have been proud!

*****

During that time in the late sixties and into the seventies there was a phenomenon within the Catholic Church called the Charismatic Movement. It caused quite a stir within the Catholic Church, for the movement's ideology was espousing a drifting away from the typical church structure. The orthodox commandments of the traditional Catholic Church were that a parishioner came to a priest for forgiveness and, in turn, the priest interceded on his or her behalf to God. These sacraments that had been held as law for centuries were being re-thought by this movement and many a priest and nun were leaving the conventional Church and forming their own type of Catholic Church. This was by no means a revolt against the Pope and his authority under God, but an attempt to "humanize" the Church's beliefs to make them more broadly appealing.

I'm not quite sure under what circumstances this took place, but my parents—in an attempt to reach out to these new, "enlightened" Catholics—met a priest by the name of Father Fagan who was part of this new movement. He was the pastor of one of the two or three Catholic Churches in Chico, and began to come out to our ranch to spend time with my family. I would say this was mid-1971.

By the way, I had married my former high school sweetheart, Charlotte Hills, in July of 1970 and we had moved into my grandparents' old home on the ranch. My grandparents were both living in an assisted living facility and the home had been vacant. And my new wife and I had a pretty decent dairy and farming operation going on, while at the same time she was finishing her degree at Chico State on the way to becoming a licensed schoolteacher, having transferred up from San Jose State.

A couple things came along as a result of my marriage to my former high school sweetheart. My parents were very pleased, and Charlotte and I were making an attempt to assimilate ourselves into the Assemblies of God Church—which wasn't an easy thing to do. It was like attempting to put a square peg in a round hole. It wasn't that I hadn't made concerted attempts in the past to abandon my resistance to the Church's teachings and join the crowd. I had— several times—but I was just a fraud for I couldn't accept the human interpretation of what had been written by inspired Men of God—if that was truly the case—and it made those efforts all the more phony the more I tried. I would speak to God, but I couldn't do it in the framework of the Pentecostal structure. It seemed to cheapen things in my mind.

So Father Charles Fagan, Charley, became a part of our lives. He would venture out to our ranch on almost a weekly basis, and all of us became very close. But that was another dichotomy. All my growing up years we had been taught by the Pentecostals to steer clear of Catholics, and now they were all around us, and in our house. But I do know one thing: Charley sure loved his wine. And my new wife and I joined him. Were we going back to becoming Lutherans again, or were we now becoming Catholic? As with most things, we were probably somewhere in between. (My-o-my.)

I operated the dairy in partnership with my dad from the fall of 1969 through the fall of 1971. I had made a good living during those two years and, after our marriage in 1970, my wife and I had really gotten into the lifestyle. But, in the fall of 1971, my father suffered a financial reversal of fortune and was forced to sell off his cows and shut down the dairy operation. Because I was so young and just really getting started in business, I wasn't able to carry on the operation, so I also reluctantly sold my cows to a dairy down in the central California town of Ceres and began to ponder what I would do next.

26

My New Career

I **had made some money on the sale of** my cows and had some financial breathing room, so I took my time looking around for my next career. I had always thought that I would spend my life in some form of agriculture—due to my background and all—but my dad had seen an ad for a carpenter/laborer in our local newspaper and I went for an interview.

John and Carl Tanner were pieces of work. More hard-headed Germans, they would argue incessantly all day about the biggest and littlest of issues. The interview went something like this: "Can you operate a shovel? *Can you pound nails with a hammer?"* I answered in the affirmative to both questions and was hired on the spot.

The brothers owned some acreage out by the freeway that they had developed as a residential community, but it was nothing fancy. They'd build and sell three or four homes a year. We did all the construction on the homes except for hanging the sheetrock and building the cabinets. They rode me relentlessly. But something happened in the year-and-a-half that I worked for them: I found that I liked and had an aptitude for the construction industry. What's interesting is that, while I was on the farm as a youngster—and in the partnership with my father—I had always been the one to build and repair things. But I had always thought that doing these things was just a part of the farming life, not a vocation. The Tanner brothers may not have thought so, but I sure had a lightbulb go off in my mind. I recall announcing, in the spring of 1972, that I would have my own contractor's license within the next year. They scoffed at me and gave me a hard time, but they were pretty good about it. I was a threat to them and it didn't sit well with their old-school mentality that a worker bee would aspire to such lofty heights. In October of 1973, at the age of twenty-five, I took and passed the test for my California B-1, General Contractor's License. It had taken eighteen months since my boastful prediction, but I had done it.

In late spring of 1973, I had an opportunity to get a job framing homes with a builder in Chico for substantially more money. I went to the Tanners and told them of my plans and what my motivation was: that I wanted to gain more experience with a larger builder and the money was far better. I tried to assure them it wasn't just about the money, but they would have none of it. Anyone who had worked for these brothers said the same thing: you couldn't work for them for an extended period of time. They treated their employees like slaves and payed them a pittance. It hadn't been quite that bad for me—and I had learned a lot—but I was not going to get anywhere staying with them. I thanked them or the opportunity, and gave my two-week notice. They told me not to come back, and said they'd mail me my final check.

So I went to work for Loris Root, a Swede, who was a nice but an unorganized man who had a son by the name of Marvin. A couple years older than me, Marvin was a momma's boy and made no bones about the fact that he was in charge—at least when Loris wasn't around. Loris's firm was building a subdivision of about forty homes and I and three other guys were in one of the framing crews, and Marvin was our foreman.

It was about a month or so after I was hired that Loris took about a two-week vacation and he left Marvin in charge. One other thing about Marvin is that he was carrying about seventy-five extra pounds and had some difficulty bending over or getting around with any speed, but he was Loris's son and now he was the "boss." And Marvin wanted to make a show for his father while he was gone.

The other thing I found out about Loris and his son—which I

hadn't known before I was hired—was that they were Pentecostals. Loris was pretty logical about his religious beliefs and only proselytized now and then and in a friendly manner, but Marvin did it all of the time. He had things all figured out and never let you forget it. In our framing crew were two atheists, a Catholic, and a mixed up Lutheran-cum-Pentecostal, but he played no favorites. The atheists told him he was full of shit, the Catholic told him he felt sorry for him, and I told him that I'd rather talk about these things another time—especially the end of the world—which for Marvin was coming next Thursday at 3:10 sharp in the afternoon. Well, it wasn't quite, but you know what I mean.

So Marvin was our boss, and I and the rest of the crew had installed the under floor structure on the first house. After the plumbing and other mechanical installations were installed, we put the decking over the floor joists. Marvin always wanted to do the layout of the walls and doors and such, and then mark out on the two-by-four plates which went on top and bottom of the walls, the proper location of these things. There were four or five foundations laid out ahead of us and so while he was doing the layout on the first house, the rest of the crew and I went on to the second and installed the under floor like we had on the first. It took about a day to complete the work and the following morning we went back to the first house to construct the walls.

Whenever Loris was gone out of town Marvin would take long coffee breaks and very long lunches. We couldn't have cared less, but it says something about the measure of him as a man. The morning we went back to start framing the walls of the first house was no exception. On average, we'd start at seven o'clock in the morning and by nine o'clock he'd be gone. This morning he left at nine o'clock and he didn't get back to the jobsite until at least two o'clock.

I was sort of the "straw boss" of our little four man crew, and so I had begun the task of determining which walls to frame first, and so on, and so on. And I had started working out how much material needed to be carried from the stacks of lumber onto the floor of the house and where to stack it so as not to be in the way of the work.

The two-by-four wall plates which Marvin had laid out were sitting on-edge on the floor decking, and I was mulling over the process and looking at the layout. Something didn't look right. Upon further investigation I determined that, in Marvin's haste to make a show for his dad and get the hell out of there, he had laid out all of the wall plates with no provision for windows or doors. I checked all of them. I summoned over Jim, the Catholic, and showed him what I'd found. He gave me an evil grin. I then summoned over the two atheists and showed them, and they did the same. So it was the consensus of the crew that we go ahead and frame that whole fifteen-hundred-square-foot house with no provision for windows and doors. And we did. After all, we were just doing what we were told, since any time Marvin was questioned on anything he acted like we were morons and just passed it off.

Because we did not have to cut large beams for over the windows and doors or make the necessary cuts for the assembling of the vertical members, it saved a tremendous amount of time and we had that sucker completely framed by the time Marvin came back from lunch. We had even straightened and braced all of the walls in preparation for the roof trusses being delivered the next morning. It blew him away. And we had already moved on to the second house and, the plumbers having finished their under floor work, were partially through with the task of laying down the decking. It was hard to contain our glee as we worked along on the second house wondering when Marvin would notice the error of his ways.

It took him about an hour. A mighty roar could be heard from inside the first house and, for a moment, we thought Marvin might be having a heart attack. For a Pentecostal, his language and demeanor got pretty colorful. "How in the f-ing world could you have framed the house with no windows or doors?!!" He screamed. He looked like a ripe beet. I calmly explained, "Marvin, we were only building it like you laid it out. You don't ever want us fiddling with your layout. So we didn't."

I snuck a grin at one of the atheists. When Marvin's roar had gone up we had scampered to the first house and so all of us were now standing in the living room area. We stood there in silence as Marvin pondered what to do next. He was furious. He paced and waddled back and forth contemplating what to do next. Periodically he would pause and look at us. We knew what he was thinking: "You mother f-ers. I'll get you." But the roof trusses were being delivered the next morning so we had to leave it the way it was and come back and fix it later. Marvin was a disciple of the religion—in addition to Pentecostal—that dictated: "you never had the time or money to do it right the first time but plenty of both to come back and do it again."

It only got worse from that point with Marvin in charge. He was just a complete nincompoop, or *dummkopf,* when it came to planning and strategy, and his mistakes just begat each other. But his dad—as good a guy as he was—suffered from much the same malady.

I recall one incident when we were building a house up in the mountains, a two-story house and, as usual, Loris and Marvin had just temporarily nailed and secured the floor support members on the second floor and we were now laying the deck over them. They trusted that one of us would remember to secure things properly before the decking was placed. Well, I was walking across the floor members carrying a four-by-eight sheet of plywood when I stepped on one of the improperly-secured floor joists and it gave way. I went right down through the floor—between the fourteen-inch space separating the joists. The plywood was ripped completely out of my hands, and I landed on my feet on the first floor. My framing hammer, which had been secured in my worker's belt, dug a deep groove into my lower rib section as it was driven against the top of the joists as I went through. When I've told people about this incident I've said that if I hadn't been so beat up by the fall, I would have killed the two of them.

There are just a couple more stories I have to tell about working for Loris.

He'd obtained a contract with a company to construct pre-cut homes that this outfit, Capp Homes, manufactured. They packaged the parts and shipped them all over the western United States. Loris had the northern California region. One Friday, Loris announced that our next assignment with that company was to frame a home up in the gold country, and that we should show up there at our typical time, seven o'clock on the next Monday morning. So the Catholic, Jim, and I drove up there together and the atheists came by themselves. Once all of us were there, the four of us reviewed the situation. Loris had told me that the building plans were in a decommissioned mailbox adjacent to a garage that the clients had previously built on the property. We found the plans and were able to orient ourselves to the foundation which a crew hired by Loris had poured. Usually we only framed these homes on foundations that were provided by an owner, but this time Loris had done the foundation, too.

The structure was a two-story rectangle shape, about thirty-by-forty feet. We took the plans and lined up the bearing points and set out to install the under floor structure. We used a builder's transit (sort of an eye-piece that focuses in on a point in the distance) to confirm the grade and to establish our bearings for the direction the house was facing. This was very wide-open mountain country, so reference points were difficult to locate. And because the house was a rectangle, this was doubly important. Front could be back and back could be front. Loris came up to visit the job a couple days later and approved what we were doing. Over the next two weeks we framed up the home and installed the windows and doors that closed it all in. Then the house sat through the winter, heavy snow. The next spring, I was instructed to take a drive up there and look at the house and see how it had fared the winter. When I arrived, the owners were there and visibly upset. It was their contention that the home had been framed backwards, that the foundation had been turned one-hundred-eighty degrees on its axis. You could see their point: the front door of the home was immediately adjacent to the side of the garage the owners had built. No windows took advantage of the view.

And, in addition, Loris had scheduled the delivery of the

sheetrock for the ceilings and walls and all of it—maybe four tons—had been stacked in the middle of the living room. It had broken floor members and settled things down a foot or more. It was a complete mess. It turns out that Loris had to buy the home from those people. I don't know whatever happened in the end.

I could go on and on. Loris was the epitome of the description of insanity that someone coined: doing the same thing over and over again and expecting different results.

The contract with the company which manufactured the pre-cut homes we were framing for Loris was coming up for renewal in the fall, and he had indicated that he wasn't planning on renewing it. With his operating style and lack of attention to detail and planning I could see why. So I told him I was getting my contactor's license in October and would like to take over his contract if he was agreeable. He talked to the company and they were all right with it, so Loris and I cut the deal. For the three months before I got my license I would operate under his license and he'd take ten percent off the top. I would run my own crews and cover my own overhead. Then, in October, I would directly take over the contract and he'd be out of the picture and we would go our own ways. It worked out fine. I passed the test for my license and took over the contract and it got me a start in the construction business.

My brother had finished his master's degree the previous June, and had come to work for me and had been a part of my crew during the summer that followed. When I was able to procure the direct contract on the pre-cut homes, he came on full-time and traveled northern California with the rest of us.

It was during this time that my wife and I were becoming more involved with the Charismatic Movement and Charley Fagan was becoming an even greater part of our lives.

27

Charley Fagan and the Monastery

Charley was in trouble with the Catholic Church. The previous summer, 1973, he had conducted marriage ceremonies for several couples whose new spouses had been married previously and the bishop in San Francisco wasn't pleased. Charley's motivation for officiating at these events was his belief that there was a new enlightenment as a result of the movement within the Church and these people could, and should, be forgiven for the error of their first nuptials. He felt that the Catholic Church's annulment guidelines were so egregious that virtually everyone who applied was granted a disillusion of their marriage, anyway. When weather permitted, Charley would ride his bicycle the eighteen miles out to our ranch, with several bottles of merlot and cabernet stashed in a carrier contraption on the back. Together, and with Charlotte sometimes, we'd sit at the table in the kitchen of the old farmhouse that we were now remodeling and drink the grape and wax eloquent on the problems of the world. Charley would drink too much and I'd tell him that he was "in his cups" and he'd argue with me in his priceless Irish brogue and then we'd finally put him to bed in the guest room. He'd get up in the morning, fresh as a daisy, and after we'd fed him breakfast he would ride his bike back to town, sans the empty wine bottles. The next week he'd do it all over again.

But the weight of his convictions and his difficulties with the Church were taking their toll. There was more and more pressure from the hierarchy within to force Charley to resign his position or renounce the new movement. He chose the former. In the spring of 1974, Charley announced he was leaving the priesthood and moving on. Coming from a revered, Northern-Irish Catholic family, having studied for the priesthood in one of their most prestigious seminaries, migrating to this country as his response to his "second child" status within his family, and then being defrocked by the very system that spawned his life, was quite a blow. But Charlie was very resilient, and he never lost his sense of humor. After all, he was a bit past fifty and in good health with much to live for. In one of the post mortems that we conducted at our kitchen table in Grandma and Grandpa's old ranch house—and in an attempt to analyze the wisdom, or lack of same, that the Church had exhibited in forcing him out—I asked Charley if he ever missed the priesthood. He set down his glass of Merlot, looked me straight in the eye with his tweed cap tipped jauntily on his head and answered, "Steve, I've r-r-risen above it."

The Monastery

About twenty miles north of Chico is a little hamlet by the name of Vina, and on the outskirts of this little village, along the Sacramento River, is a Catholic Trappist Monastery, the Abbey of New Clairvaux. It sits on land that was originally the home of the Leland Stanford Ranch (he was the founder of Stanford University), and which at one time encompassed the largest vineyard in the world, with twenty-five hundred acres. In the mid-1950s, the Catholic Church purchased about six hundred acres of what remained of the ranch and created the domicile.

Having left the formality of his role as a priest within the Church, it didn't mute Charley's search for inner peace and communion with his God. He chose the monastery as a place of solace and fellowship with the monks who lived there. This was during the summer of 1974. My parents took up his interest in the place and began visiting Charley and the other monks on a regular basis. My wife and I took up this same interest and became close friends to many of the men who lived and worked there. I became especially close to the head Abbot, Father Thomas. Former California Governor Jerry Brown was a frequent visitor, among other dignitaries and well-known people.

It was on a day in the fall of 1974 that my father was visiting the monastery when Brother Regis, head of operations, inquired of my dad as to his interest in possibly leasing the open farmland, about three hundred acres, on a "share crop" basis. The balance of the land was planted in orchards. The monastery would receive a percentage of the crop, in return for leasing the land to my dad. Dad told me about the offer and asked me what I thought. "Why not?" I told him. It was very fertile soil and I still owned a fair amount of equipment that could be used to farm the land, so my dad cut the deal. That began a relationship with the monastery and the monks who live there which has endured until this day. Some have come and gone— Father Thomas retired a year or so ago. Some have died—Brother Joseph who was an extremely close friend of my parents passed away about ten years ago.

Brother Pierre—who played minor league baseball before his calling—is still with us, the same with Brother Cashmere, the class clown with a fabulous sense of humor. "Cash," as we called him, would periodically make the twenty-mile trek to our ranch, on foot, to spend a weekend and get caught up on world events. No outside literature was allowed within the confines of the monastery, but the rules allowed the monks to venture outside the place on a periodic basis, and then they were free to do whatever they cared to. It was only a couple days but it seemed to rejuvenate them. When we would find out that Cash was going to be paying us a visit I would collect all of the newspapers I could get my hands on. The *New York Times*, Chicago *Tribune*, *Wall Street Journal*, *Washington Post* and San Francisco *Chronicle*, to name a few. And I kept all of the old issues of *Sports Illustrated* so he could read them and then go back and tell Brother Pierre what was happening in the sporting world.

These men I have mentioned were but a few of the twenty-five or so men who had exchanged their lives on the outside for a life of abstinence and meditation. Some were "running to" and some were "running from," life. It was—and is—a great privilege to have known and been a part of this experience.

It was like we were all on a spiritual highway: a busload of Lutherans, a busload of Pentecostals, a busload of old-line Catholics, and a busload of New Age Charismatic Catholics. And then there was a busload of cum-whatever that was the spiritual life as it had evolved within my family and me, hybrids. We were all on the same road, enjoying ourselves, judging each other, being mystified by each other, understanding each other and not understanding each other. Life had issued us—or we had acquired—different road maps. Even though each map had the same final destination we all were taking different "zigs and zags" to get there.

We'd sit with the monks at midnight mass on New Year's Eve and listen to them sing the Celtic Hymns, *a cappella*. And that was the joy and pain of the whole thing. For, as a card-carrying Pentecostal, one cannot sit next to a professed Brother-in-Christ and not ask the question. "Are you ready if the Lord should come back tonight?" After all, we were taught to judge first and ask questions later. On the drive back to the ranch with Mom and Dad, they would express their joy in having experienced the evening, and then ask us to pray for these men of the cloth, for they weren't on the right highway. The Pentecostals had it all figured out, but the Catholics and Charley Fagan were forgiven—and that bothered them. (Damn the logic of it all!!)

*****

It was also in the fall of 1974 that, during a visit with the men of the monastery, Brother Regis inquired of me as to whether I would be interested in bidding on some new construction the enclave was considering. They had plans to build a new refectory and a library. The refectory, in layman's vernacular, was an elaborate kitchen and dining area. The brother had learned that I had recently obtained my General Contractor's License and it was through our friendship that he was extending his hand of fellowship to invite my bid. I accepted his offer.

Over the next month or so I worked feverishly to get my bid in order. Not yet twenty-six, and with little or no experience in commercial construction, I labored mightily to bring things together. And I did get things together. The father of a friend of mine was an insurance agent and had access to the bonding, which the brothers required. All bidders were required to provide a "Performance and Payment Bond," guaranteeing the successful completion of the project. And he and I traveled to San Francisco to meet with the bonding firm.

I had absolutely no knowledge of the bonding world and entered this arena with ignorant bliss. We met with the company he had selected—actually a division of an insurance company—and I gave them my pitch on the virtues of the project and they said "yes" and wrote the bond, for about seven hundred and fifty thousand dollars. My net worth was two cats, a dog, and a loving wife. How in the world I was able to secure this guarantee is beyond my comprehension, but I did secure the underwriting and was ready for the bid opening ceremony.

The day came and all of the bidders, five as I remember, met with Brother Regis in the office area of the monastery, very formally. Each presented his written bid, from the architect's estimate of nine hundred and fifty thousand down to eight hundred and fifty thousand. My bid was around the seven hundred and fifty thousand dollars, as I've mentioned. That won me the contract. Brother Regis and the other bidders congratulated me—the other bidders somewhat grudgingly. Which was understandable since I had won the contract, but I was worried. Why the hell was my number so much lower than the other bids? I wasn't that smart and most of the subcontractors had submitted their bids to all of us, meaning that our hard numbers should have been the same. Then I learned why my bid was so much lower. I had left out a category in my numbers: the exterior block-work, which amounted to one hundred and twenty thousand dollars, or so. But adding that in still left me the lowest bidder.

I called my dad to let him know that I had screwed up, that my bid was actually much closer to the next lowest. We were farming the open ground and I didn't want to create difficulties with that relationship, but I couldn't let what I had discovered about my bid just dangle out there, and hope for the best. There was no way I could make up the error by tightening down my other costs. No way. Dad said he'd talk to Brother Regis, but I said "no." I had to face it myself. So I called the brother and told him we needed to talk.

On the drive to meet with Brother Regis I grumbled and mumbled and lamented the fact that I had probably blown it. If I had just been more careful in tallying my numbers I would have been about five thousand dollars lower than the next bid and would have gotten the job. What a great opportunity down the drain I thought to myself.

I arrived at the monastery and met with the brother. I told him of my dilemma and what my number would have been had I properly accounted for things. That I still would have been the low bidder. He extended his condolences, but informed me that I had made a formal proposal—which they had accepted—and that they were going to hold me to my number, and then he quoted some legal premise that supported his position.

Well, that's pretty neat, I thought. Here I am, spilling my guts in an attempt to be straightforward with him and he's playing hardball with me. Welcome to the real world, Steve, I thought to myself. And these were Men of God. The one hundred and twenty thousand I had left out would have ruined me, but to them it was mere chump change. But that's the way they were. They had nothing better to do. And Brother Regis had been a businessman on the outside before his calling and knew the ropes. I didn't. But, as they say, necessity is the mother of invention. I abruptly thanked him and bid him farewell, and headed down to Chico and my attorney. I told him my story and Brother Regis's response. My attorney said he'd take care of it and wrote a letter to them. The brothers took the next bid and never pursued anything with me. Regis had probably just been calling my bluff. And the incident never did negatively impact my relationship with him or the other monks. What had happened was just all in a day of business to them.

Ironically, the company that was finally awarded the bid lost their shirts on the project. The monks, having nothing better to do, would literally stand and watch every nail and bolt and board that was being installed. They did this in shifts, and would make the workers redo the work over and over again until they were satisfied. Money didn't mean anything to them. I thought the world of these guys, but they were in such a *Nirvana* state of mind that to do business with them was suicide. Someone was watching over me in my exercise to win the contract.

From 2 Corinthians 11:19 it reads, "Ye suffer fools gladly, seeing ye yourselves are wise." I guess we know who the fool was and the wisemen were. And I wasn't among the latter.

28

Now I'm a Real Estate Developer and the Pentecostals are Lurking

he Yom Kippur War in October of 1973 between Israel and Egyptian/Syrian factions, and the resulting oil embargo by OPEC that was aimed at industrialized nations of the West, tended to upset the banking system in this country. It was nothing like we've experienced in the past couple years, but it put a clamp on lending that hit our economy very hard. The embargo finally ended in March of 1974 and things began to return to normal. But, just like during the Six Day War in June of 1967 between Israel and Egyptian/Syrian and Jordanian factions, the Pentecostals seized upon the opportunity to declare that the end of the world was at hand. They opened their King James Bibles and, pointing to the book of Revelations (the last book in the New Testament), stood behind their pulpits and in front of their television cameras and quoted—chapter and verse—the description of the last battle that would take place on earth before the rapture. Predicted by the Apostle John in Revelations and also by the second book of Ezra in the Old Testament, the battle of Armageddon, "where blood would run as high as a horse's belly," was upon us. And they were ecstatic, for in their minds it validated the years of prophesies that were so dear to their hearts. "I told you so" was everywhere among these people. And, as the Bible said in II Kings 2, 11–12 in part, the "trumpet would sound and in a mighty whirlwind the believers would be taken to Heaven, as a thief in the night. There to remain for Eternity." And the believers were the Pentecostals and no one else. (But we're all still here, aren't we?)

I was in my first year of Junior College during the Six Day War in 1967, and a budding real estate developer during the Yom Kippur War in 1973, and both times I was scared to death. I was afraid because I couldn't—or wouldn't—accept the Pentecostals' view of things, and afraid because they could be right. And I wasn't ready to meet the Lord, according to what I had been taught and was still wrestling with. All those Wednesday night prayer meetings would come back to me when the Bible would be sliced and diced to infinity in an attempt to figure out what the hell was going on in the world. And to do this wasn't even biblical for it said in the New Testament: "do not ponder on these things I have told you."

But the Bible is convenient for these people and filled with contradictions that beget contradictions. And these Fundamentalists have always and still do attempt, in a mind-numbing manner, to put things in a neat little box. You can interpret the Bible any way you want and therefore anyone could be right. But those in the Assemblies of God Church have a key to the door. All these other people who worshiped in a different manner and could be kind and caring, take care of the sick and in-firm around them, give tirelessly of themselves and absolutely follow the golden-rule, were going to Hell. Mother Teresa was going there, too, they said, for she wasn't "saved" in their minds or according to the dogma they espoused.

Who would *you* rather sit beside in Heaven for Eternity, the slimy Jerry Falwell or our dear Sister? If you happen to drop by Heaven some time and look up the two of them I would venture that she has a better address than he does. Pentecostals, for the most part, have never learned to walk the walk. Watch them on television some time. God must look down from wherever Heaven is and shake his head as he observes the Pentecostals' pathetic attempts to put him in a box. You can almost hear him say, "You've missed the point, for cryin' out loud!"

Through all of this I struggled mightily to develop an identity within myself that could deal with these things. My wife was sympathetic to my struggles and did what she could to allay and discuss my fears. And when I would begin another foray to Church to try and make things right with the Lord she would join me and support my efforts, but it wasn't meant to be. As I've said before, I was just a phony when I tried these things and it only made matters worse the harder I tried. Each time I made an attempt to join the Pentecostals and failed, it made it easier to go my own way. Maybe it was the aging process or whatever, but more and more I could see the folly of their ways and could begin to trust my own judgment. It's a long process to unshackle one's childhood.

*****

It was during early summer of 1974, and before I got the opportunity to bid on the monastery work, when I came across three building lots located in a country club south of the town of Chico. They were owned by one of the developers of the golf course, a very successful farmer, and were available for purchase. Six thousand apiece, which might as well have been a million given my finances at the time. I went to talk to the farmer, Clay McGowan, anyway. I told him I really wanted the lots and had plans to build three homes on speculation. The economy was coming around after the embargo and I wanted to "get on the train." I can still hear him: "Steve, I'll tell you what I'll do. If you can get me a thousand a-piece up front I'll give you the title to the lots so you can get your financing, and I'll take the rest when you sell the homes." Things were a little different then. I told him that I thought I could come up with the three thousand dollars and we shook on it. Now, where to get the money?

As I've mentioned, I married my high-school sweetheart, Charlotte Hills, in the summer of 1970. I wasn't yet twenty-two at the time. Her dad was a successful businessman who thought I was too big for my britches and generally full of crap. I'd like to think I was just confident, but he and I were like water and oil. We never could get a relationship going. But, when I had the opportunity to purchase the building lots, I told Charlotte and asked her whether she thought her dad might be interested in investing the three thousand dollars.

She told me that she thought he'd be interested, and that I should just call him and set up a time to have coffee or something and talk it over. But then, knowing my relationship with him, she thought better of it and said she probably should talk to him first—which she did—and he loaned me the money and I built and sold the three houses. I remember the day I walked into Chico Savings and Loan to inquire about three construction loans. Ignorance is bliss! The manager of the place, a man by the name of George Loney, sat me down and listened to my proposal and then called in his assistant, Nell Cottingham. He introduced me and then instructed her to draw up the papers. She actually ran the place. George was a flaming drunk and kept a vodka bottle under his desk in plain view, but he was from a good family so everyone looked the other way. The appraisals in those days were done in-house, which he assured me would be no problem. I signed the papers the next day and we were off to the races. I made some money and my father-in-law made some money and I paid the bank—and Clay McGowan—back and all was right with the world. But not between my wife's father and me. It was obvious that he had only loaned me the money to assure himself that his daughter had a roof over her head. He couldn't have cared less about me, and he told me so. That's the way it was.

A little background into my wife's family. Her father had an older brother by the name of Liston Hills who, in the mid-1930s, had graduated from the University of California at Berkley with a degree in engineering and had taken a job with Standard Oil of California—the forerunner to Chevron. Oil had been discovered in Saudi Arabia, and the company was looking for an entrée with King Ibn Al-Saud, so as to gain favor and obtain drilling rights. Standard Oil had sent a team, including her uncle, to the Gulf and the first assignment Charlotte's uncle had when he arrived was to design and engineer an air-conditioning system for the King's main palace. This was successfully accomplished and the king was pleased and Standard Oil got the drilling rights, pretty much in that order. When the main deposits were discovered in the late-1930s a consortium of companies was put together to begin the development, production, and marketing of the oil. This entity was named the Arabian American Oil Company or ARAMCO. My wife's Uncle Liston rose to be Chairman of the Company, a position he held until his retirement in the late 1970s.

*****

It was late in the summer of 1974, and I had made a little money on the sale of the three homes and had the framing contract that I had obtained from my former boss, Loris Root. We weren't getting rich, but we were doing all right. My brother was working for me, and so was my father. It had been rough on my mom and dad since he had suffered his financial reversal in 1971 and was forced to sell his dairy herd, which—as a result—also forced me to sell my herd, as I've mentioned. My dad had found employment in the agricultural field to some degree but nothing had been really permanent. So it fell to my wife and me to provide what financial support we could to help the two of them along. We actually had been providing financial support for the previous two years or so, and this—along with the difficulties I had in dealing with my upbringing—were putting a strain on my marriage.

It came to bother me more and more that I had never experienced the "carefree days of youth." From my earliest recollections I was always looked upon to be the responsible one. Not that my brother wasn't responsible, but he was just a normal kid who did normal kid things. I, for some reason, had taken on this load of responsibility that I couldn't get out from under. And my parents ran with it, heaping more and more on me even as my emotional foundation was starting to show signs of stress. They didn't, couldn't, or wouldn't notice. I couldn't ignore them, for they were my parents and couldn't help themselves. More times than I care to remember the phone would ring and I could hardly lift the receiver for fear of it being my dad on the other end, asking to borrow money. I know it must have almost killed him to make those calls—a subject we've talked about in later years—

but he had no choice and neither did I. As I look back on things I remember it was the same with Grandma. Our family was always asking her for money, and she always had something to give out of her meager finances.

I think my parents justified this borrowing by the fact that they took care of my grandparents until the day they died, my mom especially, and her brothers and sisters didn't. Not that my aunts and uncles had abandoned them, but there was some ill-will my grandfather had created amongst my mother's siblings and they just didn't live as close as we did, either. That's a fact. So Mom was there for my grandparents at their every beck and call.

In the fall of 1974, all of these things came to a boil and I separated from my wife. Bottom line: I just needed to feel my oats. Charlotte had done nothing to warrant this, and she was a good partner and confidante, but I just needed to do it. It hurt her, for which I am— and always will be—very sorry. Charlotte's mother took it fairly well. She and I had a good relationship, one that has lasted to this day, but my wife's father did what fathers do and tried to stab me in the ribs financially. We had some business dealings that were ongoing and which were now put in jeopardy by my actions. I can't say that I blame him. I had made the decision to separate, not him. It's hard to explain, but he's handled things in such a manner so as to always have himself pitted against whoever was in the way. He's alienated his son—my wife's brother—has never made any attempt to be a grandfather to his biological grandchildren, and has treated my mother-in-law like dirt in front of family and friends. I may not have been "lily white," but it takes two to tango.

I got an apartment in Chico and did my thing and she did hers. We had no children, so that made things easier. It took three or four months, but I got everything out of my system for the time being and we put our lives back together again. But I was still my parent's keeper, and my upbringing was still lurking in the shadows, never very far off. My relationship with Charley Fagan helped in that he was going through some tough times in his excommunication from the Catholic Church and we would commiserate with each other and drink volumes of red wine. *Good* red wine, I might add. It was cabernet sauvignon and merlot in those days. He'd had more experience than I, given his role in the Church and all, but I was learning.

Something else that helped my wife and me get through this period is that, in the fall of 1974, Chalotte had secured a job teaching kindergarten in an elementary school—Mill Street School—in the little town of Orland where we had both attended high school. She's taught that class to this very day. If you looked up "kindergarten teacher" in the encyclopedia, you would see her picture beside the description. Parents in this public school would put their children's names, shortly after they were born, on a waiting list to get into her class. It's pretty neat to have that kind of recognition. It's fleeting for most of us.

The economy continued to improve into the early part of 1975, and I had been able to negotiate contracts to build three homes as personal residences for clients. I didn't mention before but I had taken one semester of architecture in junior college, years before, and had developed a knack for design. So everything we built, I had designed and created the working drawings for. Periodically, it was necessary to hire a structural engineer to work out the calculations, but for the most part the designs were ours.

It was also around this time, in the spring of 1975, that I located two more building lots in the little town of Orland, but I didn't have enough money for them. I had saved some, but not enough, and there was no Clay McGowan around to finance them out. So, again, I asked Charlotte about her father putting up the money and she said she'd ask. And, I'll be damned—he said "yes," again and staked his smart-ass son-in-law to a grubstake to build two more homes on speculation. I sold one of them part-way through construction and the other right before floor coverings were installed. I paid back the money to my father-in-law and old George Loney at the savings and loan, and even made a little for myself.

29

Hearing The Call

This is completely an aside to what I've been talking about recently—and maybe a little out of context—but I mentioned earlier in the book that ministers in Assemblies of God Churches tend to come and go on a fairly regular basis.

One of the reasons I stated for this happening, in my belief—which is supported by others—is that they hear "The Call." In other words, they feel that God is calling them to minister to another flock—or flocks—as the case may be. So here's how the conversation might go between the minister and God.

*****

Phone rings. Minister answers. Let's call him Dave.

"Hello. Hello. I can't hear you, bad connection." Silence. "That's better, now I can hear you. Who, may I ask, is calling?" inquires the minister.

"This is God, Dave," comes the booming reply from the other end of the line.

Dave gasps. "Oh, God, I didn't recognize your voice. You sound different on the phone. How are things in Heaven?" The minister asks.

"They've been better." Dave can hear the frustration in God's voice.

"How so?" The minister inquires, definite concern in his voice.

"A couple years ago we adopted a fair-entry program that was pushed really hard by the Catholics. As you know, and according to their bylaws, when a person of that faith dies they must wait in purgatory for an unspecified period of time before it's determined if they can enter Heaven. The Pope's been all over me and they've had their panties in a wad in general ever since the bill was passed, claiming that we don't process things fast enough. You know how busy we are with all the dying and such on Earth. So, under pressure from the Catholics, Peter rammed through a new program that the other disciples ratified and it was passed into law about three months ago. This new law requires that anyone making application to Heaven must be processed within thirty days. You can imagine what that's done to the quality of the people in our City."

"Yah, God, I get the picture." The minister is concerned about his heavenly reward. This doesn't sound good.

God continues, "So now, to meet his quota, Pete is letting in every Tom, Dick, and Harry, just to keep up. It's a mess. And on top of it all, Notre Dame just fired their football coach and so the Catholics are all over me and my phone is ringing off the hook with requests from the priests for help in finding another to lead their program. The school's a real money-maker, I'll admit, probably the highest donation-per-soul rate of any on Earth. And I'm getting pressure from the Pentecostals about how they think I'm playing favorites. You know how they feel about the Catholics. There just aren't enough hours in the day." Now that really worries Dave. God is talking as if he has the same problems we have on Earth. What happened to the harps, the rivers flowing with milk and honey, and "no more cares"?

He asks God about those things.

"Oh, Dave," God adds with a little chuckle, "we've had a very aggressive marketing campaign over the past several hundred years. The devil's been on our ass and he's made it look pretty good, I must admit, to live a wild and crazy life on Earth. My guys in some of the churches haven't made it much easier on me, the Pentecostals especially. All their wife swapping and fornication has certainly given me headaches. And don't get me started on Tammy Faye and

Jim Bakker. So we had to really push our marketing and downplay some of the problems we're having." God was now sounding *human* to Dave. The Big Man continues, "Not that Heaven's a bad place. I'd put it up against any other City I know of. But we just have got to get a handle on things. That's why I called you, Dave."

"What can I do, God?" Dave asks.

"Here's the deal," God continues, "I have a church, a Pentecostal Church, over in the Napa Valley—a big dollar church. The minister, a real hotshot who has increased the Sunday attendance to over ten thousand has crapped in his own nest. He's been seeing a hooker from the Mitchell Brothers strip joint in San Francisco for the past two years and it just came out in the papers. It's too late for damage control in the public eye, but I think we have a good shot at keeping the lion's share of the members from abandoning ship. Dave, I need you to take over the operation—lock, stock and barrel. You, of all people, know how long it takes to build up cash-flow in a church. In these economic times we can't afford to lose many souls. It's rough out there."

Dave mulls over what he has heard. Lately he's been thinking it might be time to move on but he hasn't come to grips with it. Having a call from God makes a huge difference.

After letting the minister think about what he has just heard, God breaks the silence and asks, "Dave will you help me out? I need you there next Sunday for the main service. If you give me your answer by the end of your day we can get it in the papers for tomorrow. With your resume it should do the trick. What do you say?"

"God, you know I'd do anything for you. Count me in!"

As they wrap up the call, the two of them chat about the details and God says he'll have Thomas, one of the disciples from the last supper, email Dave a contract. Thomas had told God that he doubted he could have the new contract out by the end of the week but says he'll try. The minister can name his price, that's how important the assignment is.

"Can you do this on faith, Dave? You know you can trust me even if you're forced to preach next Sunday without a contract. Can you do that?" Dave indicates he can.

God continues. "We get this worked out and dinner's on me. This just may be the opportunity both of us have been waiting for." God is all fired up, but Dave isn't so sure. This whole conversation didn't seem like what he'd imagined. But then, what was the alternative?

They end the call. "Thanks for your trust in me, God."

"Dave, it's a two-way street."

30

More Stuff

In May and June of 1975, my father planted his second yearly crop on about one-hundred-and-fifty acres of the land he had rented from the monastery, but this crop was different. Through his farming connections Dad had been able to acquire a contract with a mid-western outfit, Stine Seed Company, to grow vine seed. This amounted to various types of squash, melon, cucumbers and other vegetables that would be harvested and dried into seed—which would then be exported to Europe and used in various agriculture programs. The oil embargo of 1973 and 1974 had severely hampered seed production on the European continent and it had opened up a profitable market for American farmers, and my dad was able to take advantage of it. In late summer, he harvested a bumper crop which enabled him to pay off the debt left over from the sale of the ranch and he and my mother were able to purchase a home on acreage not far from the ranch. All of which eased their dependence on me for financial help.

It was also during the summer of 1975 that I decided to bring my brother into the company and we formed a partnership: Morgan Construction Company. It seemed like the thing to do, and we both had much the same vision of where our combined efforts could take us.

A year or so before my brother and I formed our partnership, he had met a gal named Shelley Hill from Palo Alto who was attending

Chico State. They developed a romantic relationship that led to their marriage in December of 1975. They were married in the grand Methodist Church in her home town and it was a very joyous affair.

Shelley's father, Lee Hill, had a good friend who was the financial advisor to several of the top executives at Hewlett-Packard, and a good number of them were guests at the wedding and reception that followed. Of course, as people will do during these types of occasions, we all engaged in conversations about what we did for a living and what our plans were for the future. I especially developed a connection with the financial advisor friend of the family, Tom Wersen. He and I spent most of our time at the reception talking business and possible real estate investments, and we made plans to talk further in the next several weeks.

Tom Wersen's interest in talking with me was based in the fact that there was a section of the IRS Code that allowed for someone making an investment in a tangible asset to depreciate the value of that asset against his earned income. It was loosely termed the "five-to-one-write-off." As an example: if you were an executive at some company and making one hundred thousand a year, and you invested ten thousand in a depreciable asset, you could take that investment and write it off against your salary at five times the amount you had invested. It was also sometimes called the "passive losses" deduction. This served to spur investment, and caused the U.S. economy to boom. It was a godsend to real estate, because of the amount of leverage that could be generated. It spurred the development of residential apartment projects until the Reagan administration pushed legislation through Congress in 1986 which killed the program in January of 1987. The write-off had been abused, and the financial pendulum swung—as it always does.

But, back in early 1976, everyone was scurrying around to find investments that qualified for this deduction. Tom Wersen was no different, so he and I worked out an agreement whereby we were able to build several apartment complexes in northern California that benefited his clients. Following that, in late 1976 and early 1977, I developed my first subdivision with Tom's clients as investors.

This wasn't a "depreciation play" but a potential profit center. It was thirty-six lots in the small town of Orland. We built and sold the homes, and the development was successful and things worked out fine. But, as luck would have it, a severe drought had taken over northern and central California, and was in its third year. We had gotten the subdivision approved and were in the process of constructing the streets and building lots when a reporter from *Time* magazine seized on the story and paid a visit to town. He interviewed several locals and paid a visit to a reservoir ten or fifteen miles west of town that was an Army Corps of Engineers Water Project which was built to collect and store rain water in the winter for use by farmers to irrigate their crops in the summer. Admittedly the water level was low when he visited. But, instead of really doing his homework, the reporter drove back toward town, spied a small canal that led from the reservoir, and stopped and took a picture of the dry water bed with a dead carp as a back-drop. He didn't bother to find out that the canal was always dry in winter.

The reporter also interviewed a local banker, a man by the misleading name of June Young, Branch Manager of Lloyds Bank California, who discussed the severity of the financial damage the drought was causing. June said that the bank was going to "hang in there" with the farmers and not foreclose on anyone. I went to high school with the banker's kids and knew him well, so about six months earlier I had made an appointment with June to discuss borrowing three thousand dollars. I was planning to use it in the purchase of constructions tools—equipment that would be needed by my framing crews during the building of the homes in the subdivision I was contemplating.

As scheduled, I went to my appointment with him and I had nicely typed out my request and method of repayment and we sat down in his office and I gave him my sales pitch. Just a couple of minutes into my speech I was interrupted by his snoring. I had been gazing out a window in his office and hadn't been looking directly at him while I spoke. Hearing his snoring, I stopped talking, which shook him awake. He sheepishly apologized for the incident and mentioned that he hadn't gotten much sleep lately. He also told me that, "I was going to loan you the money anyway, Steve."

The *Time* reporter filed his story and it came out in the March, 1977, issue of the magazine. The picture he took of the dry canal and the dead carp were on the lead-in to the article and the caption read: "A Tiny Town Near Collapse." I could have shot him. Tom Wersen called me and wanted to know what the hell was going on with his money. Thankfully, the drought passed and we sold the homes, but it sure elevated my blood pressure.

*****

Going back in time a little, the year of 1976 had been good to Charlotte and me financially, and we had planned a two-week trip to Hawaii over Christmas—a week on Maui and a week on Kauai. Mother Nature's biological clock was ticking. We had been married for more than six years and both of us had decided it was time: time to have a young'un. There's probably not a better place to conceive a family than Hawaii, and so it was that Charlotte became pregnant and we had our first child in September of 1977—a son we named Jason Heath.

It was in the early summer of 1977 that the Assemblies of God Church, which was adjacent to our home on the ranch my father had bought from my grandparents—and which was on land that had been donated by them—announced that a new shepherd would be arriving to minister to the flock. They were getting a new pastor, a man about my age, named Dennis Sylvester. He was about as "normal" as any of the pastors that had come and gone over the years—save for my cousin, Fred, whom I've mentioned before. Dennis's arrival got me involved in the Church again.

Dennis was really a good guy, in spite of his misguided religious beliefs, and he asked if I would be interested in heading up a program called the Royal Rangers: a church club of youngsters between the ages of about ten and thirteen. They were all boys—a rough crowd to say the least—full of testosterone and all that stuff. The "Royal" in the club's name alluded to the church's belief that children were the sons and daughters of the "King": God. The name may have sounded regal, but the devil had gotten through the gate.

I took the job, and it was a nightmare. Imagine trying to get the attention of ten or twelve boys who were totally content with pulling the legs off bugs and punching and kicking each other. And then imagine getting their attention long enough to even announce that it was "time for the Devotionals," which meant we had to stop whatever we were doing and read and discuss the Bible. "What's that all about?" they'd ask. The job was not possible.

So it came to pass that—being the "rugged, outdoor type" that I appeared to be—it fell to me to take these rascally, devil-inspired youngsters on an overnight field trip. Now you're talkin'. This was right up my alley, and I knew just the place to take them: Boone's Island! The "island" was really a piece of riparian land that, at the end of the summers along the Sacramento River, would become land-locked and create a sort of island—but we liked the name: Boone's Island. It was named after a pioneer family who had been among the first to settle in our area, even if it wasn't a *real* island. There were even bobcats and cougars and snakes and all kinds of critters that made their homes there, which were good stuff for kids and counselors of kids. Tom Kalb, the helpful athlete of Mrs. Ollenberger fame, had volunteered to assist me in this adventure but had to cancel at the last minute, so I was on my own.

The day came, and we headed out on our great adventure. It was a Friday afternoon. We were going to spend that night and all day Saturday, and then the kids would return home. Their parents would pick them up at the canal road which led to the island.

Most of the kids met at the church. A few had their parents drop them off down by the river—these were probably people who wanted to see what their kids were getting into, which was not unreasonable. I had loaded all of the supplies—and five or six of the kids—on the back of our old farm truck and had headed out on our adventure. We waited for the others to arrive at the meeting place that led to the island. Once everyone was there I piled them all on the back of the truck, and we made our way to our camping site.

I don't know how many of you have been around—or have had in your charge—ten or fifteen twelve-year-old boys. It's not a pretty sight. What with keeping them from falling off the back of the truck or beating the hell out of each other, it was a massive undertaking to just get them the mile or so to our camp. I had come down to the camp earlier and had set up a fire pit and the tent I would sleep in, and had mounted a makeshift container of water that could be used to clean up things; hands and utensils and faces. The boys would be required to set up their own tents and organize their own stuff.

I pulled up to the camp area and stopped the truck, and prepared to announce the order in which we would do our chores and get things set up. I no more had turned off the ignition than I heard wild banshee yells and every one of those boys took off in all directions into the wild beyond, down by the river, into the jungle of tangled vines and snakes. This was about six o'clock, and it wouldn't get dark until about nine o'clock. For the next three hours I would hear, but never see, them.

As darkness was setting upon us, one by one the boys straggled back to camp, dirty and scratched and sweaty and bedraggled. The mosquitoes had almost carried them away and they were all starving to death—as becomes all kids, right after they've told you emphatically that they're "*not* hungry!" So I had to get their dinners together. I had dug a fire pit, as I've mentioned, and had lighted several pieces of wood, which had burned down sufficiently to make a bed of coals. Each kid had brought along with them a piece of meat, maybe potatoes, and vegetables and whatever else they wanted for dinner wrapped in tin foil that could be placed down in the coals to cook until ready to eat. I finally got all of their dinners cooking, but I had fifteen boys who had to wait for their meals with idle hands. They'd gotten their second wind since returning from their adventures and they were restless. The time had gotten away from me and it was past ten o'clock and we still hadn't eaten. It would take an hour to cook their meals in the fire-pit, and I still hadn't done the devotionals. Time to tell a story, maybe?

So I gathered the "little darlin's" and finally had them seated around the campfire. Some were on pieces of wood they'd dragged in, some were on the ground, and some were just sitting on their hands. I had them quieted for the time-being, and I asked if they wanted to hear a story. "Sure, Mister Morgan," they said. "Tell us one of your stories."

When my boys were little—and my daughter in later years—I would tell them a story each night before they went to sleep. Most of the stories I told were recollections of my childhood, but when I ran out of those tales I would make them up. I would build up the story line, and change the inflections in my voice to accentuate the effect I was trying to achieve. I would scare them to death on occasion when I got too involved in the tale, and this time was no different. Watching our meals cooking in the fire pit I began to spin my yarn. Further and further I went into my tale, of things and animals and creatures lurking in the dark, of creepy things, of ghosts and things unexplainable. And it scared the hell out of them. Several began crying and asking for their parents. These testosterone-filled jungle rats who had defied nature were now scared to death, and I was in deep doo-doo.

It came to the point that most of the kids were scared enough that it wouldn't be possible for them to stay the night. So we broke camp and I loaded all of them, all fifteen or so—and their things—on the back of the old truck and took them all home. None of us spent the night. I resigned my commission the next day, and Dennis accepted. Several parents thought I was a "meanie," but what's a little story among a counselor and the kids. All in good fun, right?

More on Suffering Fools

I was a fool to think I could handle those rascally boys on my own. But you never know if you don't try. The real fool is one that can't laugh at themselves. Self-humor, in my mind, is the beginning of wisdom. And I gained much wisdom that night.

G. K. Chesterton wrote something that I think is divinely-inspired, pure genius, and much to the point. To the epistle of 2 Corinthians

11:19 that I've previously quoted and which reads, "Ye suffer fools gladly, seeing ye yourselves are wise," he responded:

> There is an apostolic injunction to suffer fools gladly. We always lay the stress on the word "suffer," and interpret the passage as one urging resignation. It might be better, perhaps, to lay the stress upon the word "gladly," and make our familiarity with fools a delight, and almost a dissipation. Nor is it necessary that our pleasure in fools (or at least in great and godlike fools) should be merely satiric or cruel. The great fool is he in whom we cannot tell which is the conscious and which the unconscious humor; we laugh with him and laugh at him at the same time. An obvious instance is that of ordinary and happy marriage. A man and a woman cannot live together without having against each other a kind of everlasting joke. Each has discovered that the other is a fool, but a great fool. This largeness, this grossness and gorgeousness of folly is the thing which we all find about those with whom we are in intimate contact; and it is the one enduring basis of affection, and even of respect.

*****

In light of the success of the subdivision we had built and sold in Orland, Tom Wersen (the investment advisor to the HP executives), wanted to invest in more real estate development, and so we began to further pursue the development of apartment complexes. We were modest in the beginning: ten, twenty, or thirty units at a time in the small rural towns in our area. Also, one of the members of my construction crew had invited his parents to invest, which they had, and we started out on our new ventures. The various projects went well with Wersen and his clients, but didn't go well for the parents of my crew member, which caused a rift between them and me and ruined my relationship with their son. It was probably my fault, because being young and full of optimism, I had given them unreasonable expectations and we were fresh off the success of the single-family subdivision which would have been hard to duplicate. But I was too "wet behind the ears" to know it. Ironically, though, my former crew member reaped a degree of revenge.

During the construction of the last homes in the subdivision I've mentioned—which was during the same time that we were building the first apartment complex that the parents of my crew member had invested in—I noticed that building materials were disappearing at an alarming rate. I knew that my crew member and a friend, another member of my crew, had been able to purchase a building lot in Chico and were constructing a home for sale on speculation, so I had a suspicion. After a couple weeks of seeing the materials disappear from the subdivision, I decided to follow these two back to Chico after work one day. As luck would have it they decided to drop by their construction project. They worked around the place for a couple hours until it was beginning to get dark and then left for the day. There was still enough daylight to see things, so I made my way from where I had hidden my pickup from their sight while I watched them, and walked around and through the house. I could tell that most of the material being used to construct the place—including the doors and windows—was from my subdivision.

The next morning when they got to my jobsite I handed each of them their final checks and told them to get off the job. They both acted indignant and I downplayed the fact that I knew what they were doing with my material, but when I did finally bring it up they both denied taking anything from my site. The crew member whose parents had invested with me was very cocky and intimated that it was only payback on his part. I let it slide. It wasn't a hill I wanted to die on. A couple years later, the second crew member who had joined in on stealing my material showed up at our place on the farm one Sunday afternoon. You can imagine my surprise. We talked out on the front porch and he said he wanted to apologize for what he had done, admitting they had taken the material, because they didn't think I'd miss it. I let bygones be bygones and accepted his apology, although he mentioned nothing about repaying the cost. Then he asked if I would give him a reference for a new job he was applying for. (Of all the nerve.) I told him to not push his luck and bid him farewell. I never saw him again.

Over the next couple of years we built several apartment complexes in small towns around the northern Sacramento Valley area. In late 1979, my brother and I had been able to acquire a piece of property in the town of Willows, in partnership with the HP guys. We were in the process of building the units when my father announced that the Assemblies of God Church had begun a program whereby they assisted Southeast Asian citizens in migrating to the United States. With the end of the Vietnam War in 1975 many families in that region had been dispossessed, and the Church was extending a hand to assist them in getting a new start in this country. It was a noble gesture, even though I judged the church members on their actual intent: to convert these folks from Buddhism to Christianity, which was quite a stretch. But these people were desperate and went for it. And I, grudgingly, give the Pentecostals credit for their humanitarian effort.

So the Church sponsored a family from Cambodia. Yung Kong, the father, and his son Boon Hi (to use our English version of their names from their native language), and two nephews, whose names I can't recall. My father brought them down to our jobsite and we put them to work as laborers. They worked their collective asses off and put our white trash laborers to shame, and that pissed our white trash laborers off. As time went on and the whites were feeling more and more inferior, it happened that we were building the second floor of one of the buildings. The Cambodians were carrying very large beams from the ground to the second floor and hoisting them up to the framers. On one particular occasion, a beam had been lifted up by the laborers and was within the grasp of the framers above when—with knowing looks—the carpenters let go and the beam fell down on the Cambodians and split Boon Hi's head wide open. He dropped as if he had been shot by a gun.

My brother and I had been reviewing the building plans on the ground floor and, observing the situation from that vantage point, scrambled up the ladder to the second floor to assess the damage. It was fortunate that Boon Hi hadn't been killed. My brother and I picked him up and took him down the ladder and got him to my pickup. As we were preparing to take the Cambodian to the medical facility, and when I realized he wasn't going to die, I walked back to the building and told the framers that I didn't want them there when I returned. They weren't. And Boon Hi recovered and came back to work. These little guys would go on the dead run and sit on their haunches at break time, drinking the strongest mixture of coffee and something we were never sure of, and they thanked us every minute of the day for the opportunity to work, which was a good lesson for all of us.

The building project I've just mentioned was deep in rice farming country, about fifteen miles south of the little town of Orland. The complex encompassed thirty-five dwelling units. We were nearing the completion of the project in mid-1980 when, one day, I happened to be operating a backhoe digging trenches for the installation of sewer lines, when a big ole Mercury Town Car pulled up to the site, burgundy with a cream colored vinyl top. That kind of car was "the cat's meow" in those days. A little fellow in a light green leisure suit got out and appeared to be looking the place over. The guy was a dead ringer for Alfred E. Newman of *Mad Magazine* fame. My curiosity getting the best of me, I shut the engine down on the tractor and, dismounting the rig, walked over and inquired of his business.

"I'm looking for the one in charge," he replied in a rather bossy tone.

"Well, I guess that would be me," I responded, and I asked what I could do for him.

"I want to buy this project from you. Name your price." Well, that was pretty neat. Interest rates were at more than twenty percent and the Jimmy Carter White House had things in a financial turmoil. No one knew what was going to happen. The Shah of Iran had been deposed and a second oil embargo was underway and the world was in a general mess. And here came this munchkin of a man saying he wanted to buy the whole apartment complex. I figured he must have been full of bull! But I listened, as all businessmen—or wannabe businessmen—do.

Talking further with the munchkin, he laid out his plan. "Steve, I'm buying everything I can find and turning them into condos." We were apparently now on a first-name basis. "Inflation has driven the price of housing up so high that no one can afford to buy anything and I can be at the bottom of the market with my pricing." (Sound familiar?!) But he was right: interest rates were through the roof and the first- and second-time buyer were out of the mix. And they are what had driven—and what drives—the housing market.

My new friend said, "Steve, I'm going to turn your project into condos and sell them for under seventy thousand. And I and my investors can make a tidy profit doing so." Well that's a fine "how-do-you-do," I thought. "What will you take for the units?" He asked.

"Forty-two apiece," I replied. We were into the project at about twenty-two thousand apiece and I had recently run the numbers with my brother.

"You've got a deal, Steve. Where do we open escrow?" He agreed, just like that.

With that, my new diminutive friend led me over to the back of his car and opened the trunk. Inside were several buckets of what looked like paint cans. But they were containers filled with gold krugerrands. At the 1980 price of seven hundred and fifty dollars an ounce, the buckets were worth thirty-five thousand dollars. "This is to show you I'm serious about the deal," he said. We headed down to Western Title and my friend, Glenn Felder.

I ushered my buyer into the lobby of the title company and told him to take a seat and that I'd speak with the manager and give him the outline of what we were going to discuss. Clara, the office manager, told Glenn I was there and I waited for him in the conference room.

"Well, Morgan, what's going on?" Glenn asked in his usual smart-ass manner. Glenn was—and is—one of the quickest wits I've ever known and among the most enjoyable people to spend time with. "Who's that sitting out in the lobby?" he inquired. "Looks like a midget."

I told him what had happened and that this fellow wanted to buy our apartment complex. And he wanted to open escrow immediately. Now, Glenn wasn't one to miss an opportunity and he leaped up and opened the door to the conference room and invited our new buyer in.

After we all introduced each other, Glenn sat down with my new friend and I and asked how this was all going to happen. My buyer explained his intent on purchasing the complex and that he had thirty-five thousand dollars he wanted to deposit as earnest money. Then he asked us to follow him outside, to the back of his car. Once again he opened the trunk and showed all of us the krugerrands. Glenn looked at the munchkin and told him that he had a fireproof document area in the office but not a burglarproof one, and that he couldn't take the gold as earnest money unless he could get a local bank to hold it while the transaction was consummated. So we headed out in the Town Car, down to the local branch of Tri-Counties Bank and Carroll Taresh, the manager—a rice farmer who moonlighted as a bank manager—and a good friend of Glenn and me.

So Taresh saw Glenn and me enter the bank and thought something was up. We're all like the "Three Stooges" and think on the same wavelength. We left our little friend out in the lobby, and Glenn and I went into Carroll's office and told him our story. He thought we were bull-shitting him but followed us out to the Town Car. Our munchkin opened the trunk and showed Carroll the krugerrands.

So, we were standing in the bank parking lot with thirty-five thousand dollars' worth of gold coins. And how were we supposed to get them into the bank and their vault for safe-keeping? Hide them in plain site is what I suggested: just pick up the containers and walk in like we own the place. And that's what we did—and it worked and no one was the wiser.

We went back to the title company and opened the escrow and signed the paperwork. A month or so later, the transaction closed and my brother and I and our investors had our money and the Alfred E. Newman look-alike had his apartments.

Inflation was runaway in the economy during 1980 and, like

I've said, housing prices were shooting up, just like in the years before this current crash—2004 to 2007. And, also just like what has occurred in the current time-frame, back then investors were thinking that by converting apartments into condominiums they could offer "affordable housing" to the masses and make a killing. But what they didn't—and don't—realize is that you can't just sell on price. Home ownership is a privilege, not a right, and it is a fickle thing and isn't just based on cost. The overwhelming majority of people in this country want to own a home with a picket fence and a backyard, unless they're in New York City, or some other major city. They don't want a nine-hundred-square-foot box that is really an apartment. And my Town Car friend and his investors lost their collective asses. They never sold a single one of the units and the bank took the whole thing back.

*****

My brother and I, through our construction company, owned a small private plane that my brother piloted, a Piper Cherokee Turbo Arrow. We used it to get around to the various projects we were involved with in northern California. One day in mid-summer of 1980 my brother had flown into the town of Willows, where we were building the apartments that Alfred E. Newman eventually bought. He had a car that he kept at the airport for ground travel, and was going to drive it back to Chico while he had some work done on the plane by an airport mechanic. I met him at the airport restaurant for lunch and, when we had finished, the two of us walked outside to my pickup and were standing there talking when a man walked up to us in what appeared to be a state of complete despair.

He was dressed in a nicely-pressed white shirt, new-looking Bermuda shorts, crisp white socks, and no shoes. He was crying and visibly upset and asked for our help. My brother, being the wiser of the two of us, would have none of it and said good-bye and got into his car and left.

So I was left standing there with this middle-aged man with no shoes in the airport restaurant parking lot. He was inconsolable, and in an attempt to help the poor fellow I asked him what I could do. He said he needed a ride to the Greyhound bus depot across town. I told him I'd take him there and motioned for him to get into my truck. He did so and started to tell me his story as I backed out of the parking lot and headed out toward the main road. I had no more than gotten underway than he grabbed my arm and broke down in a fit of tears. The guy was a mess, so I pulled over to let him talk. I wasn't sure what he was going to do next and it was better to be sitting on the side of the road than driving along in the vehicle.

Here's what he told me. This is the absolute truth. You can't make this stuff up.

My new friend with no shoes told me that he and his wife had been sitting in their living room the previous evening, in the town of Red Bluff, about forty-five miles north of where we were, when the phone rang. He answered the call and was greeted by a representative of the California Highway Patrol who told him that there had been a terrible accident on Interstate Five, about thirty miles north—near Redding—and that his son had been a victim of the crash. His son was dead. In his despair at hearing the news, he had run to his car and taken off down the highway until he had stopped in the town of Willows, at the motel next to the Greyhound bus depot. That's where he came to his senses and finally realized what he was doing and—collecting his thoughts—called his home and told his family that he'd take the bus back in the morning, which was the morning we met. He told me that he didn't trust his ability to drive back to his home and would take the bus instead, like he'd told his family. Someone would get his car back to Red Bluff.

Poor Bastard! I felt for the guy! He was very sincere. He had calmed down a bit and I decided it was safe to head out to the main road, and so we did. Driving along, my new friend asked if I could stop at a liquor store and buy him a six-pack of beer, which was not an unusual request given his state of mind. So I stopped in at a convenience store and bought him a pack of Bud Light. He told me the bus wouldn't arrive for an hour or so and he'd hang around the motel room until it did and the booze would help calm his nerves.

It made sense, I guess. He invited me to have a beer with him but I declined. He also told me that he was making plans to run for President—President of the United States. That kind of upset the apple cart and I dropped him off at his motel and got the hell out of there.

As you can imagine, I was somewhat suspicious of my shoeless friend and so I decided to stop by the local office of the California Highway Patrol and have the captain, a friend of mine, check to see if there had been any fatalities on Interstate Five in the last twenty-four to forty-eight hours between the towns of Red Bluff and Redding. He checked and there hadn't been any fatalities in more than two months. Either my man was confused about the location of the tragedy or he was full of you-know-what. Probably the latter, I guessed.

A couple weeks later I was sitting in Carroll Taresh's office at the Tri-Counties Bank branch discussing some business with him and relating the story I've just told. I glanced through the glass enclosing his office toward the main entry to the bank and there was my shoeless friend. I jumped up and excitedly pointed the guy out to Carroll. "That's the guy I'm talking about! That's him!" Carroll doubled over with laughter. He told me I'd been taken, like everyone else in town, by a guy who had been committed by his family to the mental ward at the county hospital and periodically wandered out of the unlocked facility and spun his yarns to anyone who would listen. It appeared that I had been his latest victim. It took me a while to live that one down as news traveled fast in the small town.

*****

In the early part of May, 1980, my sister, who was an active member of the Fellowship of Christian Athletes, asked if I would be willing to pick up a guest speaker at the Chico airport later that month. This person was going to be the lead attraction for a regional meeting of the group. Since I had a Mercedes SL450 convertible and they wanted a person with a *fancy* car to give him a ride from the airport to the event, they asked me. The guest-speaker was future

Hall of Fame Quarterback, Terry Bradshaw. "Well, I'd be glad to," I told her.

The day came and, shortly after lunch, I arrived at the airport to meet Bradshaw and chauffeur him around town. The meeting didn't start until seven o'clock that evening and so we had five hours or so to kill. I was waiting on the tarmac when his plane arrived and gave him a wave of my hand as he came down the stairs, introduced myself, and headed for my car. He was just as I had imagined: a big ole country boy with a big ole cowboy hat. He was dressed in Wranglers and boots, just as I was (except I was without the hat). We made small talk as I drove us out of the parking lot and I asked him what he'd like to do to kill time until the meeting started.

"You know, Steve, what I'd like is to get us a couple six-packs and a pack of Red Man and drive around and see the countryside. You drink, Steve?" he asked.

"Why yes I do." Not much of a beer drinker, more of a hard-liquor man, but I told him I'd make an exception this time. So I pulled into the parking lot of a convenience store that was on our way from the airport and we got out and went into the place to make our purchase. Well, now, it's hard to be incognito when you're as big and famous as he was—the Steelers having just won the Super Bowl the previous January—and people in the store began to notice him and were all a-twitter. He was very gracious and signed a few autographs while I got the beer and Red Man and, as I approached the counter to pay, he muttered under his breathe, "Let's get the hell out of here." And we did. But he was very good with those in the store, and showed no pretense.

We headed out into the countryside, past the almond orchards and rice fields. He was very intrigued by the orchards as he hadn't seen many in his native Louisiana. He'd grown up near Shreveport and the agriculture in that area was mostly cotton, rice, and truck farming of vegetables, but no orchards. We drank our beer and he chewed his Red Man. I stopped the car every now and then to let him spit out a big ole wad, even though I didn't chew.

"Where do you live, Steve?" he asked me.

"Oh, about twenty miles west of here," I told him, "near the ranch I grew up on." So we headed west and I took him by my place and introduced him to Charlotte. Neither she nor I were planning to attend the event that evening, but he insisted that we be his guests. And he wanted me to sit up on the podium with him. We accepted his offer, and I called my sister and told her of the plans and she passed the word along to those in charge of the event. Since it would be late when the affair ended, and there would be no flights available to take him back to San Francisco to make his connecting flight back to his home, I volunteered to fly him back to the City after the shindig. I'd arrange to have a pilot friend fly him back in our company plane and I'd ride along. He said that would be great. Since time wasn't an issue I invited him back out to our place on the ranch to sit in our hot tub for a while after the meeting, but before we flew back to San Francisco. He thought that was a great idea.

So I sat up on the podium with the future Hall of Famer that evening and he wowed the audience and introduced me as his "close friend" and we all had a ball. He pointed my wife out in the crowd and had her stand and take a bow. She blushed and thought the attention was great. When it was all over we got the hell out of there—as he suggested again—and made our way to the ranch and the hot tub. I had an extra pair of trunks I loaned my new friend and we sat in the hot water and enjoyed ourselves. My wife was only about a month away from delivering our second child so she couldn't get in the spa, but she dangled her feet over the edge and sat and talked with Bradshaw and me. We must have been in there for two hours or so before we realized it was time to get back to the airport and our plane and pilot. Terry did a tender thing as he was getting out of the hot tub. He bent over and, placing his head next to my wife's swollen belly, said, "Neil you have a good life, you hear!" Neil is the name we had picked for our soon-to-be second son.

The pilot and I flew Bradshaw down to San Francisco and we dropped him off at Butler Aviation, the general aviation area of the airport, and he took a cab over to the main terminal. He and I exchanged contact information and the two of us made periodic communication over the next couple years, since there were no cell phones or email in those days. But then we drifted apart and we haven't talked in years. I'm not sure he would even remember the occasion, but it was kind of neat for a small town boy. Two small town boys, I guess. And he hasn't done too badly for himself after football.

As we'd driven through the countryside that afternoon and sat in the hot tub that evening we had talked about all kinds of things, religion, politics, sports and such. He still has a great sense of humor that you can see during the NFL pre-game show he co-hosts on the Fox Television Network in the fall on Sunday mornings. He'd been raised in much the same religious environment as I had—although his was maybe a little less judgmental—and could relate to the difficulty I was having in shaking the unnatural attachment I had to my past. He told me his involvement in the Fellowship of Christian Athletes was as much to assuage his feelings of religious guilt as anything that could be construed as "joining the movement."

Not that the group doesn't do good things. They do. It's just that the religious bent of the organization is hard to handle when you've come from the background he and I had. He also wanted children. He was married to the skater, Jo Jo Starbuck, at the time and she didn't want kids, which was putting a strain on their marriage. He was almost thirty-two (my age) and envied my wife and me for having one son and expecting another shortly. He and Jo Jo divorced three years later and never had children between them, although he has two daughters from a subsequent marriage. He's a good guy and I wish him well.

About a month later, on June 9, our second son was born. We named him Neil, as I've mentioned, Neil Colin. The two boys are a little less than three years apart. Neil was seven weeks premature and was suffering some distress, so the doctors decided to perform a Cesarean section. Consequently, he spent the first ten days of his life in an incubator at the hospital but soon was robust enough for the doctors to let us take him home. He suffered no ill effects from his ordeal and today is a big, strapping man.

*****

About a month after Neil was born a friend of mine was having a bachelor party at his home in Chico. Several of us attended and, after a few drinks, at about two o'clock in the morning, I headed back to the ranch. I was driving my SL450 and, approaching a long straight stretch, I put my foot to the floorboard and got the thing going over one hundred and thirty miles an hour. It was a moonlit night and as I passed the intersection of Highway thirty-two and Meridian Road the moon reflected off two Butte County Sheriff's cars, parked by the side of the road, with the deputies leaning against their cars. As I flashed past them they raced to get in their rigs and took off after me in hot pursuit, but my rig was much faster than theirs and I left them in the dust. However, about a mile from the ranch, my conscience got the best of me and I slowed down and pulled over to wait for them to catch up. I could see their flashing lights in the distance and just leaned back against my car and waited for them. I don't know why. I guess I thought I could talk my way out of the situation.

They eventually caught up and, parking a hundred yards or so behind, walked up to me and my car and inquired as to why I had been going so fast. I told them I had no good reason. They went back to their cars and did what deputy sheriffs do, and came back with a ticket for reckless driving. I put up a feeble argument and then we all went on our way. They didn't even ask if I'd been drinking.

A couple days later the headline in our local paper read, "High-Speed Chase Nets Orland Man." High-speed chase, my ass! I could have been home in bed before they caught up to me, but I'd stopped and taken my medicine. My brother had seen the article in the paper and called me. Old George Loney and several of my business associates ragged on me and so I decided to fight the ticket.

I got hold of an attorney friend of mine, Paul Henry, who handled these types of things and told him my story. He filed a petition with the court and we were set for trial. Now Paul was a very eccentric man and "danced to his own drummer." But he was "dumb like a fox," a taller version of the character in the television series *Columbo*.

When the day came, I was in court and Paul was late and we

were all sitting there waiting for him. He finally came rushing in and apologized to the judge and the trial began. An Assistant District Attorney made the opening remarks and laid out the State's position that I should be hanged by the neck until I was dead. Paul made a brief opening statement and then the judge asked if the two deputies were present. They weren't. They didn't show up. And then the judge read the Assistant DA the riot act on how the cops should have called in the Highway Patrol and how they crossed county lines while in hot pursuit and didn't notify the Glenn County Sheriff's Department. Then it was Paul's turn.

He got up and thanked the judge for the opportunity to speak and walked over to the empty jury box and began speaking, as if a jury was seated before him. He waxed eloquent on the virtues of my innocence and the skullduggery forged by the two deputies who gave me the ticket. And periodically he walked back to the desk I was seated at and rummaged through some notes he'd written on the back of envelopes, and then went back to his phantom jury. He finished his dissertation and again thanked the judge and came back to our table and sat down. It could have been a scene from a movie; for the judge told the court and my attorney that the speech Paul had just given was one of the finest he'd ever heard in his courtroom. Paul leaned back in his chair, fiddled with his paperwork and uttered these words: "Purely accidental, your honor."

The judge reduced my charges to "Going in excess of fifty-five miles per hour"—which was the speed limit at that time—and I paid the seventy-five dollar fine and we went our separate ways. I wish I could have filmed Paul at work. The judge thought the world of him. And so did I. But I was thirty-two years old and still acting out in my personal life.

I'm a Guest-Speaker at Rotary

In the fall of 1980, when interest rates were twenty-one percent and the economy was in the tank, I had a small town-home project of about twenty units, also in the village of Willows, which had been complete for six months and that I couldn't sell. My sister-in-law, Shelley, had gotten her real estate license the year before and had worked her ass off trying to sell the things, but it just didn't happen. The carrying costs were killing me.

One day I was lamenting the situation to my friend, Glenn Felder—he of the title company fame—and he suggested that I make an appearance at one of the Rotary Club meetings to discuss my project. Now, Rotary doesn't allow for speakers to pitch their business ventures, but Glenn thought it would be okay if I gave a talk about the *theory* of town-home development. And I knew most of the members to boot. I was desperate, so I took up his offer and was scheduled as the guest speaker for a meeting in a couple of weeks.

The day came, a Thursday, and I dropped by Glenn's office, picked him up, and we made our way to Franco's, the local eatery that was host to the club's weekly meetings. It was about eleven-thirty and, as was customary, we met other members that we knew in the bar and knocked down a couple of drinks, and then headed into the conference room where the meetings were held at twelve o'clock sharp.

The northern California region of the Sacramento Valley is a large rice-producing area and, yearly, harvests more rice per acre than any other part of the world. The Asians, having rice as a food staple, would travel to "the Valley" and discuss with the various farmers and organizations the methods that were used to achieve such high yields. And, as luck would have it, six Japanese representatives of their rice farming industry were in the crowd to listen to my spiel.

Glenn, as the current president of the group, opened the festivities with a prayer presented by a local clergy member, and then went through the old and new business and did what leaders of Rotarian clubs do. It was sophomoric, but enjoyable. All the while this was going on we were eating our lunches and making small talk with each other, and staring at the Japanese. As we were finishing our meals, Glenn made his way to the podium and announced that a guest speaker was in our midst and would deliver a speech on real estate development. He asked that I stand, which I did, and everyone politely booed my introduction and I sat down and we finished our lunches.

While the waiters were clearing our tables, Glenn once more went to the podium and introduced me again and I stood and made my way to the front and prepared to begin my speech. Glenn shook my hand and began to make his way back to his seat. But he took a detour and, motioning to all those present, led everyone out of the room into an adjacent hallway, all—that is— save for the six Japanese farmers. This had all been prearranged. Glenn was the master of this type of thing.

I was suddenly standing at the podium addressing an empty room except for the guest rice farmers. They were excitedly talking to each other and stealing glances at me, and in their own language generally asking each other "What the hell is going on?" I just stood there and, in no more than thirty seconds, Glenn led everyone back into the room and they all took their seats. When they all had comfortably sat down again, I gathered my papers and notes and left the room by the same side door the others had previously used. Not a word was said. I stood in the same hallway, just out of the sight of those in the room, and listened to their conversation.

After a few seconds the murmur began.

In a hushed voice, someone asked, "Do you think we offended him?"

"Nah, Morgan and I do this kind of stuff to each other all the time," came Glenn's response.

Another thirty seconds passed. I could hear the shuffling of feet. It was becoming a bit uncomfortable for all involved. I decided enough was enough and came back in and walked to the podium. I thanked Glenn for inviting me and began my speech. Nothing was said publicly in the meeting about the little episode we had just experienced, but I mouthed an obscenity in Glenn's direction. Like I've said, I knew almost everyone in the room, and Glenn's shenanigans were nothing new. After the meeting ended, Glenn, I and several of our friends spent the afternoon in Franco's Bar, laughing about the day's events.

I never could sell the town-homes and gave them back to the bank. It's interesting to see how history repeats itself when you look at the current economic times. Almost thirty years ago we went through much the same thing. Maybe we'll learn this time, or maybe we'll just begin to understand that these things come around every so often and level the playing field. The Wall Street banks and AIG notwithstanding, the economic meltdown we're currently experiencing is no one individual's fault. It's the fault of all of us, as is usually the case. It's a series of calamities by the public and private sector, generated by those who hadn't—or haven't—experienced the errors of the past, as is also usually the case. As a society we can't move forward on the highway of life by looking in the rear-view mirror all the time. If we do, we'll run off the road. But, now and then, we still must give a glance backward. We can plan where we're going by where we've been. But, as humans, we always think that "this time is different." It takes many follies to learn that if something appears to be "too good to be true," it probably is.

Like P. T. Barnum said, "There's a fool born every minute," and we're on a ship of fools. All of us, as much as we'd like to think not. No one meant it to be that way, it just happened. If and when we can stop the finger-pointing and join hands and work on this thing called "Life," we'll get somewhere. If not, we'll just wander around in the wilderness like Moses and the Children of Israel, if you believe in that Bible stuff.

*****

It was late winter of 1981 and I did it again. I got itchy feet and the feeling of wanderlust and I had my head up my you-know-what so far that I had to drop my pants to chew my food. (At least that's what Roy D. Mercer said.) And I got an apartment in Chico, again, and my wife Charlotte and I separated, for about five months this time. This time, we had children, Jason, who was about two-and-a-half and Neil who was not yet a year old. And, yet, I was still compelled to live out the fantasies of my youth that I believed I'd missed. But many other men have missed their youth and haven't responded in the way I did. On one hand, I was a responsible businessman taking care of things, my family and business. And on the other hand, I wanted to hang out in bars and pick up chicks. I did a lot of crazy things over those five months and sowed many wild oats and put many "notches on my gun." There are many stories around my activities during that time that are funny and ironic. Many close friends, and my current wife, know of these episodes. I've thought long and hard about telling those tales in my book, but I'm torn between further hurt I might cause my ex-wife, my sons, and others in the family and doing so may not warrant the pleasure and self-satisfaction I might derive from the telling. So, for now, I'm going to leave it at this.

Well, there's one I'll tell. I guess it's craziness! I still needed to "sow the oats."

I was sitting at the bar in Perry's on Union Street in San Francisco, at about six o'clock in the evening, and there was an empty stool to my left. A pretty blonde walked up and asked if someone was using the stool. I told her no and she sat down next to me. We made small talk and I bought her a couple drinks and she asked me if I'd like to drive up to Sausalito and have dinner at Ondine. Yep, I would, I agreed. We left Perry's and jumped in her Porsche and headed toward the Golden Gate Bridge. We crossed it at about a hundred forty miles an hour and wound our way down into the town and our restaurant. We handed off the rig to the valet and went on in. We had no reservations, and the place was virtually impossible to get into without advance notice, but she did her thing and they gave us a table.

We had a great meal, wine and before-dinner drinks, and headed back across the bridge toward the city, once again at a hundred and forty miles an hour, slowing down just enough to pay the toll. We went past the Presidio to her place in the Avenues south of Golden Gate Park.

She invited me to spend the night and one thing led to another. It was about three o'clock in the morning and I was half-asleep and half-awake and I "felt" someone looking down at me. You've probably had someone come up to your bed at night and scare the hell out of you. This was the same thing. I opened my eyes and as they adjusted to the darkness I could see the outline of someone standing beside the bed: a man. Her boyfriend. Well, that got my attention and I got my randy ass out of bed and, apologizing, put my clothes on and made my way out of there, to the living room. Showing amazing restraint, he led me to the front door and told me I was lucky he hadn't kicked my butt, which was true.

So I was standing out in the courtyard in front of the place. I needed a ride back to my hotel. I had no cellphone in those days and I was without a car. So I went back and knocked on the front door and, in a little while, he opened it up and asked "What the hell is it now?" I told him I need a cab. So he invited me in and got a phone book out of a drawer in the kitchen and the two of us looked through the yellow pages, found a cab company, and he called in with his address. Then he told me to get the hell out of there, and I did.

I approached the gate to the street and I couldn't get it open. I had been trying desperately for about fifteen minutes when I noticed the cab pull up at the curb. But I was locked in. I motioned to the driver but he didn't see me and then I yelled out. He still didn't know where I was, but I couldn't lose that cab. He finally saw me inside the gate and I told him to wait, I'd be right back. So I had to go back to this guy's front door and ring the bell. It took him a little bit to answer the door. You can imagine his attitude when he saw me.

I ate more "crow." "Would you please open the gate for me?" I asked in a little pathetic voice. He did, and I hurried to the cab and we barreled out of there back to my hotel. I was lucky to survive that evening. Even without the boyfriend, we could have wrapped the car around a bridge abutment. Suffer the fools!

*****

You know how I feel about the Pentecostals—especially the ministers and televangelists. I've vilified them for their transgressions, and their fornication, but I was no better. I just didn't get up behind a pulpit with the television cameras running and profess my virtues. I ran around in secret and lived out my fantasies. It seemed like I just had to prove something to myself, over and over again. How much does it take? I'm not saying that my Fundamentalist-Pentecostal upbringing was the only cause of my being so screwed up. There undoubtedly must be tens of thousands of males who grew up in the same environment and who dealt with it just fine and kept their heads screwed on straight. I know I keep harping on this but I wasn't *weird* or anything, at least no more so than anyone else, and when I walked down the street no one said, "there *he* goes."

My personality is such that I believe I tend to "over-think" everything in life. I don't take much for granted. And that's been the boon—and the bane—of my existence. But, as crazy as it may sound, I wouldn't have it any other way. I like the fact that I'm inquisitive and look beneath the surface of things. It's one positive trait that I've passed on to my children and I admire that in them and know they're generally well-adjusted to things around them: motivated, but appreciative. I never got the appreciative part. But they didn't grow up around the Pentecostals.

Religion-wise, my kids knew the Pentecostals from afar: my parents, sister and her family, cousins, aunts and uncles. They observed them from the outside, in the fresh air of cognitive thought. I viewed my childhood from the inside, in "prime time." Open-minded thinking was discouraged, as I've mentioned. It was as much a death sentence in the Church as was taking out a gun and putting it to your head and pulling the trigger. The emotional gates were unlocked to most of my friends, but I didn't have the nerve to pass through, and that's why it's taken me a lifetime to get a handle on things. Thank goodness my kids don't have to deal with that. All they're faced with is dealing with life's "normal" problems. And dealing with normal problems is okay, for it hardens our resolve and makes us the responsible people we become as a result.

Like I've mentioned, the economy was in a mess in the early 80s. Business was upside-down. The result of Reagan being elected president in the fall of 1980 was growing a sense of hope but, like today, no one knew how long things would take to get back on track and—if and when they did—what track they would take. The new president's positive personality certainly had a strong impact on things and his "supply side" economic policies got things going in a much shorter time-frame than was originally anticipated. The economic policy that Reagan espoused has been a source of very spirited debate within my immediate family as my younger son, Neil, graduated from the University of California at San Diego with a Degree in Economics from the Thurgood Marshall School, and takes great exception to my support of that theory. Many hours over good tequila and great cigars have been spent arguing the perceived good and evil of both sides of the theory. But, in 1981, we needed to get people back to work, just like today, and we did. This country began to produce things again, and sell them and pay taxes on the profit, and that got us going again. We need that traction today. Hopefully there's a "Reagan" somewhere in Washington as I write this.

As real estate developers and builders, it was out of the question for my brother and me at that time to pursue residential development. We would have been lucky to get a mortgage for seventeen percent and inflation had skyrocketed. But commercial development was another thing. There had been such a "feeding frenzy" in housing that commercial development—office buildings and retail and the like—had been somewhat ignored. Housing is quick money when things are good, but in a good location commercial/retail is generally profitable for the long haul. Contrarian investments, one might say.

In the area we all lived in was the city of Chico, about one hundred miles north of Sacramento. About twenty-five miles to the southeast of Chico was the town of Oroville, which was on the edge of the 1850s gold country—and the county seat for Butte County—of which Chico was a part. My brother had been out looking around for property to develop and had come upon a couple acres in downtown Oroville that was zoned commercial and adjacent to a rather vibrant area of town. After having told me about the property, the next day he and I took a drive from Chico to Oroville and looked at the site. I liked it and so we decided to build an office complex on the property. This would be the last deal we did with the Hewlett-Packard executives, and I called them up and told them about the opportunity and they said they were in.

So, using the HP guys' money, we bought the property, and hired the architects and engineers to design the buildings and—through our collective efforts—came up with a complex of two, two-story buildings with a sort of Asian look. It might sound a bit "out there," but the complex was really very attractive, about twenty-five thousand square feet. We simply had to finance the construction.

We had a strong relationship with Lloyds Bank of California and their local branch in Orland, whose earlier manager, June Young, had been quoted by the reporter in the article *Time* magazine had done several years before, during the severe drought. He was now retired and a new man was in charge. Over the few months since June's retirement and the new guy's elevation to manager, the new guy and I had developed a good relationship. I dropped in one day and told him about our deal in Oroville and he told me, "Steve, if you can get me a long-term loan committal (a 'take out,' in the vernacular) I'll make the construction loan." This was still in the heyday of the Savings and Loans and an outfit in Stockton by the name of State Savings was making long-term loans all over the place. There were high interest rates, about seventeen-percent, but the money was flowing and just maybe things would turn around and rates would drop and we could refinance.

Shortly after my conversation with the Lloyds banker, my brother and I hopped in our plane, flew down to Stockton, and came back with a "takeout committal." We were in business. The next day I took the committal to the bank and they accepted it, and we discussed the construction loan. What he proposed was the most convoluted, jerry-rigged construction loan I had ever—or have since—been involved in. Any banker in these days, setting things up in the manner I'm going to describe, would be put in San Quentin.

The dollar amount of the construction loan was about seven hundred and fifty thousand dollars. What our banker proposed is that—instead of funding a conventional construction loan and our firm taking monthly draws against the funds that would be set aside— the bank would just charge an overdraft to our company checking account each month to cover the amount of the bills that were due. And, once the buildings were finished, we'd fund the takeout from State Savings and pay off Lloyds Bank and all would be right with the world. And that's what we did.

It took us about six months to construct the project and, once it was done in early 1982, my brother and I once again took our plane down to Stockton and picked up a check to pay off Lloyds. We landed at the airport, parked the plane, and took a cab to State's office. We chatted for a couple minutes, they handed us a cashier's check for the seven hundred and fifty thousand dollars, and my brother and I took a cab back to the airport. We fired up our plane and flew back to Chico.

We could have headed for Mexico, for all the guys at State Savings knew. They just handed us the cashier's check, made out to our company, negotiable almost anywhere. But we didn't head out and, the next morning, handed the check over to the title company and they paid off Lloyds and everyone was happy. The interest rate on the State Savings loan was seventeen percent and we were glad to have it.

But we couldn't rent the buildings for one month, two months, then three. Nothing rented. And at seventeen percent the interest payments were heavy. Cash was dwindling. In the early part of March our whole family, my mom and dad, my brother, my sister-in-law, her parents, her sister, my wife, kids and I, my sister and her boyfriend, and a seeming cast of thousands, had made plans to make a skiing trip to Bear Valley at Mount Reba (a resort south of Tahoe at which my sister-in-law's family had a large, pole cabin). The Lloyd Bridges family, Clint Eastwood, and Robert Conrad and his family all had cabins near their place.

So we all got there and did our thing for the first couple days and then I got a phone message from a realtor in Oroville who had been trying to lease or sell our buildings, on the message machine in the cabin. It's amazing how we conducted business without fax machines and cell phones in those days—let alone email and the internet—but we did. And, somehow I got his message and called him back. He said that the Butte County School Department was interested in buying both our buildings, and wanted to know if we would be interested in selling? Well, you know the answer to that question: Yes! And the HP investor pretty much wanted out, so a sale would be great. Leaving everyone at the cabin to finish-off the rest of the week skiing, I headed out down to Oroville and cut a deal with the School Department.

The sale wouldn't leave much leftover to stick in our pockets, but it paid off the debt and took the HP guy out of the mix. Holy Cow, what times those were! The husband and wife who had founded State Savings were on an episode of a popular television show later that spring, during which one of the guys from the show interviewed them and the founding pair wowed him and the viewers with the virtues of private banking. And then, within a year, the two were indicted on federal banking charges and sent to the *hoosegow*, but we had gotten our takeout and lived to fight another day.

31

Steve's Great Adventure

Acouple of weeks after we had closed the office building deal with the School Department, I got a call at our office in Chico from an attorney in San Francisco. He had been referred to me by our old friend, Tom Wersen, the HP investment guy. He was inquiring of my brother and me as to our interest in getting involved in the commodities business, specifically, the production of Appalachian coal in West Virginia and eastern Kentucky. Now, once again, that was a switch and a stretch. My brother wasn't interested, but I was curious and discussed the matter at length with the guy. With the high interest rates, real estate development was tough and maybe we needed to look at other options, or at least that's what I was thinking at the time. The attorney told me that, within a week, he and a partner were going to take a trip back there and investigate things. Over several conversations I developed a raport with him and agreed to go with them.

I've mentioned before that the federal tax laws in those days favored speculative investment, the losses from which could be used to shelter earned income gained from whatever daily pursuit or job a person might have or be involved in. This was all part of the passive losses segment of the IRS Code, as we've discussed. It was thought that, given the instability of the Middle East, oil prices would skyrocket and thereby make investments in our own country's fuel production lucrative. The price of coal generally followed the price of oil, and profits could be sheltered at a five-to-one ratio to boot, using depletion allowances.

So the three of us flew back to West Virginia, stayed in the capitol, Charleston, overnight at the Holiday Inn, and then rented a car and drove the fifty miles down to Beckley where we were to meet a man by the name of Odell Herron. Herron, a graduate of the Colorado School of Mines and a highly-thought-of mineralogist, had been referred to us by Mellon Bank as a potential manager of our local operations. As my contribution to the possible venture, I had used my relationship with Lloyds Bank of California to provide a letter of introduction that I would use with Mellon, the bank that was also, sort of, the "broker" on the deal we were contemplating. This introduction would give us the impetus to negotiate lines of credit with the bank to provide the capital necessary to finance our contemplated purchase, and additional lines of credit to be used to finance the daily operations.

Everything was leveraged in those days. And Mellon's senior coal specialist, a man by the name of George Shelley, was contemplating his retirement from the bank and was available to work for our group, and had inquired about handling the business side of the operations. It seemed like things were lining up for us.

*****

But, first, another story: the night we stayed at the Holiday Inn in Charleston the three of us each had separate rooms, as one might imagine, on about the third floor. We'd eaten dinner at a restaurant suggested by the concierge and, after a couple of drinks, had returned to the hotel and retired to our rooms at about 11:30. I was just dozing off and there was a knock on my door. I threw a bathrobe on and answered the door. It was my attorney friend, Bill. He was in his underwear, scratching himself all over his body. He'd been attacked by fleas. My room was right next door, and I had experienced none of this. I invited him in and sat him down, found another bathrobe for him, and then called the front desk and told them about the incident. The young guy I talked to sort of chuckled and told me that there had been a dog convention in town the previous weekend and many of the exhibitors had stayed at the hotel. "Must have left some fleas behind," he joked. It *was* West Virginia, after all. I told him to get all of us new rooms, pronto (at near midnight that's not what I really said, but you get the idea), and he did. I woke the third member of our party, Allan, and told him what the deal was and we all sleepwalked to our new digs. Bill recovered, the hotel compensated us for our room costs, and we headed out after breakfast the next morning, without the fleas, as far as we knew.

*****

It took us about an hour and a half on the tollroad to make it down to Beckley and the Ramada Inn that would be our headquarters for the week. It was not yet noon when we arrived and strode up to the registration desk. We gave our names and informed the attendant that we had reservations. Well, we might as well have been from the Moon, for when we spoke it was in that funny language that westerners use, according to the gal that was checking us in. "Where ya'll from?" Not the Moon, but California we informed her. We dared not say San Francisco—it would have been too much of a shock. We finally got checked in, but it was too early in the day and our rooms weren't ready.

The attendant said we could take our things up to the third floor and leave our bags by the doors to the rooms. They'd be safe, she assured us, and the rooms would be ready for us after lunch and we could then take our things in. It sounded fine. We took the elevator to the third floor and exited and began to look for our rooms. Now, at this point in my life, I hadn't been out much and surely not around many black people. As we searched for our rooms and encountered these housekeeping folks I would acknowledge each one as we would in our "*western* culture," as we would have when we encountered Hispanics in our hallways out West. I always enjoyed the banter with them and the attempt by each of us to address the other in their native tongue. "Buenos Dias," we'd say. "Good morning, sir," they'd reply.

But not in the Ramada Inn, in Beckley, West (By God!) Virginia. Not only would the staff not meet our gaze, but they would make no response when spoken to—something which was foreign to the three of us. After noticing their consternation in seeing us leave our bags unattended, and wanting to assure them that things were fine, I finally took one of the ladies aside and told her that we were leaving our bags outside our rooms until they were cleaned. That the front desk had told us to do so, and that we'd return after lunch. And that she was not to worry. We weren't worried. I tried to tip her, but she wouldn't take it. Cultures.

A little before six o'clock that evening the three of us met in Bill's room and then together we made our way to the elevator and down to the lobby, to meet Odell Herron. There he was. You couldn't miss him. Proud as a peacock in his beige, three-piece polyester suit, with his Samsonite briefcase and a lump under his left breast pocket. A man of fifty-six, he told us later, and about five-foot-five in height, with a chunky build. He immediately noticed us and we acknowledged him and each of us exchanged handshakes and greetings. He had a drawl that was so thick it made it very difficult for us "city boys," as he came to call us, to understand what he was saying. During the evening we had to ask him to repeat himself numerous times, and we apologized profusely each time we did.

We'd made the introductions and we were standing there making small talk with each other and the very next thing Odell said was, "You know I'm packin," and he patted the lump under his left breast pocket. Bill and Allan gave me a perplexed look—they really were "city boys." Odell looked at me and slightly opened his left breast flap to reveal a shoulder holster containing a snub-nosed pistol. Upon observing the weapon Bill, who had a dry sense of humor, looked at Odell and uttered, "Holy-moley!" followed by a nervous laugh. Then our new acquaintance made a gesture to a man standing off by himself—he was about the same age as Odell but much bigger— and the fellow came over to where the four of us were standing.

Odell introduced him, in that thick drawl I wish I could get on paper, saying, "Gentlemen, this is a good friend of mine. This here is so-and-so (I can't remember his name), Sheriff of Raleigh County. And he knows I have a permit for the sidearm I'm carrying. His office issued it to me." We all shook hands and exchanged greetings and probably appeared to look like the *five* stooges, especially Bill and Allan. They were completely out of place in this environment: Bill, a tall, gangly Norwegian; and Allan, a short little Jewish man who I came to be very fond of. I was as much a country boy as these locals, but without the firepower I guess you could say. And as time went by I became sort of a liaison between my two partners and the local folks. If nothing more, I was there to translate what the hell they were saying *and* what they meant by it, which weren't always one and the same thing.

Immediately after we'd all finished our greetings and convivial small talk, Odell marched over to a low table in the lobby, set down his plastic briefcase, fished a key out of his pants pocket and unlocked it to expose another firearm in a holster. He looked up at all of us and, with a slight grin to Bill, Allan and me, said, "If you ever need anything, just let me know and the sheriff will take care of it for you." We didn't know what to say, but thanked him. It sounded like "frontier justice" to me. And, with that, he closed and locked the briefcase and escorted us out to his Jeep Grand Wagoneer and the four of us were off to dinner, without the sheriff. The whole episode took only about five minutes, but it sure was an eye-opener.

Odell took us to a surprisingly-good restaurant on a small lake just outside of town: The Char. As we entered, an elegant black lady, the *maître d'*, greeted us and she obviously knew Odell. They exchanged pleasantries and he introduced his new "big boys" from the West Coast and she showed us to our table, where we had a great meal, great service, and good and informative conversation. We had finished eating and were sipping a very good dessert port when Odell asked if, after we finished dinner, he could show us where he lived and introduce us to his wife. "Of course," we replied.

I was riding in the front seat with Odell as we navigated the streets to his home. And as we were entering a very nice section of town I asked him where the elegant *maître d* might have lived.

The racial overtones in the city were very blatant and, during the evening, I had developed the sort of repartee with him that would allow me to ask the question. Turning and looking at me in a very serious manner he replied, "They don't live in this part of town, they know their place."

To which I shot back, "But you and she seem to have such an obviously good rapport."

"Steve, if she and her husband—a really good *nigger* who owns the best boat shop in town—were to move into a home next to mine, I'd be forced to sell and move. The people in this town don't tolerate niggers living next to good white-folk. Not even *good* niggers."

Man-o-Man! I can't judge racism for I have absolutely no experience with it. But it was a shock to me to see *this* racism so up-close and personal. And it always affected my view of things while I was involved in this business venture.

We arrived at Odell's home in the same section of town I've just mentioned and were taken inside to meet his wife. As we'd pulled up in front of his very elegant place he leaned over and quietly told me, "You know I've got a young wife, Steve." (Remember the drawl as you imagine hearing that statement.) Well, I guess I do now, I thought to myself.

His "young wife," truly an attractive woman, met us at the door and ushered us into a parlor area of the home and offered us refreshments. We settled on Grand Marnier, heated in brandy glasses, which was very nice and we made polite conversation as we sipped our beverages. Mrs. Herron could have been no more than in her early twenties and was at least thirty years younger than Odell. During our sipping and talking, Odell announced that his beloved wife was about to finish college and get her degree. Bill, Allan, and I applauded her accomplishments and I inquired of her what she planned to do with her new degree. She deferred to Odell.

Once again, we heard the drawl. "Steve, our women don't work outside the home if we're businessmen here in West Virginia. Their place is to take care of their husbands and children." He was dead serious, and she followed orders. Her degree was just "window dressing" in their culture. The two of them didn't have children. Why didn't that surprise me? Poor Bill and Allan had been reeling from the conversation all evening and hadn't spoken unless spoken to. Culture shock had gotten them. After finishing our drinks and mentioning to Odell that we'd best be getting back to our hotel, he took one last chance and showed us his collection of guns that were displayed in his basement: a very impressive setup that showcased more than five hundred weapons, from brand new high-powered rifles to valuable antiques. Bill and Allan were squeamish, but I thought it was neat and I kind of rubbed it in to my city friends. Odell took us back to the hotel, and we turned in for the night.

The next morning the three of us discussed the previous evening and their culture shock as we ate breakfast in the dining room, before we met Odell and had him tour the mining operations with us. I dressed in Wranglers, boots, a denim shirt, and leather jacket—pretty snappy if I do say so myself—and Bill and Allan were in suits and ties. They stood out like sore thumbs. I asked them what they had expected. "Not this," they said. I told them to just sit back and let me handle things, and they did.

Mellon Bank had suggested that we look at two operations as possible purchases. The first one was owned by a man by the name of Freddie Haddad. A Lebanese immigrant who had founded the Hex Supermarket chain with stores in West Virginia, Virginia, eastern Ohio and Pennsilvania, which were very successful. He had a mine, an above-drainage drift mine, near the town of Slab Fork, about ten miles outside of Beckley. This mine produced steam coal, used in electric power generation. So that's where Odell took us first. Freddie had his main office in Beckley and so we stopped by and met him on the way. All I can say about this man is, "Yikes!" You can read in between the lines, yourselves. We got to the mine and tromped around and took pictures and got back in Odell's jeep and headed to the other mine, near Summersville, West Virginia, on the New River Gorge. It was in a beautiful area that was just emerging from the "Appalachian" stigma. (If I have time, I'll tell a story about filling up a rental car that we used to tour this area the next time we visited with gas. Let me just say the movie *Deliverance*, comes to mind all over again.)

But, on this day, Odell was our chauffeur and I asked him on the way to Summersville, "Ya think there's coal in Freddie's mine? Enough coal to make buying it worthwhile?" He answered with "Could be, Steve," which is what he always said. It's what they *all* said. We finally got to the mine near Summersville and pulled up in front of the office of the two brothers who owned the operation, Jack and Carl Grayson. They were producing twenty million dollars' worth of coal a month out of their open pit mining operation. They were producing coking-coal for the steel industry, high BTU, thirteen-thousand BTUs (British Thermal Units which is the measure used in the energy business) and more, and neither of them had more than a third-grade education and they could barely read or write, but with the smarts of river boat gamblers. This whole affair freaked Bill and Allan out and they, after the brief introductions, left the office and stayed in the jeep for the duration of the meeting (I know I'm making them sound like big weenies, but that's how they were, out of their element).

Jack and Carl had brought their accountant to show us the books and I spent an hour going over things. The numbers could mean anything or nothing, but what I did know was that Jack had just bought *his* young wife, said to be no more than sixteen, a two-million-dollar diamond ring. Which was not bad if you don't have to pay taxes. And later we found out that they hadn't done that for years and Uncle Sam had come knocking. We didn't do that deal.

When Odell and I had left the Graysons' office and gotten in his Wagoneer, he told us a story about Carl's young wife and her diamond ring.

Shortly after giving his wife the ring, Carl had returned home and found her inconsolable. Asking what the matter was she had told him that, during the washing of the lunch-time dishes, she had lost her new ring down the kitchen drain, all two million dollars' worth. Well, that wouldn't do, according to Carl, and he commenced to pull the drain under the sink apart and search for the damn thing.

Not finding it, he went out behind the house and opened up the septic tank. Now what? He couldn't just reach his hands down in the thing, so he rented a pump and a filter, and pumped all of the liquid out of the tank, to no avail. Then he had a friend bring his backhoe over and dig up the drain lines that led to and from the septic tank. Nothing. They never found the ring. The young wife didn't look so good after that episode.

We left Beckley a couple days later and took a flight through Pittsburgh on our way home to San Francisco. We stayed at the old, but elegant, William Penn Hotel across from Mellon Bank and had dinner with George Shelley and a couple other coal guys, and then went our way, having had a very nice time. They were very cordial. I spent the next six months in trying to figure out the coal business.

When we had first arrived, steam coal was at thirty-four dollars a ton, loaded, stowed, and trimmed on a barge floating on the Kanawha River in South Charleston, where Union Carbide and Dow Chemical have two of the largest plants in the world. By the time I had finished my exploration journey—which included a jaunt to the north coast of Colombia, near the old town of Cartagena; and then up the coast to Barranquilla, where an Exxon/Morrison-Knudsen partnership had a major mining operation—and after spending hundreds of thousands of dollars, the same coal was at twenty-two dollars. We packed our bags, licked our wounds, and headed home. We were left with good, but painful, stories.

*****

It was 1983 and I was back to what I knew best: building and developing real estate. We had gotten to know a company from the Midwest that wanted to get into the apartment business and had built several projects for them in northern California. I also had been able to meet, through a mutual friend in San Francisco, one of the heirs to the Beaulieu Wine empire in the town of Rutherford in the Napa Valley. Walter Sullivan, the great-grandson of the founder Georges de Latour, was a member of the Bohemian Club in San Francisco. The Club was hosting a reception for the Australian Team that had taken the America's Cup from the United States for the first time in one hundred and thirty-two years, in this, the most prestigious yachting race in the world. (John Bertrand, piloting *Australia II*, had defeated American Dennis Connor in the finals to take the Cup. Connor won it back four years later.) Walter invited me to be his guest, and it was very special to sit in their magnificent club that night to honor the Aussies.

Sitting there as an invited guest among such luminaries as Steve Bechtel and his son, Riley—scions of the international construction company that bears their name; the newly-appointed Secretary of State, George Shultz; and former Chairman of Bechtel, the Chairman of the newly-formed Chevron Oil, George Keller; and many others. The cigar smoke was so thick in the room that it actually dimmed the projection of the films of the race that were being shown on a screen at the front of the massive ballroom. And I was smoking those cigars right along with them. Much good-natured heckling went on between the Australians and Americans as they each gave their version of the race. It was a special time for me, a small-town boy, child of Pentecostals. And then we adjourned to Trader Vic's, just down the alley, for more libations.

32

Sunday School

It wasn't long after my foray in San Francisco** that my oldest son, Jason, came to me and asked if he could begin attending Sunday school at the Assemblies of God Church next door to our house on the ranch. The minister, Dennis—whom I've mentioned— and his wife had three boys. One, a year older than Jason (who at the time was almost six), one the same age as my second son, and one two or three years younger. They were like peas-in-a-pod with my sons and all of them played together everyday. Kids that age don't play politics or religion. Jason said that the oldest neighbor boy had told him it was a lot of fun and they did all kinds of neat things. I told him that it would be okay with me until, or when, they began feeding him the judgmental dogma I had grown up with. (I didn't quite say it like that but that's what I meant.) Jason understood, and my wife agreed.

One day that summer, after having attended Sunday School five or six times, Jason was walking home from Church and found me out in the front yard, mowing the grass. He looked dejected. I shut the mower down and asked what was bothering him. He hesitated. Then he looked at me with pain in his eyes and said, "You're going to Hell, Dad. They just told me in Sunday School." It hurt me to hear him say that. Not that I believed Hell was where I was going when I died, but that it hurt *him* so much to have heard it said.

I put my arm around his shoulder and inquired, "Why do you

think they said that?" He had told me "they" referred to his Sunday school teacher at Church.

We sat down on a stump, and he continued. "She said because you drink beer."

So that was it. It had been only a matter of time before he started hearing about the do's and the don'ts. It brought back painful memories for me, so I hugged him and asked, "Do you think I'm going to Hell?"

He cried and emphatically said, "No!"

"You know what this means, Jason?" I asked him.

"Yah, I do," he answered. "I can't go to Sunday School anymore."

"That's right. That was our deal. Are you okay with that?" I asked.

"Yah," he replied, "but I just don't know why she said that."

"Because that's just what they do, Jason," I said, and we hugged each other.

(Damn them!)

33

The Construction Business

Into 1984 we were building apartments all over northern California, but had taken on two particular jobs that had become cause for concern. One was about two-hundred-fifty units in the East Bay area and one was about three hundred in the South Bay. The first one was a development undertaken by a company run by a retired Air Force General. The company's main business was selling life insurance policies to members of the military. That might sound risky but, in the 1980s, we weren't at war with anyone in particular and the military was a relatively safe haven, and the company appeared to be very profitable. We haggled over costs and bid prices, as is always the case, and finally signed a contract in late spring. I hired a good project manager and we were on our way.

Things went along in a fairly normal manner until we were about eighty-percent complete. Payments to us by the developer had been relatively slow all along but had begun to move into the sixty-to-ninety-day arena. Cashflow is king to any company, and this slowdown was draining our cash reserves. Finally, we reached the point of being owed about three and a half million dollars by the developer, and were told that it was all their bank's fault. Their lender was a large, minority-owned bank in San Francisco. The developer gave us authorization to talk directly with their bank, and I did. When I called them I was greeted by the most unbelievable set of redtape. The bank was being taken over by the FDIC—the

Government. This was in the midst of the great savings and loan and banking scandals that swept this country's financial institutions during the mid-to-late-1980s. Construction loans were at the bottom of the pile. Being desperate for cash and being legitimately owed the money, my brother volunteered to jump in our plane and fly down to San Francisco to see if he could get a check out of these people.

He landed in Concord, took BART (Bay Area Rapid Transit) into the city and walked into the bank. He said it was total chaos, but he finally got someone's attention (he had taken with him a complete copy of the paperwork we submitted every month), and a person with enough juice authorized a payment to us of about eight hundred thousand dollars and they cut him a check. It was not the whole amount we were due, but it sure helped. He got his fanny back across the Bay and flew back to our office and we deposited the money in our bank, pronto-like! We never heard from the bank or the developer again. It was a very smelly operation.

The other project I mentioned—in the South Bay—was a development by a company headquartered in Southern California. This was a different situation. The financing for the apartment complex was through the use of tax-free bonds—a popular method of financing multi-family housing at that time—and was underwritten by a major West Coast bank. This method had really picked up steam in the early '80s. With interest rates so high, if a developer could make the costs pencil out, this bond-financing was at an interest rate of around eleven percent. That sounds high now, but at that time it was little more than half the interest rates on conventional financing.

The hook was that twenty percent of the dwelling units were required to be rented to low-to-moderate-income people and families. It was a dicey proposition if you didn't know how to play the game, because the "low-moderate" units were typically monitored by a public housing entity within the city government. Not that they shouldn't be, but that meant sixty of the three hundred dwelling units in the project had to be rented at the reduced rate. And the ratio between the "market" units being occupied and the low-moderate apartments had to be maintained. In other words, as developer/owner, you couldn't rent up all of the market-rate units and then throw your hands up in frustration as a response to your inability to rent the below-market units. If you had more market-rate applications than low-moderate ones you would actually have to turn people away or put them off until, or when, the ratio had been stabilized. The interest rates that made the program attractive were also part of the carrot and stick. As we all know, there is no free lunch.

We began the project in mid-summer. The negotiations for the contract had been fierce. There was stiff competition from other builders—and the northern California Vice-President of the company was trying to make a name for himself within the organization, but we won the contract. I use a saying that probably makes my family and friends cringe because I use it so much but, it's kind of like the dog that finally catches the car: "Now what do I do with it?" And our brown-noser, the VP, liked to use the term "Kleenexed-them," as in, "I used them as far as I could (financially), and then I wadded them up and threw them away." This style catered to his massive ego and should have been a major red flag in our negotiations, but we were expanding our company into these geographical areas and some of what this fellow espoused just came with the territory.

Our negotiations were completed and we hired a competent project manager and were off. We no more than got the foundations poured for the first group of buildings than our site manager was visited by a union representative. In the bidding documents there was no mention made of a requirement to bid the job to *union* sub-contractors—which would have increased the price—or that the project was a federally-mandated, prevailing-rate, job. Our arrogant friend had withheld this information from my brother and me and we were caught in the middle. And—like most young entrepreneurs—I hadn't been as careful in reading the fine print as I should have. So, by virtue of the construction contract we had signed, our company was responsible for any changes in right-to-work conditions, such as the necessity to bid the project at union rates. We were caught in the middle. We consulted with our attorneys who felt we were in a strong position with the contract we had signed and that we could prevail in court, and we felt we were safe because they were from a major law firm that specialized in construction contract law. But the bills kept coming and the cash didn't flow. It's one thing to have righteous indignation with cashflow and a much different sensation to be right and financially dead. We were heading toward the latter.

All of our projects were interconnected through an endless web of necessary cashflow, meaning that all of our projects were affected if *one* was doing poorly. And we had two of them. I had meeting after meeting with the northern California "big dog" and got nowhere. And, even if he had no scruples, he had something even better than that, which protected his ass: a Performance and Payment Bond written by a Triple-A rated insurance company that guaranteed the completion of the project. Almost every one of the projects we had under construction, as the general contractor, required us to provide the bond I've mentioned. We had around twenty-five million dollars of bonding on the line, and that was a lot of money back then. We/I had stretched our company's ability to meet the cashflow requirements of this aggressive push we were on, even in the best of circumstances. We had now met up with people who were one step ahead of us or lacked scruples and knew they could use and then "Kleenex" us. Either way it was painful to our wallets.

So the project in the South Bay was shut down and we all went to court. The attorneys made a lot of money and our cash was dwindling and our names were on millions of dollars of performance bonds. Interestingly enough, the northern California guy I've mentioned that liked to Kleenex people was fired right in the middle of all the litigation. And, through all of this, I actually got to know the president of the parent company in Southern California quite well, who lamented what his guy had done. That was all well and good, I told him, but things had been pushed so far that we wouldn't be able to complete the job even if we prevailed. And that could be years away.

It was March of 1985, and I set up a meeting with our bonding company. The two jobs I've mentioned had taken at least four and a half million dollars out of our cashflow and we had no reasonable expectation of getting to that money. To keep up with this cash drain we had extended our lines of credit at our banks, which put all of the projects in jeopardy. Even if we prevailed—as I've said—it would be years before we saw any cash. So I told the bonding company that we had to pull the plug. It was very painful. These bonding guys had gone with us and believed in our plan and we had worked our collective asses off to make things work. But, even going into these projects, we were undercapitalized and depended on our button-down system of paperwork to elicit prompt payment by our clients. For the most part it had worked, but we were highly leveraged. My aggressiveness and the bad apples ruined the barrel.

We also had a property management company that managed several hundred units throughout northern California and complemented our construction business. The business was run by my sister, mother, and father—although my father was beginning to move away from property management and into onsite project management. My sister had come to work for my brother and me in 1977, after two years at Chico State, and was a very competent manager and businesswoman. She complemented my brother and me.

In 1982, we had built a new office building in Chico to be occupied by our company and had outfitted it with the latest technology. Each desk was outfitted with a computer, from a new firm, Compaq, tied to the others in the building with a Hayes Modem. We had centralized printing, since there were, as yet, no personal printers. There were no fax machines, and the printers used rolls of paper on which anything that was printed would fade in a day or two. So everything had to be recopied using a Xerox machine that was the first to use plain paper. The Project Managers on our jobs were also outfitted with computers and, at the end of the day on every Friday, would send a report to our office on off-peak-hour phone lines to update the status of each job and prepare for the coming week. This was 1982. The Apple 2E had just come out, and personal computing was a mere infant in terms of technology. But something had triggered the notion in me that, in order to handle all of this expansion, we needed technology. I was right, but we also needed cashflow. And that need eventually sunk our ship.

After my meeting with the bonding company, I returned to Chico and met with my brother and sister, and told them we had to shut things down. It was a sad moment. All the great hopes and expectations were going up in smoke. We had such a good organization, but I'd extended things too far. We were in a Rolls Royce, so to speak, and were going down a highway at a hundred miles an hour with bald tires, and then two of them blew and it killed us financially. Given my position in the company, and my responsibility, I spent the next six months trying to work things out, sometimes successfully, sometimes not.

My brother and I would now have to seek other employment and both of us were successful. My brother found work within the real estate division of a legitimate savings and loan in the San Joaquin Valley, and I found work with a nationwide builder headquartered in Dallas, heading up their development division in Los Angeles.

34

New Careers

little story about how I got my eventual position in
Southern California.

In late summer of 1985, I answered an ad in the Wall
Street Journal for a development director in the commercial/retail
development field, with a company located in Santa Fe Springs. They
would be building "strip centers" in Orange County and the "Inland
Empire." They hired me, and I worked for about three months in
the position when I realized it wasn't a good fit. My entrepreneurial
instincts were lurking.

After work one day I was driving back to my apartment in Yorba
Linda when I needed to use a bathroom. (Stay with me! We've all
been there!) I spied a mid-rise, black glass building off the fifty-five
freeway and pulled into the parking lot. Figuring there must be some
facilities in the lobby—or accessible in one of the offices—I entered
the building. Coincidentally, an employment agency specializing in
the construction and development industry was located in the lobby
and I inquired as to what they could do to help my bladder problem.
The gal at the front desk took pity on me and gave me a key to the
restrooms. When I'd finished, I took it back to her and inquired as to
what, if any, openings were available as I was somewhat disillusioned
with my current employer. Hearing my voice, Kathryn Bren, owner
of the agency—and widow of Chuck Bren, and sister-in-law of
Donald Bren—the clairvoyant purchaser of the Irvine Ranch and a

heavyweight in the real estate development industry, invited me in. We chatted a bit and she told me that a major nationwide apartment developer was looking for a director of development in their Van Nuys office in the Valley. Would I be interested? You know what I said. I interviewed and got the job. Figure that one out. Is someone looking over me?

I had interviewed for the position with the company in Los Angeles in October of 1985, and after being hired went down the first of November to set up an apartment and get things organized. My family would remain in the house on the ranch in northern California and I would commute by air back and forth on weekends. Sometimes I would do this every week and sometimes every two weeks. This living arrangement doomed my marriage to Charlotte. I was still struggling with monogamy and this tended to open the floodgates. What with the feelings of letting everyone down in my family as it related to the business decisions I had made on behalf of all of us, and the prevailing curiosity left over from my life as a Pentecostal, the flames of Hell began once again to nip at my heels, for there was a smorgasbord of sin in "La La Land." You can't put a dog in a meat market and expect him to not sample of the riches displayed before him. I was no different—and no one was watching.

Things were successful at the company I had hired on with and we built several thousand apartments and rented them and sold most of them to Japanese investors and all was fine. I would fly home on Friday afternoons and back down to work on Monday mornings. The joy of greeting my family on Friday was always blunted by the sorrow of leaving on Monday. Each morning I left the boys— and sometimes my wife—would gather on the front porch and we would hug and I'd get in my car to drive to the airport. I'd look back at them as I drove away, this wonderful family, these wonderful children, and see them crying and waving. At times it almost broke my heart. Then the next week we'd do it all over again.

We did this for five years, during the most formative times of my children's lives. And that was a terrible burden on me. I was making very good money by doing what I was in Los Angeles, but the concern over what I might be doing to my children was a heavy burden to bear. I resisted moving everyone down with me. The environment on the ranch in the country where the boys lived was irreplaceable and I knew in my heart that it was only a matter of time before my marriage would end. I thought it was better for the family to be on familiar ground if, and when, it happened than to be in a strange land, but it took its toll on everyone. I don't want to downplay the effort my wife Charlotte made to keep things together, but it wasn't meant to be. I knew trouble was coming and didn't know what to do about it.

Over the next couple of years we did what we had to, to survive. We had some good times and not-so-good times. I tried to be around as much as I could and my boys would say that they would rather have quality time with me, than a pat on the head as they told me other full-time fathers of their friends did. "Son, this," and, "Son, that," they'd say. "You don't do that, Dad. You always listen to us." But I wasn't so sure, and my heart was heavy.

It was early 1986, and my dad was still dependent on me for a job, while I was carrying the weight of financial support as always. I needed something that he and I could do together that employed him. I still had "manure on my boots" from the days on the ranch— an affliction my brother didn't suffer from—so I decided to go into the sheep business, and have my dad run the operation. (Wouldn't you? Makes sense, doesn't it?)

Sheep ranching was something I was familiar with and something my father could manage with his experience, and a venture that could shelter some of the income from my job in Southern California. And maybe it would make a little something to boot. I purchased about four hundred head of ewes and we set up shop. For the next three years I worked my ass off on every weekend I came back, which exacerbated the problems in my home life to a greater extent. There built up a resentment in my wife, and to some extent my boys, of the time I spent working on the operation. Although I complain about it, there still were many good times and good memories, lots of rack-of-lamb and lambchops on the grill. We had lots of barbecues out on the ranch in the west hills of the northern Sacramento Valley, land leased from Cal Worthington, the big auto dealer. This was the old Earnest Michaels Ranch that my grandfather and uncles had worked on fifty or sixty years before, when they were tending the massive mule teams that pulled the threshing machines which cut and harvested the thirty-five thousand acres of wheat that was grown on the place.

But it became too much and I sold the whole operation in late 1989. I came out of it okay. And, even though I complain, it was some of the best times that were had between my father and me. There's an incident that took place three or four months before I cashed-in my chips that I must tell you about.

In the United States, sheep are raised—for the most part—to produce lambs that are bred for meat and ready to go in the spring. But the Australian sheep industry, with their government support, is a severe financial test to the industry here, making it hard for U.S. producers to compete. Shearing the ewes for their wool is a necessary evil, as there isn't any money in it, but it must be done to help them cope with the heat of the summer. To address the meat production—and in an effort to compete with this foreign threat—industry scientists have developed new breeds that produce more "meaty" lambs in a shorter period of time, and less wool. To that end, I was notified by my father that there was a "high-powered" operation, as he called it, up near Red Bluff that was raising a relatively new breed of sheep and were producing this new, more desired, lamb—and they had some rams (male sheep) that were available for purchase. So I decided to take a look, and on one particular Saturday morning in April—during the height of the sheep-mating season—I jumped in my pickup and drove north to check things out.

Arriving at the sheep ranch I looked up the manager and told him what I was looking for, one of his "high-powered" rams. He showed me around the operation and then took me over to the pen where they were kept. They were Dorset rams and they were meaty. I looked them over and, with his input, picked out one of them and bought the sucker, for eight hundred dollars. I cut him a check and we loaded all three-hundred-fifty pounds of the thing into my truck and I headed out, back down to our ranch. I had called my dad on the way and he was going to meet me at the barn by the corrals.

Arriving, I backed my pickup up against the loading chute and we opened the back gate and let "lover boy" down the ramp into the corral. To get him acclimated, we fed him some alfalfa hay and rolled oats with molasses, which was pretty good stuff. But there was "love" in the air and he was agitated. The barn and corral were located down wind of about three hundred ewes that were pasturing about a half-mile from where we were. They were bedded down under a grove of oak trees as shelter from the midday heat.

A little background: we normally ran about one ram to fifty ewes during the mating season, mostly Suffolk, black-faced rams. But, knowing that most of the ewes had already been impregnated, we had moved them out in order to introduce the new guy. We wanted to ease him in, gentle-like. And further, like most males of the animal kingdom, the rams are very territorial and many times we had experienced fights to the death and we obviously weren't excited about that happening this time. So our big guy had the girls—such as they were—all to himself.

He was all fired-up and, after waiting a few minutes to get him oriented to the layout, we opened the gate of the corral and he headed out toward the ladies on a dead run. (Well, all-right then!)

The next morning, my dad and I had coffee in town and then headed out to the ranch to check on our new boy, and things in general. We pulled up to the barn and got out and gazed into the fields. The ewes were scattered as usual and we looked for our new ram. We couldn't detect him, so we and our two border collies headed out on foot toward the oak grove. As we neared the trees we detected something, an animal, lying next to one of them. It was our new boy, lying flat on his back with his feet in the air. Stone dead. He had f-ed himself to death. There's no "money-back guarantee" on this sort of stuff, but he was smiling.

*****

In August of 1988, I was managing the completion of a project for my firm in Malibu Canyon, on Las Virgenes Road, which was south of the 101, Ventura Freeway. It was on an old Bob Hope Ranch, just north of the tunnel that leads to the Pacific Coast Highway. The apartment/town-home development encompassed thirty-four acres and six hundred dwelling units. In addition to handling development and construction, our company provided the leasing and management services for the projects we developed—several thousand units just in the Los Angeles area. On a weekly basis I would visit the various complexes we owned or managed to monitor the efficiency of the operations.

It was on one of these visits to the Malibu Canyon project that I had stopped in at the management office to use their phone. I had a car phone, but reception in those days was very spotty and the hills around the place tended to block the signal. I had finished my call and was making small talk with one of the leasing agents when she suggested that I meet the newest member of the marketing team, a gal by the name of Annette LaRue. Well, shut my mouth! Standing in front of me was a blonde-haired vision of loveliness who, with her perfect Texas drawl, announced, "It's so good to meet you, Mr. Morgan." Holy cow! I was smitten.

This happened at a time during which it was evident that my marriage wasn't going to last and my wife and I were separated by distance and emotion, but I had not made my true feelings known to her. There was still a strong attachment, but it was one that I had let lie, fallow, for a long time in my search for inner piece. Might sound like BS, but it's true. How could I be anything to someone else if I couldn't be that person to myself? And this Ms. LaRue awoke something within me. It scared and excited me, and it hurt my wife deeply, absolutely, and for the last time in our relationship. For I now was forced to be honest with her. An emotion I had not come to grips with but now had to.

Before I go on I want to say that after we ultimately divorced, my ex-wife met and married a fine man, who is also a good man. He is a man I have a lot of respect for, and my boys love him, too, and he loves them in spite of their pimples and warts. Ms. LaRue, whom I married, and I have a good relationship with my ex-wife and her husband. And I have a good relationship with my ex-mother-in-law and sister-in-law and ex-brother-in-law. And my ex-wife and current wife get along very well. They even, from time to time, sit on the patio with a glass of wine and kick the old boy around a little, the bastard that's been married to both of them.

Ms. LaRue, Annette, told me later that she had gone home the evening after she met me and called her mother in Dallas and told her that she had met the man she was going to marry. Her mother wasn't quite convinced, and her father especially wasn't when he heard the news. And I was a slow learner.

I went from pillar to post emotionally: from extreme guilt over how I was treating my wife and kids, to the enjoyment I felt when I was in Annette's company. My boys were nine and twelve and professed that the struggles I was dealing with were not affecting them, that they loved me no matter what happened, and that I would always be their father, of course. But a child loves his father even though he might be an axe murderer. The damage to the psyche is what's unknown. And I know there is some, because we wouldn't be human otherwise.

In the fall of 1988, I had been invited to a Halloween party at the Ambassador Hotel in Los Angeles, where Bobby Kennedy had been shot by Sirhan Sirhan twenty years before, by an Arab friend of mine, Michael Omary. It was sponsored by the Arab-American Society of Southern California, and hosted by Casey Kasem, the radio and television personality. I had invited Annette to go with me and we were decked out in our costumes, I as a pirate, and she as a mermaid. I was smoking a cigar, as were most of the men, when a fellow seated at the next table and dressed as a sheik tapped me on the shoulder. I had been smoking some cheap cigars that I normally purchased at an offbeat smoke shop. The fellow reached under his robe and produced a Cuban and said to me, "Here, son, have a *good* cigar." It was Danny Thomas, the Hollywood impresario, he of Lebanese descent. We spent the rest of the evening kibitzing and, when the night was over, he gave me a card and an introduction to the smoke shop on Ventura Boulevard where he and George Burns bought their tobacco. Somehow, mysteriously, this was a place where Cuban cigars were available.

My romance with Annette went on for another two years and, due to the California economy, the company I was with was winding down their Southern California operation and I was contacted by a headhunter who had a position he was trying to fill in northern California, in Napa County. It was in, essentially, the same real estate development industry I'd come from. I was interviewed and I took the job and Ms. LaRue and I moved to northern California.

More to Annette.

I'm not sure why, but for the first time in my life I had met someone of the opposite sex who I could be honest with. I feel this is a tribute to her, as I didn't at the time—and have trouble with now—believing I was, and am, worth it. The term "soul mate," I think, is overused. But that's what she was for me. She would laugh at my goofball humor and cry with me when I was overcome with guilt. She would listen and council me in ways to deal with my family, in ways that might be to her detriment. She was selfless. We partied together and did business together. But, in the fall of 1991, I still couldn't make up my mind and she moved back to Southern California, and I moved to southern Oregon, pursuing an opportunity offered to me by a cousin whom I had done business with years before: Duane Smith. Yet Annette still loved me even though I had my head "where the sun don't shine," again.

When I moved to Oregon in the fall of 1991, the California economy had tanked, which affected southern Oregon, and so I put my nail bags back on and became a carpenter, again. There was no development going on, and I still had my work ethic and ambition, and no one had stolen my brain.

Not having much cashflow and needing to send money down to my family, my Springer spaniel, Barney and I found accommodations in the old Mark Anthony Hotel in Ashland, for three hundred bucks a month. I dried my clothes on the old radiator heaters, and strung wire around the room in an attempt to get television signals, and fought Barney for room on the bed.

One evening we were lounging around and watching the snow-covered picture on the television when there was a knock at the door. Getting up, I walked over and answered it. Standing before me was a middle-aged man, stark naked. What next?! He apologized for his appearance and asked if he could come in. What was I supposed to do? Leave him in the hallway? I let him in and got a towel from the bathroom so he could at least cover his genitals. Then he explained his predicament. He had ordered room service for his dinner meal and after finishing it he had opened his door to set the tray outside in the hallway. During this exercise, the door had closed on him, and it was locked. I guess he must have eaten in the nude, for now he found himself stark naked in the hallway, where he had knocked on my door at random. I called the front desk and they said they'd send someone up with a key. My new friend and I sat there in relative silence for about ten minutes. What do you say to a naked man?

*****

I started networking with people I met and got small construction jobs and Annette visited me periodically. But her biological, marital, clock was ticking and I knew it was only a matter of time before I had to "fish or cut bait." And that day came in the summer of 1992 when, on a visit to southern Oregon, she said, "You're either going to take me to Palm Springs and buy me an engagement ring, or I'm going back to Texas and I'll never see you again." That was pretty straight forward, I guess. I'm no fool, well not completely anyway, and I went down to the travel agent and bought two plane tickets to Palm Springs and made hotel reservations for three days at the Grand Marriott—over my budget, but necessary. Then I went to the jewelry store and bought her an engagement ring. And that night I got on my knees and asked her to marry me. You know what she said, of course. It had been only four years coming. But, as I was getting up from my knees and watching her examine the ring, she looked at me and uttered, "I love you dearly, but this looks likes it came from a Cracker Jack box." To be fair to her she was absolutely right and didn't mean what she said to be cruel. She just had waited so long, and her expectations had been so high.

On my carpenter's wages I couldn't afford much, and had gone to a fly-by-night jeweler against my better judgment, and what I had bought *was* a piece of crap. So I went back to the guy and told him what had happened, that the diamond was flawed. He basically told me, "tough luck, it's yours now," but I was bigger than him—with all those muscles from swinging a hammer—and we had a little chat and he gave me my money back. And I gave the money to Annette and she put in more of her own money and bought herself a real engagement ring which, a couple nights later, I dutifully and— even more so—*willingly* knelt and put on her finger. She had already agreed to marry me, but how romantic I was! What a knucklehead! And we went to Palm Springs and she called her mother, we had a great time and all was right with the world. The deal with the ring was hard on my ego but, as they say, "Pride goeth before the fall."

A wedding date was set for June of 1993, in the Highland Park Presbyterian Church in Dallas. In the meantime, we did our thing and I swung a hammer and made a living and Annette sold real estate. She was good at it and was very energetic and diligent. She was able to do some subdivision sales for a developer we had met, which is what she was used to doing in Southern California.

I had gone through with my divorce from my first wife, Charlotte, and my boys told me they were okay. I surely hoped so, as I've mentioned. My parents were very close to Charlotte and were reluctant to even acknowledge Annette, and I don't blame them. They didn't realize at the time—and don't even realize to this day—what pressures they put on my first marriage. Charlotte hung in there like a trooper, but it just flamed out. To try and explain to them that I needed to get away from everything and make a new, clean, start was not possible. My parents are very childlike and take everything personally. They don't have the ability to look at things arbitrarily, but I felt they did need to meet Annette, at least before our marriage. So we made arrangements to meet them halfway between their home in northern California and ours in southern Oregon, at a Burger King in Mt. Shasta City. This was in early April of 1993, and the snow was still piled high and it was still cold and blustery, but not as cold as the reception my parents gave Annette. We worked through it, though, and they grudgingly made conversation and we spent an hour or so talking. Then they went back to California and we went home.

In preparation for our wedding, each of us put together a guest list and invitations were sent out to those we'd invited. Annette sent out about two hundred fifty and I about one hundred. My invitees were mostly made up of close relatives I enjoyed and friends from my past. There were not many new acquaintances in southern Oregon, as we hadn't lived there long, and Oregon to Texas is a ways to travel if you don't know someone very well.

It was getting near the date of the wedding and Annette had gotten the RSVPs back from her invitees, and I had only received correspondence from a very close cousin—one who was in the wedding—and his wife, from Seattle, and a cousin and his daughter from southern Oregon, the cousin that had been the impetus for moving up from California. And a co-worker of mine in the construction crew, Dennis Ochoa, a Native American, bought a new suit and came to the wedding. Dribs and drabs came back from old friends, but I heard absolutely nothing from my immediate family or invited relatives. That was a bit disappointing, but not unanticipated. My brother and sister had their own lives and still held resentment against me for having to shut our company down years before. My parents were childlike and the rest of my relatives wouldn't travel more than a hundred miles unless someone else paid for it. I must say that, even though my immediate family and relatives have— by now—warmly accepted Annette, I harbor some resentment. I believe that over the years I have been one of the most generous people I've known—and without strings—just because. It might sound self-serving, but you'll not find many who disagree. I've probably reaped the rewards and pain of that generosity, but I think the cosmos has generally given me peace with it. Probably, but not altogether. I guess when they read this book we'll find out.

My sons and I traveled to Dallas two weeks before the wedding. Annette's parents and friends had scheduled numerous parties to honor our marriage and I wanted my children to experience these occasions with me. Annette's parents—wonderful and kind people—took me in like a long-lost relative. It did take me a little while with her Dad as he needed to do "the father thing" and put me through the ringer a bit, but I understood where he was coming from and we've become close over the years.

We attended all the pre-wedding parties and my boys enjoyed things very much. These occasions were something they weren't used to, and it was very special for them. The wedding in the magnificent church was very elegant as was the reception, held at the Dallas Petroleum Club downtown. A little chuckle: My friend, Dennis Ochoa—the Native American who traveled from southern Oregon to attend the wedding—upon having exited the thirty-eighth floor onto the viewing deck and observing the magnificent view and how far above the ground we were, uttered these words, "I haven't been this high in twenty-five years." An obvious reference to his days in the drug culture of the 60s. But he was a solid human being. Then we gave my boys a hug and shipped them back to California. Annette's parents had made them feel like their own, which I'll never be able to adequately thank them for. We took a week's honeymoon to Mexico and then headed back to Oregon, and no job.

Before leaving for Dallas I had put in a bid on a town-home project in Ashland and wasn't sure how it was going to work out. I was up against some heavy competition, but I had a shot. If I didn't get the contract I would have to really scramble to keep things together. A week after we came back from our honeymoon I got the call that I had won the job.

Using the town-home project as a springboard, I was able to network with developers in the area and built up a fairly decent portfolio of work. When we had first moved to southern Oregon, and after I moved out of the old hotel and Annette joined me, we rented a home in Ashland. In the spring of 1994, we moved to the City of Medford, fifteen miles north. It was a good move for us and led to the development of good business relationships.

35

Life

In June of 1995, my oldest son, Jason, graduated from high school in Chico and was accepted into Chico State College. He studied there for a year, and then moved to the Southern California town of San Clemente, where he studied at Saddleback College for two years. He then moved back to Chico in the summer of 1998 to continue his studies at the college where he had begun, but after a semester he expressed his desire to attend culinary school. He always had a fascination with cooking and had taken a couple jobs in restaurants while he attended college. When he came to me and expressed his desire to do this, we sat down and talked it over. I wanted to impress upon him that Annette and I were completely supportive, but that he would have to really buckle down if we were going to continue to pick up the tab, as she and I had been doing. He had been bouncing around in his pursuit of higher education and we needed to put a limit on things. He assured us that this was his ultimate goal—to attend culinary school—and thereafter work for a great restaurant and then start his own business. It was a risky plan, but what isn't?

So, in the spring of 1999, Jason, Annette, and I traveled to San Francisco and enrolled him in the California Culinary Academy. Culinary schools don't get much better than that one. We got him set up in the dorms the school provided, met the dean of the school and developed a good rapport with him. A school like that is different than a conventional college in that the students are on their own. You have renowned chefs who have returned to hone their skills, mature men and women who have been successful in other walks of life but want a career change, and then people like Jason who have a dream. It's incredibly competitive and every student needs to be prepared, and we hoped Jason was.

In June of 1998, my younger son, Neil, had graduated from the same Chico High School that his older brother had, and then enrolled at Butte Junior College, a local school that was a good place for a kid like him to bring his grades up to allow for acceptance into a good four-year college. It took him four years, but he made it and was accepted into the University of California at San Diego, majoring in economics. He had also been accepted at UCLA and UC Santa Barbara, but he chose UCSD.

For Jason, the program at the Culinary Academy covered eighteen months. It was spendy, but it would result in a resume that could get him in any door. He buckled down and did well with the program for the first eight months, or so, then I began to get calls from the dean. Jason was missing classes, and showing a general lack of interest. He told me that Jason was a brilliant student and was very advanced in his understanding of things, but that these problems he mentioned were rearing their ugly heads, and the school didn't give the students a lot of slack. So Annette and I made arrangements to visit my son and the school to see for ourselves, and have dinner in one of their fantastic restaurants, of which there were three of different levels of food and service.

We arrived and met Jason. I had called and expressed my concerns, and he was prepared to give a defense of his position. Having met, we adjourned to a library area reserved for these types of things.

"How are you doing?" I asked.

"I'm not being challenged. It's very mundane and I don't feel I'm really experiencing what it means to be a chef." You must realize that Jason is eerily intelligent. He can analyze things from most perspectives and give a thesis on each. But, at the time, he was still a twenty-two-year-old kid who couldn't seem to get his act together.

"What can we do for you?" I asked.

"I want to be thrown into the mix. To be involved in what it means to run a kitchen. What it *really* means. Not the continual practice that we get every day, over and over."

I told him I would talk with the dean about this and the three of us then left for one of the restaurants and had a delightful meal, which was very, very good. We drank wine and had good conversation, but I ended our evening on a serious note. I explained that, if he didn't get very earnest about completing the course, we wouldn't be able to continue our financial assistance. He assured us he would. I met with the dean the next morning and told him of Jason's dilemma. The dean said that Jason wasn't the first to complain about these things and they were addressing the issues. He felt that this feedback could actually improve things at the school. He was very positive.

For the next two months and heading toward the end of June, 2000, it appeared that Jason had gotten serious about things at the academy. The dean and I exchanged fairly frequent phone calls and the dean was generally pleased. Then, the Saturday morning before we were to leave for California and a boating excursion over the July 4th holiday, I received a call from Jason's mother, Charlotte, telling me that Jason had been arrested and was being held in the San Francisco City Jail. He had called his mother, and—telling her what had happened—had given her his case number and the phone number of the jail and she asked if I would do what was needed to post his bail. I said I would.

Hanging up the phone, I wasn't sure what to do. Not having been through this type of situation before, I had no experience. On a whim I called the jail and gave them Jason's info and asked what I should do. They gave me the names and numbers of three bail bondsmen in no particular order, and were very helpful. I called the first one and got bad vibes. The second seemed okay, so I gave him my credit card number and my address, and he said he'd go bail Jason out.

A couple of hours later, Jason called me. As part of our collective attempt to get things straightened out at the institute, we had moved him into an apartment with a couple of other guys on Scott Street,which was a decent neighborhood. The dorm that the school owned was east of the main campus, which was located in the old German Embassy at 625 Polk Street, and was in the heart of the Tenderloin District of the city. Hookers, drug addicts, and other unsavory characters plied their wares in the area. It was not a good place for someone trying to get his life going. By moving Jason we felt it would lessen his temptation to partake of these things, but it wasn't meant to be. He had returned to his old neighborhood to pick up some things he had left in the dorm, and had solicited the purchase of cocaine from an undercover cop who had arrested him.

"Did you do it, Jason?" I asked.

"Yes I did, Dad. And I'm sorry. That's all I can say."

"Where do we go from here?" I inquired.

"Thanks for bailing me out, Dad. I'll do whatever it takes to make this right."

We had been sending money down to him every month and it was never enough. Not that any college kid ever has *enough* but he was spending a lot of money. And I asked him about it.

"How long have you been using?" I asked.

"Since right after I moved here," he answered.

"Just cocaine? No hookers or anything?"

"Yah, just cocaine."

We'd also been paying his AOL bill every month, which was debited against a credit card, and these bills had been dramatically increasing. I asked him about that.

"What's the deal with your online bills? They've really increased."

"Yah, I know they have. I've been using the internet a lot for school."

"Have you really, Jason?" That was a stretch.

I needed an attorney to plead Jason's case in court, so I called a friend of mine in the City and he gave me the name of someone to use, the former District Attorney for the County of San Mateo, a hard-nosed, but fair, guy. I traveled to San Francisco and met with

Jason. I took him to Union Square and we sat on a bench among the pigeons and the homeless and talked. He said that he needed to get out of town, and back into his more familiar environment of Chico.

"What about Culinary School?" I asked him.

"It's just not working for me," he said. He told me he was sorry, and I inquired as to what he wanted to do with his life. He said he wanted to stay in the restaurant business and work in the real world, not the continual practicing of the school. I didn't want to bring money into the equation, but I did. I told him we had spent a lot of money on this. And he said he knew and appreciated what we had done. I felt we had been honest with each other, but you never know.

We met with the attorney in San Mateo and he frankly asked Jason if he was guilty and Jason said yes. The attorney said, "I can get this case dismissed on technicalities if you want." Jason and I had discussed this and I'd told him that he had to take his medicine. He realized that and agreed. He told the attorney he wanted to plead guilty and suffer the consequences. He had no choice.

I gave the attorney a check for his retainer and Jason and I headed back to the City. It was a little uncomfortable for both of us. His mother and Neil had come down to lend support, and we met at their hotel and went to dinner. The next morning all of us headed back to our homes, leaving Jason in San Francisco. His hearing date came up a month later. The dean told me that Jason was doing better at school—not perfect, but better. When the hearing date came, Jason missed it. The bail bondsman called me and asked what I knew. I told him I didn't know anything about why he had missed the date. He said he'd go by Jason's place and see what he could do. I know what you're thinking, but this bail bondsman—who weighed about 300 pounds, with a pony-tail to his waist, and rode a motorcycle about two sizes too small—was one of the neatest people I met in this whole ordeal. He really cared about those he bailed out and was a primary reason Jason met his obligations.

The bondsman located Jason and read him the riot act. The attorney was able to get a continuance. Both he and the bail bondsman told him that he had one more chance and—this time—

Jason held up his end of the bargain. At the next hearing the judge gave him a suspended sentence and community service. He had no record, which helped.

With his stepped-up concentration at the Academy and the development of his obvious skills, shortly after his brush with the law he was able to get a job as a *sous-chef* at one of the top five restaurants in the City, helped by a letter of recommendation from the dean. He was doing his community service and things seemed to be going well. Then, a couple of months later, he called his mother and said he needed to move back to town. He was worried about his behavior. There were "too many temptations in San Francisco" is what he said. I think he had gotten back into cocaine but he never admitted it. I called and talked to the manager of the restaurant where he worked and got a glowing report. He said Jason was very good at his craft and was surprised he was leaving. I didn't go into the details with the man.

We had the attorney petition the judge to remand the case to Butte County so Jason could move back to Chico as he desired, and he was able to finish his sentence there. During all of this, he had the misfortune of having his Nissan pickup towed from a no parking area on one of the streets in the City—which isn't hard to have happen in San Francisco. He was afraid to tell me that he needed four hundred dollars to get it out of the impound yard. Eventually, he waited too long and the City sold the thing. That meant that he had no vehicle, so his mother and Neil went to San Francisco and moved him and his things back to Chico. I won't even tell you what all of this cost. Parents do what they must. And Annette supported me.

Jason was back in Chico around his support system and with a job at an up-and-coming restaurant in town, this time as an assistant chef. He liked the place and our family ate there several times. The eatery seemed to do well for a year or so but, as with most restaurants, its popularity waned and tastes changed, and it closed its doors. Jason was lucky enough to find another job almost immediately as co-chef at another trendy restaurant and it seemed to be a good fit.

It was the fall of 2002, and Neil had graduated from Butte

College with his AA Degree and—having been accepted by UCSD—was making plans to move down to San Diego. His major was economics, which he liked and excelled at, and things went well. In his second year there, his last, he was accepted into the Thurgood Marshall School of Economics and graduated in June of 2004, with honors, as I've previously mentioned. He's a good man.

While at Butte College, Neil had met a gal by the name of Tierney Kramlich, from Minot, North Dakota, and they fell in love. Tierney also graduated from Butte College in 2002, and chose the University of California at Berkley to finish her studies. And, like Neil, she also graduated in June of 2004.

One day, in early December of 2003, Neil called me and asked, "Have you ever thought about me coming to work for you?" You could have pushed me over with a feather. I didn't even think my children knew what I did for a living. I quickly thought about his question. With his economics degree, it could be a good fit. "Hell, yes!" I replied after the brief pause. We made plans to talk over the Christmas holidays, which we did, and Tierney also expressed her interest in moving to southern Oregon with Neil. I wasn't sure how her English degree might be extrapolated into employment in our area, but I told her we'd sure try—and that we'd love to have the both of them. I mentioned to Tierney that we had a need for a real estate broker and if she was interested she could take the course and pass the test online in the spring before they moved up.

Tierney liked that idea, and by the time they had moved to southern Oregon in July of 2004 she had her Oregon Real Estate License. She excelled at real estate and helped tremendously in our subdivision sales; and my son was a tremendous help in our real estate development and construction company.

Miss Girlie

When Annette and I were married in 1993, I promised her that I wouldn't prohibit us from having children. Even though I was fourteen years older than she and had two of my own, she had none.

She wanted a child between us, and so did I. All that I asked is for us to wait five years to get our feet on the ground and provide for a solid marital foundation. She agreed.

One thing led to another and, a little more than five years after we married, in September of 1998, Annette gave birth to Natalie—"Miss Girlie" as she came to be called. Parents and fathers gush about their kids and go on and on about them. I'm no different, although I believe I have better cause to do so. (Also like all parents.) But when they made Miss Girlie they broke the mold. I have so utterly enjoyed my two boys and wouldn't trade them for anything, but to have a little blonde girl come along after all these years is beyond compare. And she's an "old soul." That pretty much says it all. But I'll add in that she's smart and witty and funny and serious and silly. I don't know what Annette and I did without her. She's been a source of joy and comfort to the both of us. She's now eleven years old, eight more years before she goes away to college—and we're going to make the most of every minute.

*****

On the morning of September 6, 2003, a Saturday, I was sitting in our den and the phone rang. It was my ex-wife on the other end. She was obviously upset. I asked her what the matter was.

Earlier that morning, federal marshals had taken Jason from his apartment in Chico and he was being lodged in the Sacramento County Jail, about a hundred miles south. What a shock it was to hear that. The severity of what she had told me was indeed a shock, but I guess I'd have to say it wasn't surprising. Over the past several months Jason had been withdrawing more and more from the family and even his closest friends and his brother. Neil had commented several times about his concerns. All of us had tried to pull the reasons for this behavior out of him, but he wasn't willing to talk about things much. Depression runs in our family to some degree and we had offered to help him along those lines, maybe with the help of a doctor or psychologist, but none of us got anywhere. And then this terrible tragedy happened, and it forever changed all our lives: Jason had been caught conducting illegal activities on the internet during a nationwide FBI sting.

The following Monday, Annette and I drove down to Sacramento to see him. Going through all of the security and the redtape of a prison was a real eye-opener. Sitting there on the phone in the visitor's section, thick glass between the two of us and Jason, tears rolling down our cheeks, it almost broke our hearts. We each put a hand up to the glass and touched each other through it, if only in our hearts. I was barely able to speak, but when I was able to I began by telling him how sorry I was. Telling him that I had let him down in life and that I somehow felt responsible for this. He stopped me in mid-sentence and said, emphatically, "This is not your fault. I take full responsibility for my actions. Don't you dare blame yourself!" But I do.

We hired a top attorney and spent two years fighting the charges, but to no avail. Our two families, Charlotte's and mine, rallied around Jason and her brother was—and has been—especially supportive, as well as my parents and her mother and sister, and my sister and brother-in-law and their kids. They've all visited Jason often.

In October of 2005, Jason was sentenced to fifteen years in federal prison. He'll serve ten or eleven with good behavior. He's a model prisoner. He's so smart and the others look up to him and ask him for advice and he runs the library at Lompoc, the federal facility where he's being held. We see him a couple times a year, other family members see him more or less often, but we're a long way away. He's said many times since he was taken that this whole thing has saved his life—and you can see it in his eyes and actions. He's fit and trim. He runs ten miles a day and plays soccer and works out in the gym. When he comes out to meet us in the pleasant visitor's area at the prison—a nice, grassy place with picnic tables— with his dark glasses and khakis he looks more like an FBI agent than a federal prisoner. The facility is a beautiful place, just forty-five miles north of Santa Barbara on the coast. A medium security facility, we joke about it being the place to be if you have to be on "the inside." But, like Jason says, it's a little bit like the Eagles' song,

"Hotel California": "You can check out any time you like, but you can never leave." He'll be thirty-eight or thirty-nine when he gets out. What a shame. What a waste. Maybe then he can do something good with his life.

During quiet times, I think about singing him to sleep when he was little. He loved my songs and made requests of his favorites. When he was just learning to talk he'd ask, in that little voice, for "Railroad," "Swing-low," or "She'll be comin' round the mountain." I'd sing 'em until he fell asleep, and then I'd tuck him in and gently kiss him on the forehead.

I'll carry this with me for the rest of my life, along with "The Guilt," and so will he. I hope both of us can accept things and give to others, the way others have given to us.

*****

We married-off Neil and Tierney on June 30, 2007, at a grand affair in the Napa Valley, at the Silverado Country Club. Being avid golfers and with the wonderful courses the resort offered, Neil and I played the south course with two of his friends—big, long and lanky boys—twice. During the second round we were approaching the eighteenth and one of his friends, who's a two handicap, pulled out his three metal and hit a two hundred and eighty-five yard shot that landed fifteen feet from the pin, but he three-putted and lost by a stroke. Driving for "show" and putting for "dough" were never more prevalent. Good memories.

What's neat is that my ex-wife and her family and I, as I've mentioned before, have a good relationship, which was very evident at the festivities. Neil and I sat and laughed and cried and smoked cigars afterwards and wished his brother could have been there. Tierney worked in real estate until the fall of 2007, and then took a position with a major drug company, which was a very lucky move for her. Neil worked for our company until this past summer and now they both work and live in San Francisco. I had them close for a while and tried to make it up to Neil for the times I was gone during his childhood. He gets angry when I mention the subject, saying I have nothing to make up for, but I think I do. I can't make it up to Jason.

*****

Annette, Natalie, and I, in preparation for Neil and Tierney's wedding, went down to Silverado a few days early. Several relatives and friends joined us. About a week before we had left southern Oregon, Annette had found a lump in her left breast. Immediately after her discovery she scheduled a mammography, the results of which wouldn't be known for a couple weeks, which ended up being two days after we returned from Napa. She hadn't mentioned anything to anyone. There was a message on our answering machine from her doctor asking her to come in for a conference about how to proceed. The doctor scheduled an ultrasound, which then led to a needle biopsy—something she wouldn't wish on her worst enemy. I sat and watched it. Annette had no sedative of any kind, which they told her would interfere with the reading. The next day we found out it was malignant. It was very emotional for all of us. It's as if time stood still. Everything around us paled by comparison to Annette having to deal with this—all of us having to deal with this—on the heels of one of the happiest times for our family.

Annette consulted with several friends and acquaintances who had experienced breast cancer and researched her family background and potential options. She found that on her father's side of the family the cancer was rampant. As recommended by two close friends and the oncologist, an MRI was conducted within a week and surgery a week thereafter. It was decided that, as a precaution, both breasts would be removed. It was a somewhat painful decision for Annette and me, but we tried to make some humor out of it as we lamented being short-changed on her breast augmentation five years earlier. Chemotherapy followed three months later and she lost her hair as is normal with that treatment, but all of us around her thought she was the best looking bald woman we'd ever seen.

Annette is a very pretty, vivacious woman and having a part of her womanhood removed was a bitter pill, but she hung in like a trooper and has made the best of it. She now laughs about being able to wear blouses and tops she couldn't before. It's been two and a half years with no sign of the cancer returning. She's very athletic and keeps in great shape, which I think helps, but it's always in the back of our minds. But we were fortunate that Annette pays close attention and knows her body. We caught it early, and we'll have her around for a looooong time.

My Dad's Family

I haven't mentioned anything about my dad's family. Not because they didn't play a role in my life, but mainly because they weren't among the Pentecostals that I've talked about. They weren't "dyed in the wool" Pentecostals. Not that they weren't religious folk. They were, but they were more "middle of the road." They were Methodists and Baptists and such, which are middle of the road compared to Pentecostals, and I wasn't around them nearly as much as I was my mother's family.

Dad was the youngest of six, and there were four boys and two girls. They were all born in Minnesota, about one hundred miles north of Minneapolis, to Frank and Effie Morgan, my grandparents. They moved to northern California in 1933, all eight of them crammed into a two-door Chevy coupe. All their belongings were tied to the fenders and roof of the car, like so many of that era. Everett, the brother closest to my dad's age, and my father were very close.

My dad wasn't close to his two older brothers—blood isn't always thicker than water—but he was very close to his older sister, and our family would visit them on their dairy in southern Oregon. Those were fun times. We were also fairly close to the younger of the two sisters and her family, but she died too young and we drifted away from the rest of her family, to some degree.

Aunt Merna, Dad's oldest sibling, married Floyd Smith and they had the dairy I've mentioned. Neither of them were five feet tall. Uncle Floyd had one of the top milk-producing Holstein herds in the United States. Other dairymen would come from far and wide to buy the offspring of these cows, which were rarely offered for sale. It was amusing to watch my diminutive uncle move among the mammoth beasts, each weighing fifteen hundred pounds or more. But they knew who was boss and he was a very articulate handler of these cattle.

In later years, after they'd retired, my mom and dad would come up from California and visit the two of them on a regular basis and talk of the old days and have a ball. Once, when the four of them were watching a movie in the living room of Floyd and Merna's home, my uncle fell asleep, and—becoming angry with him—my aunt got up and marched into my cousin's old room in the house and got one of his leftover fire crackers. She lit it and threw it under my uncle's chair. That woke him up. Luckily, it didn't burn the house down. Those Morgans are a feisty lot!

EPILOGUE

Well, that's it! That's my story. I hope you could make some sense of it. It seems like I've led many lives, especially when I put things down on paper, but I wouldn't change a thing. I can't imagine life without those stories. And I have so many more. Like I said earlier, maybe I'll get around to telling them. Some are only lockerroom fodder, and some only for adults, and some are tales everyone could hear. I wonder if all that has befallen me in my life is a result of renouncing my Pentecostal upbringing. Wouldn't that be something?! But I don't know, and will never know what impact the Fundamentalist, Pentecostal, upbringing had on my life.

I've dealt with things "straight on" in my business life—as most of my partners and associates would confirm—but have never come to grips with opening myself up and being disarmingly honest in my personal life. I'm still secretive. No bodies are buried in the basement or anything but my wife has said many times, "Boy, Steve, I just wish I knew who you are." I'm not one for dishonesty, but not openness, either. I wish I had that. But what I do know is that writing this book has been a great tonic for me and that I'm the luckiest guy in the world to have lived—and to be living—this life of mine. Now most of my stories are out in the open so my friends won't think I've been pulling their leg all these years.

And the world *isn't* flat and *wasn't* made in six-days. But I still think God probably had a hand in things.

Like Billy Joel said in his song, "Piano Man": "It's sad and it's sweet and I knew it complete, When I wore a younger man's clothes."

Thanks for listening.

In the fall of 1991, during one of the lowest points in my life, I wrote two poems to Annette. Maybe a person should read these before he reads the book.

The Call

The day, the night, September bright,
Of joyous seasons, of sad refrain,
My heart recalls such wondrous sight,
And sweeps away all hint of pain.

A dream, a vision, it builds inside,
To bring its joy, its hope of the 'morrow,
But fades at last from force of pride,
And lives its day amid the sorrow.

Arise my dream, my joy, my hope,
Take up the cause so loud and clear,
Hold the day that love awoke,
And put away all doubt and fear.

To touch, to hold, to feel inside,
Amid life's storms, tossed on the shore,
Take up and follow, abandon all pride,
And feel the dream, it calls once more.

Hope

Oh, could I know of heart so torn,
Of kindled flame, swept by the wind,
The sound, so silent, of pain is born,
No joy my soul and self to mend.

Shall hope be carried in mind and soul,
To hold the promise, its embers glow,
Or does it lie, in silence, fallow,
No sound to hear, no voice to know?

Hope lives, I think, in silence driven,
In eyes, and touch, and kindness shown,
To rise and take the life it's given,
And bring that heart to love's sweet home.

Greta

Darrel (Grandpa)

Carol

Nicki

Mrs. Roberts

Sharon

Lawrence

Richard
(The Bastard)

Author

Grandma and Grandpa Gottschalk

Tierney, Neil, Author, Annette, Natalie

Tierney and Neil

Annette and the Author

Author and the Shearing

Miss Natalie

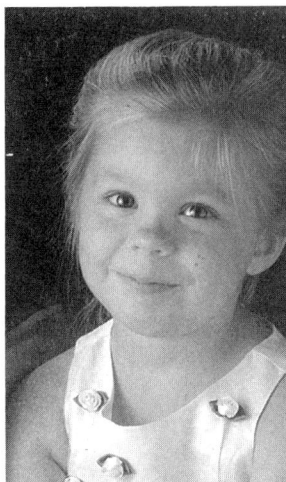

Miss Girlie

Jason

Jason's prison photo

Dad, Mom, Author, and Brother

Yearbook